PROBLEMS OF THE MODERN ECONOMY

Inequality and Poverty

PROBLEMS OF THE MODERN ECONOMY

General Editor: EDMUND S. PHELPS, *University of Pennsylvania*

Each volume in this series presents
prominent positions in the debate of
an important issue of economic policy

Inequality
and
Poverty

Edited with an introduction by

EDWARD C. BUDD

PENNSYLVANIA STATE UNIVERSITY

NEW YORK

W · W · NORTON & COMPANY · INC ·

How Should Income Be Distributed? from *An Introduction to Economic Analysis and Policy* by James E. Meade and Charles J. Hitch. Published by Oxford University Press. Reprinted by permission of James E. Meade, Professor of Political Economy in the University of Cambridge, and Charles J. Hitch.

The Ethics of Redistribution from *The Ethics of Redistribution* by Bertrand de Jouvenel. Reprinted by permission of Cambridge University Press.

Equality from *Equality* by R. H. Tawney (London: George Allen & Unwin, Ltd.), 1952. Reprinted by permission of the publishers.

The Distribution of Income, Government Measures to Alter the Distribution of Income, and The Alleviation of Poverty, from *Capitalism and Freedom* by Milton Friedman. Copyright © 1962 by the University of Chicago Press. Reprinted by permission of the University of Chicago Press.

Inequality and Growth from *The Cost of Freedom* by Henry C. Wallich. Copyright © 1960 by Henry C. Wallich. Reprinted with the permission of Harper & Row, Publishers, Incorporated.

Income Inequality since the War by Robert M. Solow in *Postwar Economic Trends in the United States* edited by Ralph E. Freeman. Copyright © 1960 by Massachusetts Institute of Technology. Reprinted by permission of Harper & Row, Publishers, Incorporated.

Changes in the Size Distribution of Income by Selma F. Goldsmith in *American Economic Review, Papers and Proceedings,* May 1957. Copyright 1957 by Selma F. Goldsmith. Reprinted by special permission.

Changes in the Concentration of Wealth from *The Share of Top Wealth-holders in National Wealth* by Robert J. Lampman. A National Bureau of Economic Research book. Reprinted by permission of Princeton University Press. Copyright © 1962 by Princeton University Press.

Determinants of the Distribution of Labor Incomes from *The Theory of Price* by George J. Stigler, Copyright 1942, 1946, 1952 by The Macmillan Company. Copyright 1966 by George J. Stigler. Reprinted by permission of the Macmillan Company.

Determinants of Inequality in the Ownership of Property, and Toward a Property-owning Democracy from *Efficiency, Equality, and the Ownership of Property* by James E. Meade, Copyright 1964 by George Allen & Unwin, Ltd. Reprinted by permission of Harvard University Press and George Allen & Unwin, Ltd.

Capitalism, Socialism, and the Distribution of Wealth and Income from *Capitalism and Socialism* by A. C. Pigou. Reprinted by permission of Macmillan & Company, Ltd., and St. Martin's Press, Inc.

The Invisible Poor reprinted with permission of The Macmillan Company from *The Other America* by Michael Harrington. Copyright © Michael Harrington 1962.

Changes in the Number and Composition of the Poor, by Herman P. Miller from *Poverty in America,* edited by Margaret S. Gordon. Copyright © 1965 by Chandler Publishing Company. Reprinted by permission.

The Poverty Band and the Count of the Poor from *Poverty Amid Affluence* by Oscar Ornati. Reprinted by permission of The Twentieth Century Fund.

Approaches to the Reduction of Poverty: I by Robert J. Lampman, and Approaches to the Reduction of Poverty: II by Harry C. Johnson, in *American Economic Review, Papers and Proceedings,* Vol. 40, no. 2, May 1965.

On Improving the Economic Status of the Negro, by James Tobin from the Fall 1965 issue of *Daedalus,* Journal of the American Academy of Arts and Sciences. Reprinted by permission of the publishers and the author.

Acknowledgment

I am indebted to Wilbur L. Avril for assistance in preparing this volume.   E.C.B.

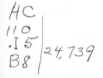

Contents

PART FIVE: Poverty

Introduction

IF AMERICANS were asked to list those economic problems they considered most important, income distribution might not appear high on the list. But it has received an increasing share of the headlines recently, as public attention has come to be focused on the problem of poverty. And it is clear from reactions to other public policy issues—full employment, inflation, tax policy, the farm question, collective bargaining, social security, rent control, even tariffs—that questions of income distribution are barely hidden below the surface. Much of the struggle appears to be between groups organized along occupational or other lines, between farmers and the nonfarm population, labor and management, landlords and tenants. But incomes accrue to individuals and families, not to groups, and our ultimate concern must be with the distribution of income among the rich, the less well-to-do, and the poor. Thus, as George Stigler claims, "the size distribution of income—the distribution of households by size of income—has been the most important question of public policy over long periods and in many countries." [1]

THE GOAL OF EQUALITY

How we choose to modify the prevailing distribution of income depends on our knowledge of the extent of existing inequality, the forces determining it, and the effects of the measures proposed for modifying it. But it also depends on our ideal of a just distribution. Equality is far from the only goal that has been proposed, but it is one that has always had strong support, and a number of arguments have been presented on its behalf. One of the most famous is that drawn from utilitarianism, set forth by the English philosopher Jeremy Bentham some two centuries ago, that the appropriate goal of a society is to maximize the total

1. G. J. Stigler, *The Theory of Price*, 3rd edition, Macmillan, p. 288.

satisfactions experienced by the individuals comprising it, and that a given total income yields the most satisfaction (or utility) when it is equally distributed. The argument, together with the assumptions underlying it and possible alternatives to it, is developed in more detail in the selection by James Meade and Charles Hitch. While Meade and Hitch distinguish between the economic principle and acceptance of the underlying ethic, the latter has been implicitly if not explicitly accepted by a number of other economists. The selection from A. C. Pigou in Part Four, for example, contains a sophisticated, if qualified, statement of the doctrine.

A criticism of the utilitarian argument for equality is offered by Bertrand de Jouvenel. He does not choose to rest his case on the grounds suggested by Meade and Hitch—that individuals may not have the same capacities for satisfactions, so that equalizing incomes would not necessarily maximize total utility, or that the satisfactions of different individuals cannot be added or compared. Rather, he stresses the social and cultural benefits of the activities and products supported by the demands of a wealthy minority—quality goods, new products, artistic creations, cultural activities. Any attempt to replace by collective consumption such losses which might result from redistribution is, he argues, inconsistent with the utilitarian emphasis on individual consumption.[2] Although echoing faintly some of de Jouvenel's arguments, Henry Wallich draws a somewhat different moral. While rejecting any case for equality on the grounds of distributive justice, he nevertheless accepts the utilitarian argument for equality on functional grounds, as simply one means among several for increasing total welfare or satisfaction. He then argues that increasing total income through economic growth is a superior means of increasing welfare, particularly when redistribution and growth are competing objectives.

Utilitarianism is not the only rationale that has been provided

2. For a further examination of the issue of individual versus collective consumption, particularly the extent to which reliance can be placed on individual choice as expressed in markets even when, as in utilitarianism, the satisfaction of individual preferences is taken as the goal, see Edmund S. Phelps, ed., *Private Wants and Public Needs*, revised edition, Norton, and F. M. Bator, *The Question of Government Spending*, Harper, ch. 6.

for equality. Indeed, utilitarian ethics as a justification for equality was explicitly repudiated by Simons, whose own egalitarian position is forthrightly stated in the selection in Part Four. A different kind of case for equality, more in the tradition of egalitarian socialist thought, is made by R. H. Tawney. While his book *Equality* was written more as an attack on the British class structure of the late twenties, much of what he has to say, particularly his emphasis on the importance of the development of all individuals, rather than just the members of an elite, is of enduring quality.

Milton Friedman presents a contrasting argument. As an alternative to equality of income as a social goal, he suggests the market principle, "to each according to what he and the instruments he owns produce," which he feels has wide acceptance as an ethic in a capitalist system such as ours. While professing neutrality in regard to both ethics, Friedman finds other instrumental merits for the productivity principle, and no ethical justification for collective redistribution of whatever distribution may happen to prevail. Any distributive ethic, he argues, must be instrumental to the role of individual freedom.

If a contrast is indeed to be drawn between the ethics of freedom and of equality, the precise meaning to be attached to "freedom" by each author must be clearly understood. Friedman would appear to emphasize the freedom of individual action from governmental control, whereas Tawney would choose to emphasize the greater freedom and widened scope for action permitted to lower income groups by government intervention in redistributing income. In Tawney's words, "Freedom for the pike is death for the minnows."

Two comments on the relevance of the readings in Part One to questions of public policy are in order. First, there are other goals than distributive justice, however defined; the selections suggest several—allocative efficiency, economic growth, economic and political freedom. Goals for particular policies are not necessarily competitive; increasing outlays on education, for example, may simultaneously reduce inequality and increase the rate of growth, and reducing monopoly restraints may improve both efficiency and income distribution. If the goals are in conflict, however, the choice involves not simply a matter of personal preference for one goal, such as equality, over the others, but consideration of the cost of moving closer to one goal in terms of the sacrifice which must be made of progress toward other objectives. The second point is closely related to the first. Particular policies frequently involve a choice between more or less inequality; complete equality remains a utopian alternative. Perhaps this is as it should be, for, as Henry Simons suggests, there may be more of a consensus on the direction of movement toward less inequality than on the ultimate goal of equality itself.

THE MEASUREMENT OF INEQUALITY

Inequality may be measured with respect to either the receipt of income or the ownership of property. Income is a flow, measurable only over a period of time, such as a year; property, a stock, is measurable at any given point in time. The former may be thought of as the flow of claims on the value of goods and services produced, accruing to individuals or institutions, such as governments or businesses; the latter, as the stock of claims or rights to the value of wealth, whether it be natural resources, man-made capital goods, such as business structures or equipment, or consumer durable goods, such as automobiles. While human beings are sometimes considered as part of wealth, they are not included in the statistics on wealth cited in this book.

In simple cases, the concepts of wealth and property may be closely identified with particular objects, as in a person's ownership of his mortgage-free house. But the structure of property claims in a capitalist economy is generally a complex one; individuals' claims on wealth owned by corporations, for example, may be represented by common or preferred stock, by corporate bonds, by notes and mortgages held by persons. Ultimately, property rights or claims can be traced to the objects of wealth underlying them or to claims on income to which the wealth gives rise.

Much of our knowledge of the extent of inequality in the distribution of income and of changes in inequality over time is based on the work of the Office of Business Economics (OBE). Some of its findings are summarized in the selections from Robert Solow and Selma Goldsmith; a more complete presentation, for the full range of years covered by the series, may be found in Table 1. This table gives the shares in total income of consumer units (families and unattached individuals), when ranked from lowest to highest by income and grouped into fifths or quintiles, and the share of the top 5 per cent of all income recipients. Thus, in 1962 the poorest fifth of consumer units obtained less than 5 per cent of total income, and the richest fifth, nearly half (46 per cent). Had income been equally distributed, each group would, of course, have had 20 per cent of the total.

Alternatively, the data in Table 1 could be cumulated from lowest to highest; on this basis, the lowest two fifths received 15.5 per cent of total income in 1962; the lowest four fifths, 54 per cent; the lowest 95 per cent, 80 per cent of total income. When shown graphically, the resulting curve is called a Lorenz curve. Were income distributed equally, this curve would correspond with the 45° line or diagonal; the latter may therefore be appropriately termed the line of equality. A widely used measure of inequality—the Gini concentration ratio, or coefficient of inequality—is the ratio of the area between the Lorenz curve and the line of equality, to the entire area lying under this line. Lorenz curves for the 1929, 1935–36, and 1962 distributions are shown in Figure 1;[3] concentration ratios for these and other years are given in Table 1.

A somewhat different way of presenting the underlying distributions, in terms of the average (mean) income of one group relative to the average for all groups taken together, is shown in Table 2. The mean income of all consumer units in 1962, when measured in dollars of 1965 purchasing power, was $7,640. The poorest quintile, however, had incomes which averaged only 23 per cent of this figure, or $1,760; the mean income of the richest quintile, on the other hand, was close to 2.3 times the mean for all units (and hence about 10 times that of the lowest quintile), or about $17,400. The top 5 per cent enjoyed incomes which averaged 392 per cent of the average income for all, or close to $30,000.

3. The Lorenz curve for 1941 lies between those for 1935–36 and for 1962; Lorenz curves for years from 1944 on are virtually identical with the 1962 curve.

FIGURE 1. *Lorenz Curves for the Distribution of Family Personal Income*

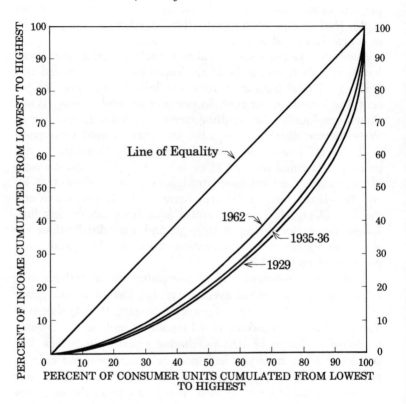

TABLE 1.   Per Cent Distribution of Family Personal Income[1] by Quintiles and Top 5 Per Cent of Consumer Units,[2] Selected Years, 1929–1962

Quintiles	1929	1935–1936	1941	1944	1947	1950	1951	1954	1956	1959	1962
Lowest	3.5	4.1	4.1	4.9	5.0	4.8	5.0	4.8	4.8	4.6	4.6
Second	9.0	9.2	9.5	10.9	11.0	10.9	11.3	11.1	11.3	10.9	10.9
Third	13.8	14.1	15.3	16.2	16.0	16.1	16.5	16.4	16.3	16.3	16.3
Fourth	19.3	20.9	22.3	22.2	22.0	22.1	22.3	22.5	22.3	22.6	22.7
Highest	54.4	51.7	48.8	45.8	46.0	46.1	44.9	45.2	45.3	45.6	45.5
Total	100	100	100	100	100	100	100	100	100	100	100
Top 5 per cent	30.0	26.5	24.0	20.7	20.9	21.4	20.7	20.3	20.2	20.2	19.6
Gini concentration ratio	.49	.47	.44	.39	.40	.40		.39	.39		.40

1. Family personal income includes wage and salary receipts (net of social insurance contributions), other labor income, proprietors' and rental income, dividends, personal interest income, and transfer payments. In addition to monetary income flows, it includes certain nonmonetary or imputed income such as wages in kind, the value of food and fuel produced and consumed on farms, net imputed rental value of owner-occupied homes, and imputed interest. Personal income differs from national income in that it excludes corporate profits taxes, corporate saving (inclusive of inventory valuation adjustment), and social security contributions of employers and employees, and includes transfer payments (mostly governmental) and interest on consumer and government debt.

2. Consumer units include farm operator and nonfarm families and unattached individuals. A family is defined as a group of two or more persons related by blood, marriage, or adoption, and residing together.

SOURCE: For 1944–1962: Office of Business Economics, U. S. Department of Commerce; figures from *Survey of Current Business*, March 1955, p. 20; April 1958, p. 17; and April 1964, p. 8. Comparable estimates for years following 1962 are not available at this time. For 1935–36 and 1941: S. Goldsmith, *et al.*, "Size Distribution of Income Since the Mid-Thirties," *Review of Economics and Statistics*, vol. 36 (February 1954), p. 9. For 1929: S. Goldsmith, "The Relation of Census Income Distribution Statistics to Other Income Data," *Studies in Income and Wealth*, vol. 23, p. 92. For this year Mrs. Goldsmith gives a figure (12.5 per cent) for only the two lowest quintiles combined; this percentage was allocated between the two percentiles by using the reversal of a Gini curve, as described by M. J. Bowman in *Readings in the Theory of Income Distribution*, Blakiston (1951). I am indebted to Alan MacFadyen for suggesting and carrying out this allocation, and for computing the Gini concentration ratios from the underlying OBE distributions by a method described by J. N. Morgan, "The Anatomy of Income Distribution," *Review of Economics and Statistics*, vol. 44 (August 1962), p. 281.

TABLE 2. *Mean Family Personal Income per Consumer Unit, and Mean Income of Each Quintile and Top 5 Per Cent of Consumer Units, Expressed as a Percentage of the Mean Income for All Consumer Units, Selected Years, 1929–1962*

Mean Income per Consumer Unit	1929	1935–1936	1941	1947	1950	1954	1959	1962
Current dollars	$2,340	$1,630	$2,210	$4,130	$4,440	$5,360	$6,620	$7,260
Constant (1965) dollars	4,460	3,940	4,900	5,740	5,820	6,190	7,160	7,640
Mean Income of Quintile Expressed as a Per Cent of Mean Income of All Consumer Units								
Lowest	18%	21%	21%	25%	24%	24%	23%	23%
Second	45	46	48	55	55	56	55	55
Third	69	71	77	80	81	82	82	82
Fourth	97	105	112	110	111	113	113	114
Highest	272	259	244	230	231	226	228	228
All quintiles	100	100	100	100	100	100	100	100
Top 5 per cent	600	530	480	414	428	406	400	392
Highest quintile minus top 5 per cent	163	168	165	167	165	166	171	173

SOURCE: First part: *Survey of Current Business*, April 1964, p. 5. Converted to constant (1965) dollars by use of the OBE implicit price deflator for personal consumption expenditure. Second part: Computed from Table 1, by dividing the income share of each quintile by .20 per cent (or .20), the share of the top 5 per cent by .05, and the share of the highest quintile minus the top 5 per cent by .15.

These figures are averages, of course, not the incomes making one eligible for membership in the class. In 1962, anyone with an income below $3,100 (again in dollars of 1965 purchasing power) would have found himself in the lowest quintile; on the other hand, it would have taken an income of over $10,400 to have placed him in the richest quintile, and over $18,000 to have put him in the top 5 per cent. The range between $3,200 and $10,400 included the remaining three fifths of consumer units in 1962.

The income concept underlying the distributions in Tables 1 and 2 is not that arising directly from productive activity, or so-called national income, but already reflects some of the redistributive effects of governmental and private institutions. For example, it excludes from labor earnings social security taxes paid to government and includes only a portion of corporate income—that part paid directly to stockholders in dividends, not the portion paid to the government in taxes or retained by corporations themselves in undistributed profits. Included are other items of a nonproductive character: interest payments on consumer and government debt and transfer payments (largely social insurance benefits and veterans' payments). While size distributions of national income would undoubtedly be useful in analyzing sources of inequality resulting directly from the operation of the market, empirical estimates are not at present available. As Mrs. Goldsmith's article suggests, the share of the top 5 per cent is no doubt greater in national income than in personal income.

The importance of the personal income tax as a redistributive device can be determined by comparing distributions of personal income (Tables 1 and 2) and disposable income (Tables 3 and 4). As might be expected, the income tax pushes the after-tax distribution in the direction of more equality, although the effect is rather modest. In 1962, for example, the share of the top 5 per cent was reduced by about 2 percentage points, with this increase spread over the four lowest quintiles. On a before-tax basis, the mean income of the richest quintile was 10 times that of the poorest quintile; on an after-tax basis, 9 times. The top 5 per cent had before-tax incomes which averaged 17 times those of the bottom quintile, and after-tax incomes averaging 14 times those of the bottom.

TABLE 3. *Per Cent Distribution of Family Personal Income after Federal Individual Income Tax Liability by Quintiles and the Top 5 Per Cent of Consumer Units Ranked by Size of After-tax Income, Selected Years, 1929–1962*

Quintiles	1929	1941	1950	1951	1954	1956	1959	1962
Lowest }	12.6	{ 4.3	5.1	5.4	5.3	5.2	4.9	4.9
Second }		9.9	11.4	11.9	12.1	11.9	11.5	11.5
Third	13.9	15.9	16.8	17.2	17.4	16.9	16.8	16.8
Fourth	19.5	23.1	22.7	22.8	22.8	22.6	23.0	23.1
Highest	54.0	46.9	44.0	42.7	42.8	43.4	43.8	43.7
Total	100	100	100	100	100	100	100	100
Top 5 per cent	29.5	21.5	19.2	18.4	18.2	18.1	18.0	17.7

SOURCE: Same as for Table 1. Estimates for 1929 from S. Goldsmith, "Impact of the Income Tax on Socio-Economic Groups of Families in the U. S.," *Income and Wealth*, Series X (Bowes and Bowes), 1964, p. 268.

TABLE 4. *Mean Family After-tax Income per Consumer Unit, and Mean After-tax Income of Each Quintile and Top 5 Per Cent of Consumer Units, Expressed as a Percentage of the Mean After-tax Income for All Consumer Units, Selected Years, 1929–1962*

Mean Income per Consumer Unit	1929	1941	1950	1954	1959	1962
Current dollars	$2,320	$2,110	$4,070	$4,840	$5,940	$6,220
Constant (1965) dollars	4,430	4,680	5,330	5,700	6,440	6,840
Mean Income of Quintile Expressed as a Per Cent of Mean Income of All Consumer Units						
Lowest	n.a.	22%	26%	25%	25%	25%
Second	n.a.	50	57	59	58	58
Third	70	80	84	86	84	84
Fourth	98	116	114	114	115	116
Highest	270	235	220	216	219	219
All quintiles	100	100	100	100	100	100
Top 5 per cent	590	430	384	363	360	354
Highest quintile minus top 5 per cent	163	159	165	166	172	173

n.a. — Not available

SOURCE: First part: *Survey of Current Business,* April 1964, and S. Goldsmith, *Income and Wealth,* Series X, p. 268. Second part: Computed from Table 3 by the method described in Table 2.

Other taxes, such as sales, excise, property, and payroll taxes, appear to have an opposite effect on income distribution. A study by Professor Musgrave for 1958, the results of which are summarized in Tables 5 and 6, indicates that the percentage of income paid in taxes of all kinds was actually smaller at higher incomes. Only for the top 5 per cent of consumer units with incomes above $15,000 did taxes take a larger proportion of income than at lower levels; the bottom group paid almost as large a percentage as the top one. While some of Musgrave's assumptions with respect to the shifting and incidence of certain taxes might be questioned, modifying them would not materially alter the results. In contrast to transfer payments, the evidence suggests that tax policy has not had a broadly redistributive effect.

TABLE 5. *Taxes As a Per Cent of Income for 1958*

Tax source	Under $2,000	$2,000–3,999	$4,000–5,999	$6,000–7,999	$8,000–9,999	$10,000–14,999	$15,000 and over	Total
	%	%	%	%	%	%	%	%
Broadly-defined income concept[1]								
1. Total taxes	33.1	29.6	28.6	27.7	25.4	25.2	36.3	29.5
Federal taxes								
2. Individual income	2.1	5.0	6.6	8.8	8.3	9.6	15.8	9.4
3. Corporation income	3.5	2.9	2.6	2.7	2.8	3.6	10.5	4.6
4. Excises and customs	4.6	3.6	3.5	3.3	3.2	2.9	1.7	2.9
5. Estate and gift	—	—	—	—	—	—	1.6	.3
6. Social security	8.3	6.5	5.4	3.6	2.6	1.7	.8	3.3
7. Total	18.6	18.0	18.1	18.4	16.9	17.8	30.4	20.8
State and local taxes								
8. Individual income	.6	.9	.6	.3	.2	.3	.6	.5
9. Corporation income	.1	.2	.1	.1	.1	.2	.5	.2
10. Property	6.8	5.1	4.6	4.1	3.8	3.0	2.1	3.7
11. Excises and customs	5.5	4.3	4.2	4.0	3.8	3.4	2.1	3.5
12. Estate and gift	—	—	—	—	—	—	.4	.1
13. Social security	1.5	1.1	1.0	.8	.6	.5	.2	.7
14. Total	14.5	11.6	10.5	9.3	8.5	7.4	5.9	8.7
Money-income concept[2]								
15. Federal, Total	19.5	19.3	19.2	19.3	17.8	18.9	31.8	21.9
16. State and local, Total	15.2	12.3	11.1	9.9	9.1	7.8	6.2	9.3
17. Total, all levels	34.7	31.6	30.3	29.2	26.9	26.7	38.0	31.2

1. Family personal income (as defined in footnote 2 to Table 1) plus social security contributions, corporate retained earnings and profits taxes, and realized capital gains. (Including both the latter may involve some double counting.)

2. "Broadly defined income" minus nonmonetary or imputed income as described in footnote 2 to Table 1.

SOURCE: R. A. Musgrave, "Estimating the Distribution of the Tax Burden," *Income and Wealth*, Series X, 1964, Table II, p. 192. The estimates are based on the following assumptions with respect to tax incidence: all sales and excise taxes, one third of corporate income taxes, and one half of employers' social security contributions are shifted to consumers in the form of higher prices.

TABLE 6. *Differential Incidence, 1958*

Tax source	Family Personal Income Class						
	Under $2,000	$2,000–3,999	$4,000–5,999	$6,000–7,999	$8,000–9,999	$10,000–14,999	$15,000 and over
Broadly defined income concept							
Federal, Total	+2.2	+2.8	+2.7	+2.4	+3.9	+3.0	—9.4
State and local, Total	—5.8	—2.9	—1.8	—0.6	—0.2	+1.3	+2.8
Total, all levels	—3.6	—0.1	+0.9	+1.8	+4.1	+4.3	—6.6
Money-income concept							
Federal, Total	+2.4	+2.6	+2.7	+2.6	+4.1	+3.0	—10.1
State and local, Total	—5.9	—3.0	—1.8	—0.6	+0.2	+1.5	+3.1
Total, all levels	—3.5	—0.4	+0.9	+2.0	+4.3	+4.5	—7.0

SOURCE: Musgrave, *op. cit.*, Table III, p. 194. "Table III repeats the overall results of Table II in the form of differential incidence. The figures show the loss (—) or gain (+), expressed as a per cent of income, which results as the actual tax structure is substituted for a general proportional income tax" (pp. 193, 195).

Contrary to the conclusions of some earlier investigators, including the famous Italian economist Vilfredo Pareto, the distribution of income does not remain constant over time. Indeed, an examination of Table 1 will disclose a rather significant reduction in inequality in the United States since 1929, the earliest year for which data are even close to being adequate. Between 1929 and 1962, for example, the share of the top quintile fell by a fifth; that of the top 5 per cent, by a third; that of the top 1 per cent, by more than a half (from 16 to under 8 per cent). The share of the two bottom quintiles, on the other hand, rose from 13 to 16 per cent, or by approximately a quarter. These figures imply in turn that the average income of the top quintile was 9 times as great as the average in the two bottom quintiles in 1929 and only 6 times as great in 1962. The reduction in inequality is also shown by the fall in the concentration ratio from .49 in 1929 to .40 in 1962.

The change has been so striking that some writers have referred to it as an "income revolution." If a revolution it was, it was largely over before the end of World War II. Since the end of that war the degree of inequality has shown relatively little change; if anything, the poorest fifth as well as the top 5 per cent may have lost a little ground to the third and fourth quintiles. This is not, of course, to say that changes in the postwar period have been entirely absent; rather, the changes there have more or less offset each other in their effects on size distribution. For example, fewer farmers and self-employed businessmen are currently found in the ranks of the top 5 per cent; their places have been taken largely by professional people and managerial personnel.

Some of the reasons for the reduction in inequality between the prewar and the postwar years are analyzed in more detail in the selections from Solow and Mrs. Goldsmith. Major factors were a rise in the share of income going to wages and salaries, which are more equally distributed than self-employment and property incomes, the increased importance of transfer payments, a reduction in the inequality of wealth-holdings, a matter explored more fully in the selection from Robert Lampman, and a narrowing of wage and salary differentials resulting from the shift from substantial unemployment to the full employment economy of World

War II. Several of the authors in this volume, James Tobin, for example, emphasize the importance of full employment in narrowing the dispersion of wage incomes as well as in raising the incomes of poorly paid and previously unemployed workers. One of the most important elements in the reduction in the property share was the increase in corporate income tax rates, which tended to depress both dividend income and corporate saving, the benefits of which accrue largely to the top income groups. The change in the share of the top 5 per cent is analyzed more thoroughly by Mrs. Goldsmith.

Data on the distribution of wealth are even scantier than on the distribution of income, but what there is suggests an even higher concentration of wealth-holdings than of receipt of income. Based on his study of estate-tax returns, Professor Lampman finds that the top 2 per cent of families, when ranked by size of wealth, owned 28½ per cent of all wealth in 1953; in contrast, when ranked by size of income, the top 2 per cent received about 12 per cent of family personal income in the same year. Lampman's study, which is of necessity restricted to the very top group, is our only source of information on changes in inequality in wealth-holding over time. The behavior of the wealth share of the top wealth-holding groups broadly parallels that of the income share of the top income-recipient group, although there are some differences. For example, his series for the postwar period shows a rise in wealth inequality which is not reflected in the income data, partly because the share of the top 1 per cent in wealth is much more sensitive to changes in stock prices (which have risen sharply since the late 1940's) than is the corresponding share in income.

Findings from the Survey of Financial Characteristics of Consumers, the Federal Reserve Board's sample survey of consumer units for 1962, throw further light on inequality of wealth-holdings and its relation to income inequality. Some of the relevant data are presented in Table 7. Several conclusions can be drawn from that table. First, the degree of inequality in the ownership of wealth as estimated by this survey is even greater than Lampman's estimate, with the top 1 per cent owning a third of total wealth. For corporate stock, which is more closely held than any other type of asset with the possible exception of tax exempt bonds, about the same degree of concentration is shown by the two studies.

Second, inequality in wealth and inequality in income, although by no means the same thing, are closely related, with a tendency for large wealth-holdings to be associated with high income. For example, the top 1 per cent of consumer units when ranked by size of income held one quarter of total wealth, compared with

TABLE 7. *Per Cent of Wealth Held or Income Received by Consumer Units When Ranked by Size of Income or Wealth, 1962*

Consumer Units Ranked by	Lowest Quintile	2nd thru 4th Quintiles	Highest Quintile	Top 5%	Top 1%
A. *Size of Wealth-holding:*					
1. Total wealth	*	23%	77%	53%	33%
2. Corporate stock	*	3	97	86	62
B. *Size of Income:* [1]					
1. Total wealth	7	36	57	38	25
2. Total income	4	50	46	20	8
3. Wages and salaries	2	53	45	15	4
4. Self-employment [2]	1	36	63	42	26
5. Property income [3]	5	29	66	47	33
6. Dividends [4]	2	15	83	65	49

* less than ½ of 1 per cent

1. The income concept used in the Survey differs somewhat from the concept of family personal income underlying Tables 1 through 4; in particular, it excludes imputed income and includes social security contributions of employees and private transfer payments (private pensions, for example).
2. Income of farm and nonfarm self-employed proprietors.
3. The sum of interest, dividends, rent, and income from estates and trusts.
4. Includes dividends from small, closely held corporations as well as those whose stock is publicly traded, and income from estates and trusts.
SOURCE: *Survey of Financial Characteristics of Consumers.* The shares of the top 5 per cent, ranked by the size of wealth, and of the top one per cent have been interpolated by the editor from the underlying distributions and may therefore differ from "true" values by one or possibly two percentage points; the Federal Reserve Board staff has kindly made available the remaining percentages. The reader should recognize that data in this and in other tables are subject to some undetermined margin of error. To illustrate, respondents in field surveys usually underreport the amount of their income and wealth to interviewers. Since there is evidence that this behavior is more characteristic of the bottom and the top income groups, the shares of the lowest and highest groups in this table may be understated relative to those in the second through the fourth quintiles, that is, the middle 60 per cent.

one third when consumer units were ranked instead by size of wealth. This relationship is what we would expect. For one thing, the rich save a larger proportion of their income than the poor and hence are able to add more to their wealth. For another, wealth itself yields income; the concentration of wealth implies in turn an equivalent concentration of property income (dividends, interest, and rent); it is no accident that the shares of income recipients in total wealth (line B1 of Table 7) and in property income (line B5) agree so closely.[4] Corresponding to the concentration of stock ownership is the concentration of dividend income in the very top income groups, with the top 1 per cent receiving half the total.

Third, the extent of inequality varies by type of income. Wages and salaries are less unequally distributed than property income, with income from self-employment intermediate between the two. This in turn implies that wage and salary income is less important to the top income group than it is, say, to the middle three quintiles, and self-employment and property income considerably more important. Only three eighths of the income received by the top 1 per cent comes from wages and salaries; the remainder is from self-employment (three eighths) and property income (one fourth). The three middle quintiles, on the other hand, rely mostly on earnings, with wages and salaries accounting for over four fifths of their income, and self-employment income, another 8 per cent. Transfer payments are the major source for the bottom quintile, constituting over half the group's income, with property and self-employment income relatively minor, perhaps 10 per cent of the total, and the remainder from wages and salaries.

4. The concept of wealth used in the Survey includes such assets as owner-occupied dwellings, automobiles, and checking accounts; the income concept, on the other hand, is limited to money income and hence excludes the nonmoney income, such as imputed interest and rent, that such assets yield. In addition, the income realized from investment in unincorporated enterprises is included in self-employment income rather than property income. If these forms of wealth are excluded from the wealth concept underlying line B1 of Table 7, so as to make the concept of wealth strictly comparable with the concept of property income, and the shares of the income groups in wealth recomputed, the shares would be virtually identical with the corresponding shares in property income shown in line B5.

The broad picture that emerges from these studies—substantial inequality in the distribution of income and wealth, and differential dependence of lower and upper income groups on income from labor, from property ownership, and from transfer payments —is not likely to be altered by future research, although many details remain to be filled in.

DETERMINANTS OF INEQUALITY

More than ethical and factual questions are involved in the issue of inequality. In an economy such as ours the distribution of income is to a large extent a market-determined phenomenon, the outcome of which depends not only on the pattern of ownership of productive resources, but of a price system, which places relatively high values on units of resources in scarce supply relative to the demand for them, and lower values on relatively more abundant resources. While transfer incomes are largely independent of the market place, being determined for the most part by government policy on income redistribution, they are a rather small proportion, no more than 8 or 9 per cent, of personal income. The other two sources—labor income and income from property—must be analyzed within the framework of market forces.[5]

Labor income is the most important single source of income for most recipients, accounting for close to four fifths of the total, whether it be in personal or national income. Sources of differences in the earnings of individual workers have been analyzed by economists, since the days of Adam Smith, in terms of demand and supply. George Stigler emphasizes those sources of dispersion in earnings which would be present even in a fully employed economy with an efficiently functioning, competitive price (and wage) system and a high degree of labor mobility. Under these

5. Self-employment income—income from an unincorporated business or professional practice—contains elements of both labor income (from the labor of proprietors or partners actively engaged in the business) and property income (from the use of assets owned by the self-employed in their own businesses). This type of income need not be discussed separately; the analysis of inequality in terms of labor and property income can be applied to these corresponding components in self-employment income.

conditions the forces of competition will tend to equalize rates of pay for equally attractive jobs requiring the same degree of training and ability and subject to the same uncertainties, such as the risk of temporary unemployment or disability. But the latter factors can produce substantial inequality in wage and salary incomes even in a competitive equilibrium, as Stigler points out. Some inequality is a consequence of the fact that our measures are usually expressed in terms of money rather than real income or "utility," and leave out of account such things as nonmonetary advantages or disadvantages of the occupation, differences in hours worked because of differing preferences for leisure, geographic differences in living costs, and differing preferences with respect to taking risks (a point emphasized in the article by Friedman). Another part arises because wages are taken gross of occupational expenses and costs of training (a point similar to that raised by de Jouvenel), although, as Stigler observes, the dividing line between occupational, and even educational, costs on the one hand and ultimate consumption expenditures on the other is fuzzy at best. Some inequality, however, would be present no matter how we chose to modify the income concept or how perfect the degree of competition (for example, those differences in "ability" which limit the supply of workers in particular occupations relative to the demand for them).

An explanation of competitive differentials in labor earnings in a fully employed economy is far from the whole story. The exercise of monopoly power may serve to raise the earnings of organized groups relative to others already below them in the income scale. Discrimination may push down the earnings of minority groups. Technical progress or changes in tastes may make the acquired skills of some workers obsolete. A whole series of barriers to mobility, which are subsumed under the heading of "imperfections to competition," may prevent the kind of earnings equalization the competitive theory presupposes.

Another force affecting the extent of inequality is the overall level of unemployment. As Professor Tobin eloquently argues in his essay on the Negro poor in Part Five, the failure to preserve full employment and a consequent tight labor market through the exercise of monetary and fiscal policy widens the dispersion of earnings, particularly for those at the bottom of the distribution. Not only does a deficiency of aggregate demand push some workers into part-time or full-time idleness or even out of the labor force entirely, but it widens wage differentials between skilled and unskilled workers and makes it more difficult to absorb low-paid agricultural workers, particularly from the South, into industrial employment. The reduction in unemployment is one explanation Solow offers in Part Two for the reduction in inequality from the Great Depression to World War II.

Inequality in the distribution of labor income among families depends not only on forces affecting inequality among individual earners, but on those influencing the number of earners per family. Empirical findings generally point to less inequality in the distribution of earnings among families than among individual persons. This latter aspect of the problem has received considerably less attention from economists, and Stigler's discussion of it should be viewed as suggestive rather than as a definitive treatment of the problem. It does not follow, for example, that distribution of family incomes in a world in which some wives as well as husbands work is necessarily more unequal than the family income distribution in a world in which only husbands work and wives stay at home, even if in the first world a wife's decision to work is independent of whether her husband does so. Only if there is a very close and direct relationship between the amount earned by a working wife and the corresponding size of her husband's earnings would the degree of inequality of family income be greater in the first world than in the second.[6] Of course, the tendency of wives to work more when their husband's incomes are less or are temporarily reduced is, as Stigler points out, an equalizing force.

6. The change in dispersion in this context may be measured by either the Gini concentration ratio or the coefficient of variation. The precise relationship between the inequality of husbands' earnings and the inequality of family earnings after husbands' and wives' incomes have been combined depends on the degree of inequality in the distribution of wives' incomes relative to that of husbands', the ratio of the mean incomes of the two distributions, the correlation between husbands' and wives' labor force participation rates, and the correlation between the amounts of their earnings (if both work).

Meade, in the other reading in this section, focuses his attention on inequality in the second component of market-determined income—income from property. Inequality in this instance is not primarily the result of differences among income groups in rates of return on units of property, although Meade does point to the fact that the rich appear to obtain a somewhat higher rate of return on their wealth than do the less well-to-do.[7] On the other hand, while the distribution of "ownership" of workers among families appears to have an equalizing effect on family income, the distribution of property ownership is clearly disequalizing in its effect.

One force tending to perpetuate inequality in property ownership is the fact that the rich save a higher proportion of their income than do the less well-to-do, and the poor save almost nothing at all. As Lampman observes in Part Two, a given income size group, such as the top 1 per cent, can preserve its share of total wealth, say a third, over time, only if it does one third of all saving. If, say, it saves only a quarter of the total, its share in the annual increment to total wealth will be only a quarter, and its share of total wealth will gradually decline from a third to a fourth.

Meade's analysis is expressed somewhat differently. He finds that differential rates of growth of individual property holdings, which influence the extent of wealth concentration, depend for each individual on the ratio of his earnings to his receipt of property income and on the proportion of his income which he saves, the latter in turn being an increasing function of the size of his income and a decreasing function of the amount of wealth he has already accumulated. Two restraining influences on the indefinite growth of an individual's property that Meade finds are the decline in the ratio of his total income to his holding of property, as his property grows (since a smaller proportion of his income will come from earnings), and a decline in the proportion of his income which he saves (since his motive for further

7. This is explained by the fact that the composition of wealth shifts from consumer durable goods, houses, and bank accounts to higher yielding assets as the wealth of the family increases. For evidence, see the selection from Projector and Weiss, pp. 89–90.

accumulation is weakened as his wealth grows). The analysis is of necessity complex, and Meade is more concerned with outlining the forces at work than in laying down precise solutions to the questions he raises.

The institution of inheritance undoubtedly tends to perpetuate inequality, although the precise outcome, assuming parents pass on their property to their children in more or less equal shares, is, as Meade observes, dependent on such sociological and demographic factors as the "degree of assortative mating" (the tendency of the rich to marry within their own class) and the "degree of differential fertility" (the tendency of rich parents to have fewer children than do poor parents). There may also be some genetic factor, as Meade suggests, which associates high wealth with high earning power, thus serving to preserve inequality in property ownership from one generation to the next.

Nothing has been said about the factors affecting the division of total income between labor income on the one hand and property income on the other. Answers to this age-old question in economics are beyond the scope of this volume. While the distribution of income between labor and property is usually considered to be relatively stable, there is evidence that the share of income from labor has been rising gradually, and the share of income from property falling, at least in the United States over the last forty years. The share of wages and salaries in national income rose from 57 per cent in 1929 to 60 per cent in 1948 and 66 per cent in 1965; the share of labor income inclusive of an allowance for the labor earnings of self-employed proprietors rose from 68 per cent in 1929 and 70 per cent in 1948 to 76 per cent in 1965.[8] Such a trend, if it continues, can be expected to have some equalizing effect on size distribution.

8. Computed from data published in *The National Income and Product Accounts of the United States, 1929–1965, Statistical Tables,* by the Office of Business Economics. I am indebted to James Caplan for carrying out the computations for these and other years by a method too detailed to describe here.

COMBATTING INEQUALITY

Each of the four authors in Part Four is concerned with the classical weapons for combatting inequality within the framework of a capitalist system—progressive taxation of income and wealth and the provision of social services, such as medical care and education, of particular benefit to the lower income groups. A common element in these articles is the progressive personal income tax, which has always been viewed as one of the most important redistributive devices. The contrast in views is sharpest, perhaps, between Friedman and Simons, where differing ethical positions are again brought to the fore. Friedman emphasizes the limited effectiveness of the tax in redistributing income in the United States and the need for reform of the tax structure to reduce its uneven incidence, a matter on which there is less controversy than on the appropriate degree of progression in the tax itself.[9]

All of the authors, as well as Wallich, earlier in the volume, are concerned with the effect of the income tax on incentives to work, take risks, and save, although Simons is inclined to dismiss all but the last.[10] Even if successful in reducing inequality, the tax attacks the previously examined sources of inequality only indirectly, largely by reducing the extent to which additional wealth can be acquired through saving. In this respect, it is more a tax on becoming wealthy than on being wealthy, as Friedman points out. One possible alternative which would mitigate this consequence is to tax property income, which comes from already accumulated wealth, at a higher rate than income from earnings.

9. The 1964 tax reduction reduced the degree of progression below the rates referred to by Friedman; the maximum rate is now 70 percent instead of 91 percent, and the marginal rate for taxable incomes in excess of $36,000 for married taxpayers filing joint returns is 45 percent instead of 50 percent. Simons, in the book from which the selection in this volume was drawn, also emphasized the need for tax reform.

10. A recent study of high income individuals indicates that tax considerations are of minor importance in their working and investment decisions. Cf. R. Barlow, H. E. Brazer, and J. N. Morgan, *Economic Behavior of the Affluent*, Brookings Institution (1966).

Another suggested by Meade is an annual tax on the value of wealth itself, although the latter form of the tax has rarely been used in the United States, except for real estate taxation at the state and local level.

Taxation of wealth at the time of death rather than annually has been much more important in American tax policy, although it would probably be fair to say that, along with income taxation, its redistributive effect has not been great. Death duties may take the form of estate taxation, where the tax is imposed directly on the wealth of the decedent before it is passed on to heirs, or inheritance (bequest) taxation, where the tax is imposed on the amount received by each heir. Such taxation has been of interest to economists since the days of Jeremy Bentham and John Stuart Mill; Pigou refers to refinements in inheritance taxation suggested nearly a half century ago. Meade examines several plans, favoring those that would tax bequests according to the size of the beneficiary's wealth or to the amount he has already inherited or received by way of gift. These, according to Meade, would encourage property-holders to pass on their property in small parcels to those without much wealth, producing less inequality in wealth-holdings even apart from the amount taken in tax.

Simons is more concerned about the effect of progressive taxation on the amount of private saving and wealth accumulation. He considers it likely that a progressive rate of taxation will lead to lower private saving, not so much by reducing the incentive to save out of a given income as by reducing the ability to save through the consequent reduction in after-tax income.[11] Here again a question of goals arises, with Simons questioning—and Wallich in an earlier section arguing for—the importance of economic growth to which private capital accumulation contributes. If the reduction in private saving does prove to be a problem, a possible solution would be an offsetting increase in government saving. Such a policy need not, at least for some time, lead to any

11. Redistribution from high to low income groups by a combination of progressive taxes and transfer payments so as to leave private disposable income unchanged will reduce total private saving only if the poor save less out of each *additional* dollar of income than do the rich, that is, if the marginal propensity to save of the poor is less than that of the rich. Statistical evidence indicates that this difference, if any, is small, except perhaps for the very top income groups.

increase in government ownership of privately controlled wealth; as Simons points out, revenues from progressive taxation could simply be used to retire privately held government debt.

Professor Pigou gives a sympathetic account of the way in which inequality might be reduced by the establishment of socialism (where the latter is defined as government ownership and operation of the means of production), despite the fact that its introduction by other than confiscatory means would leave all the claims to wealth, although perhaps indirect ones, in private hands. The solution would ultimately be one of government saving taking the place of private saving.

Only Meade deals at any length with policies designed to reduce inequality in the distribution of labor incomes. One of the most important equalizing forces has undoubtedly been public investment in education and training. Insofar as jobs requiring more education and training are the more highly paid, such policies, by increasing the supply of those in higher paid occupations and reducing the supply of those in the more poorly paid fields, serve to narrow wage and salary differentials. Meade points out, however, that there are limits to the effectiveness of such policies in reducing dispersion by equalizing the future earning power of students and nonstudents. As emphasis on higher education and graduate training is increased, the process of education will become increasingly selective, with investment being concentrated in the ablest students, who will thereby be able to qualify for the highest paying jobs. Meade is concerned that the net effect may be to increase inequality, despite the fact that there would be a closer association between earnings and "ability." Again, conflicting goals, this time between equality and efficiency, may well be involved.

POVERTY

There is a close relation between the problems of poverty and of inequality; indeed, the former can simply be interpreted as a concern with the lowest part of the distribution, roughly, the lowest fifth (quintile) of income recipients. There is undoubtedly an ethical case for concern with poverty that cannot be made so eloquently for other parts of the distribution. The creation of a consensus on the need for undertaking policies to raise the incomes of the poor was unquestionably assisted by Michael Harrington's book, *The Other America*. In the first selection in Part Five he argues that the misery of the poor has become increasingly hidden from public view, and that much of our so-called welfare state legislation, such as social security, has failed to aid today's poor minority.

Harrington was also one of the first to attempt a measurement of the number of poor. Herman Miller summarizes more recent efforts to determine the size of the poor population; these measures do a better job of taking into account differences in the needs of farm and nonfarm families, of families and unrelated individuals, and of families of different sizes. The effect of these refinements is more on the composition of the poor than on their numbers, although other investigators have used a lower cutoff in determining the number of poor than did Harrington. In order to minimize the arbitrary character of a specific cutoff point for defining poverty, the study by the New School for Social Research, summarized in the selection from the book by Oscar Ornati, measures its incidence in terms of bands defined by three (instead of just one) income levels: minimum subsistence, minimum adequacy, and minimum comfort.

Since the American economy has experienced a rising standard of living, one would expect to find a historical decline in the number of the poor, or at least in their proportion to total population. If a fixed standard of living is used for measurement, such is indeed the case, as evidence cited by Miller shows. But disagreement exists on the appropriate standard to apply over time. If poverty is indeed a relative concept—relative to the kind of standard that society is able and willing to provide to the less fortunate at any particular moment of time—then the appropriate definition will vary from one year to the next. The New School poverty index, which is based on definitions of adequacy as embodied in social policy (for example, granting of relief) prevailing at the time, shows a much smaller decline in poverty, at least as measured by their minimum subsistence standard; for the other, higher standards, there has been virtually no reduction during the postwar period. Even more stringent standards for measuring a decline in poverty could be applied. One measure (not discussed in the readings) would in effect require a rise in the *share* of total income received by those in poverty; a fall in Ornati's poverty index, on the other hand, could occur even if the poor's slim share of the income pie were constant, provided society's aspirations for the poor were to rise less rapidly than society's real income. Such a criterion would virtually eliminate any distinction between a reduction of poverty and the redistribution of income.

Economic growth, even if it leads to some decline in poverty, is likely to do so only gradually, and positive measures are required if a faster rate of decline is desired. The important contrast in policy measures is between income transfers to the poor and efforts to raise their earning power. In the former vein, the solution proposed by the Ad Hoc Committee on the Triple Revolution is to guarantee everyone a minimum income as a matter of right. The short selection reproduced here does not give the Committee's complete rationale for the proposal; namely, that automation leads to increasing unemployment with the consequent necessity for a break in the traditional link between jobs and income, rather than to the need for providing a minimum income for the already existing poor. Their plan, however, does not depend for its validity on their own particular diagnosis of the causes of low income. In his comment on Lampman's paper on poverty, Harry Johnson also emphasizes the income guarantee approach in the war on poverty.

Other economists, however, are concerned with the effect of such income guarantees on the willingness to work: few people would have an incentive to take a job if its pay fell at or near the minimum guaranteed, since each dollar of earnings obtained would mean sacrificing one dollar of income through transfers. A possible solution might be a rate of subsidy less than 100 per cent, set at some bare minimum well below what those supporting an income guarantee would favor. An administrative scheme for handling the payment of such family allowances, as they are characterized by several authors, is the negative income tax, first proposed by Friedman. With the conventional income tax, not only do the poor have little or no tax to pay, but their incomes are usually less than the exemptions and deductions to which they would otherwise be entitled. The plan is simply to "refund" to them some proportion of the difference. Aspects of such a scheme are also discussed by Lampman and Tobin. Tobin is particularly critical of the disincentive effect of the present system of public assistance, although, unlike Friedman, he does not consider the plan a substitute for the social security system and unemployment insurance.

The income maintenance or supplement programs described above simply provide the poor with cash income and let them decide how to spend it. A case can also be made for using tax revenues to provide free public services to the poor instead of cash grants—public housing may be one, and Tobin points to medical care as another. Tawney's *Equality*, in fact, contains a strong argument for the use of revenue from redistributive taxation to provide free social services, rather than cash grants, for the lower income groups.

Income transfers are not the only, or even the best, solution, although Tobin's statement that "the reduction of inequality in earning capacity is the fundamental solution, and anything else is a stop gap" may not command universal assent. Tobin emphasizes the importance of creating a tight labor market through the use of monetary and fiscal policies. Such policies will in turn reinforce other policies designed to reduce unemployment among the poor, to assist the movement of workers out of poorly paid agricultural pursuits, to encourage employers to take a more flexible view of their job requirements, and to break down restrictive and discriminatory practices, which limit the earnings opportunities of other poor groups beside the Negro. Educational and manpower policies are also important elements in a program to increase the earning power of lower income groups. Other suggestions are contained in the paper by Professor Lampman.

The attack on poverty requires action on both the income maintenance and earning power fronts. In many cases—for example, families in which the potential breadwinner is aged, disabled, or needed for the care of minor children in the home—the appropriate emphasis would appear to be on the former. But many others can and want to earn an adequate living by their own efforts; for these, the appropriate task of public policy is to realize that potential.

PROBLEMS OF THE MODERN ECONOMY

Inequality and Poverty

PART ONE   The Goal of Equality

How Should Income Be Distributed?

JAMES E. MEADE and CHARLES J. HITCH

James E. Meade is currently Professor of Political Economy at the University of Cambridge. In this passage from An Introduction to Economic Analysis and Policy, *published in 1938, he summarizes the old utilitarian argument for equality. Charles J. Hitch, now Vice President for Business and Finance at the University of California at Berkeley, adapted Professor Meade's book for use by American readers.*

IN DISCUSSING THE PRINCIPLES on which the national income should be distributed we are concerned with many questions of an ethical nature, which it is not our purpose to discuss. Whether certain types of people 'deserve' more than others is not a question on which the economist can pass any significant judgment. It is held by some that people with greater ability deserve to earn more than people with smaller ability, while others hold that people with greater needs deserve more than people with fewer needs; these two principles are not necessarily compatible, since a man may have little ability and great needs or great ability and few needs. It is not an economic problem to decide between these two principles, although economic problems are involved as soon as the choice has been made and means are required to give effect to the choice. But in choosing the fundamental principle upon which income should be distributed there is one important economic consideration; the larger the income of any one in-

1

dividual in a given situation, i.e., with unchanged tastes, knowledge, and needs, the less important will it be for him to receive a given addition to his income. This is a fairly obvious rule, to which there are probably no important exceptions. If a man possesses an income of $1,000 a year, a $500 increase in his income will add a great deal to his satisfaction; whereas if he starts with an income of $100,000 a year the $500 increase will mean a much smaller addition to his satisfaction. This fact is expressed by saying that the marginal utility of income diminishes as income increases.

It is an easy extension of this argument to say that if there are two persons *with the same tastes and the same needs,* and if there is a certain income to be distributed between them, this income will 'go farthest' and will give the greatest total satisfaction if it is equally divided between them. This argument is not ethical; it does not assert that it is just or fair to divide the income equally between the two, but only that it is *economic* to do so, since the greatest amount of satisfaction can be derived in this way.[1]

The argument can be demonstrated by means of an example. Suppose that of two men with the same tastes and needs one has $2,000 a year and the other $3,000 a year. $1 will mean more to the first than to the second, and if we give the first man $2,001 instead of $2,000 we shall add to his satisfaction more than we subtract from the satisfaction of the second by giving him $2,999 instead of $3,000. We can go on increasing the combined satisfaction of the two men in this way until both have $2,500. If we transfer another $1 from the second to the first we shall diminish the satisfaction of the second by at least as much as we increase the satisfaction of the first; and as we continue to transfer income from the poorer to the richer we shall more and more certainly

1. The term 'economic' is here being used in a sense which has the sanction of ordinary usage, i.e. that it is 'economic' to act in such a way as to obtain the maximum satisfaction from limited resources. Some writers insist that 'economics' should deal only with the means of obtaining any given end, without implying that one particular end (i.e. maximum satisfaction) is itself 'economic.' The question is merely one of definition, and any reader who objects to this use of 'economic' may substitute an adjective more to his liking.

diminish the satisfaction of the poorer by a greater amount than we increase the satisfaction of the richer. If, therefore, the marginal utility of income diminishes as income increases, and if there are a number of persons with identical tastes and needs and a certain income to be distributed between them, the total satisfaction to be gained from this income will be greatest if the income is equally divided.

This argument must be modified if different persons have different needs and tastes. Let us suppose that of two persons with the same tastes one has greater needs than the other, because the one has dependents to support while the other has not. If both have the same income, it will be possible to increase the total satisfaction by transferring income from the person without dependents to the person with dependents, since the man with dependents will have unsatisfied needs which are more urgent than many of the desires which the independent person is able to gratify. In this case, if we wish to make a given income go farthest, the ideal principle of distribution is that the man with dependents should receive just so much more than the man without dependents that an extra $1 would add an equal amount to both men's satisfaction.

This argument can be extended to cover the case of persons with different tastes. If one man's pleasure is to work in his garden while another's is to travel abroad, the greatest satisfaction to be obtained from a given sum to be divided between them will not necessarily be achieved by an equal division. For, if the income were equally divided, it might be possible by transferring income from the gardener to the traveller to cause an increase in the traveller's satisfaction which is greater than the decrease in the gardener's satisfaction. It is not the task of the economist to determine whether in such circumstances it is just to divide income unequally. Some people may urge that—apart from differences in needs which arise from differences in the number of dependents and in expenditure upon medical services made necessary by differences in health—the state should distribute income equally, although this division means that the man with inexpensive tastes can satisfy his desires more fully than the man with expensive tastes. For it may be held that the state should aim at providing equality of opportunity for the satisfaction of desires. The economist can, however, aid clear judgment by pointing out that there is a divergence between an equal distribution of income and that distribution which will insure that the greatest total of satisfaction is obtained from the national income.

Let us consider the case of men with different tastes more fully. It may be that the gardener with simple tastes can get a great deal of enjoyment out of a simple life, while the traveller with expensive tastes is extremely unhappy if he cannot travel. To transfer income from the gardener to the traveller, and so to distribute income less equally, would in this case both increase the total satisfaction to be obtained from the sum to be divided, and would also make both men more nearly equal in their real enjoyment of life. But it may equally well be that the gardener with simple tastes is by nature unable to get as much out of life as the traveller, who can enjoy life a great deal even with a small income, but could add to his enjoyment very considerably by having still greater opportunities. In this case to transfer income from the gardener to the traveller, and so to distribute income unequally, will increase the total satisfaction obtained, but at the same time will increase the inequality in the real satisfaction which the two men are getting from their incomes. The gardener was at the start less satisfied than the traveller because he was unable to get so much enjoyment out of the same income, and he will remain so.

These simple examples show that there is a divergence between the principles involved in distributing income:

1. so that every one has the same opportunity of satisfying his needs;

2. so that every one gets the same real satisfaction; and

3. so that the total satisfaction obtained is the greatest possible. The first involves equal money incomes, after allowances have been made for needs such as dependents and ill health; the second involves giving more income to the man who is hard to please and less to the man who is easily satisfied; and the third principle involves distributing income in such a way that the last $1 received by every one satisfies equally urgent desires.

There is a possible objection to the whole of this argument. While it may be admitted that the marginal utility of income diminishes as income increases in the case of each individual, it may be denied that the marginal utility of income to different persons can be compared. It would then be meaningless even to ask whether total satisfaction could be increased by transferring income from one person to another. If, therefore, it were decided that one man's enjoyment cannot be compared with another's, the whole foundation for any economic arguments about the distribution of income would be removed. Yet common sense demands that we should compare different men's satisfactions. If there is any meaning in saying that to take $1 from a millionaire and to give it to a starving man does more to satisfy the starving man than to dissatisfy the millionaire, then logically we must admit that the feelings of different men are commensurable. It may be that in innumerable cases there is too little evidence even to guess whether $1 means more to A than to B; but this must be because we have not got the necessary information and not because it is nonsense to attempt to compare A's feelings with B's.

The economist can therefore argue that, if it is considered desirable to maximize total satisfactions, the third principle mentioned above should be chosen. This is a purely economic judgment. We shall assume that it is desirable to make total satisfaction as great as possible and that the national income should, accordingly, be distributed in such a way that the marginal utility of income is the same to every one. As we have shown, if all men had the same tastes and the same needs, this principle of distribution would involve an equal distribution of income. It is difficult to make fair allowances for differences in tastes; but there is one important difference in needs—namely the size of the dependent family—for which allowances can and should be made. In order to get the more out of a given national income, this income should be distributed in equal amounts to each *person* rather than in equal amounts to each *family* regardless of its size.

The Ethics of Redistribution

*Bertrand de Jouvenel is a contemporary French political philoso-
pher. In this passage from his book,* The Ethics of Redistribution,
he criticizes the utilitarian argument for redistribution.

REDISTRIBUTION STARTED with a feeling that some have too little
and some too much. When attempts are made to express this
feeling more precisely, two formulae are spontaneously offered.
The first we may call objective, the second subjective. The objective formula is based upon an idea of a decent way of life
beneath which no one should fall and above which other ways
of life are desirable and acceptable within a certain range. The
subjective formula is not based upon a notion of what is objectively good for men but can be roughly stated as follows:
"The richer would feel their loss less than the poorer would
appreciate their gain." Thus Professor Pigou: "It is evident that
any transference of income from a relatively rich man to a relatively poor man of similar temperament, since it enables more
intense wants to be satisfied at the expense of less intense wants,
must increase the aggregate sum of satisfactions."[1] This statement, by virtue of its informality, is more readily accepted than
Professor Lerner's imposing: "Total satisfaction is maximized by
that division of incomes which equalizes the marginal utilities
of income of all the individuals in the society."[2]

Marginal utility of income is really a fancy name for the satisfaction or pleasure derived from the last unit of income. Let
this be £10. Professor Lerner's statement means that income is
well distributed when the loss of £10 would cause the same dis-

1. A. C. Pigou, *Economics of Welfare*, 4th ed. (London, 1948), p.89.
2. A. P. Lerner, *The Economics of Control*, 3rd ed. (1947), chap.II, p.29.

comfort to any member of the society. Professor Pigou's statement means that the shift of £10 from one individual to another is justified as long as in new hands the £10 will yield more satisfaction than in the former.

Professor Robbins has argued,[3] with his usual elegance, that the stretching of diminishing marginal utility to income is unwarranted, that marginalism in this field involves a comparison of the satisfactions of different persons, and thus falls into the very trap that in its legitimate applications it had sought to avoid. Satisfactions of different persons cannot, he says, be measured with a common rod.

This argument, however, turns out a boon in disguise to the welfarist who had saddled himself with the impossible task of equating the marginal utilities of different individuals. By proving this a stalemate, Professor Robbins unwillingly induces a new move: "The probable value of total satisfactions is maximized by dividing income *evenly*" (Lerner).[4] It is not necessary to dwell upon Professor Lerner's demonstration, which rests upon the highly artificial assumptions that the initial condition is one of equality and that moves away from it are haphazard. The strength of the case for even distribution does not lie in this formal reasoning. It lies in that, as soon as equal distribution is proposed as the solution to the maximization of satisfactions, those who oppose it have laid upon themselves the burden of proving that those who in fact draw the greater incomes have the greater capacity for enjoyment—an undertaking in which they cannot fail to shock every presupposition of a democratic society.

Therefore, in a discussion of the maximization of satisfactions, however the ball is set rolling, it must come to rest on the solution of even distribution. That, however, is on the assumption that the holders of incomes have not developed their lives and tastes in accordance with their incomes, a qualification rightly stressed by Professor Pigou.[5]

3. Lionel Robbins, *An Essay on the Nature and Significance of Economic Science,* 2nd ed. (London, 1935), chap. VI.

4. Lerner, *op. cit.* pp. 29–32.

5. Pigou, *A Study in Public Finance,* 3rd ed. (London, 1947), p.90.

Let us however notice a certain consequence of equalization. Let us grant that any differences in tastes due to social habits have been erased. Men will not however be uniform in character; some differences in tastes must exist among individuals. Economic demand will not any more be weighted by differences in individual incomes that will have been abolished: it will be weighted solely by numbers. It is clear that those goods and services in demand by greater collections of individuals will be provided to those individuals more cheaply than other goods and services wanted by smaller collections of individuals will be provided to these latter. The satisfaction of minority wants will be more expensive than the satisfaction of majority wants. Members of a minority will be discriminated against.

There is nothing novel in this phenomenon. It is a regular feature of any economic society. People of uncommon tastes are at a disadvantage for the satisfaction of their wants. But they can and do endeavour to raise their incomes in order to pay for their distinctive wants. And this by the way is a most potent incentive; its efficiency is illustrated by the more than average effort, the higher incomes and the leading positions achieved by racial and religious minorities; what is true of these well-defined minorities is just as true of individuals presenting original traits. Sociologists will readily grant that, in a society where free competition obtains, the more active and the more successful are also those with the more uncommon personalities.

If, however, it is not open to those whose tastes differ from the common run to remedy their economic disadvantage by an increase in their incomes, then, in the name of equality, they will be enduring discrimination.[6]

Four consequences deserve notice. Firstly, personal hardship

6. Reading offers a minor but clear instance of the discrimination referred to. Say that the Primus household acquires every month twelve books of the shilling kind: the total cost is 12s. The Secundus household has different tastes which run to less popular books, costing from 7s. 6d. to 21s. If the Secundus household is to have the same amount of reading matter, it may have to spend something like £6.: ten times as much as the Primus household. This means, if incomes are equal, that in fact the Secundus household will be at a disadvantage for the satisfaction of its other needs (without having a greater quantity of reading-matter).

for individuals of original tastes; secondly, the loss to society of the special effort these people would make in order to satisfy their special needs; thirdly, the loss to society of the variety in ways of life resulting from successful efforts to satisfy special wants; fourthly, the loss to society of those activities which are supported by minority demands.

With respect to the latter point, it is a commonplace that things which are now provided inexpensively to the many, say spices or the newspaper, were originally luxuries which could be offered only because some few were willing and able to buy them at high prices. It is difficult to say what the economic development of the West would have been, had first things been put first, as reformers urge; that is, if the productive effort had been aimed at providing more of the things needed by all, to the exclusion of a greater variety of things desired by minorities. But the onus of proving that economic progress would have been as impressive surely rests with the reformers. History shows us that each successive enlargement of the opportunities to consume was linked with unequal distribution of means to consume.

THE EFFECT OF REDISTRIBUTION UPON SOCIETY

No one has attempted to draw the picture of the society which would result from radical redistribution, as called for by the logic of reasoning on the maximization of satisfactions. Even if one were to compromise on the extent of redistribution in such a society, it would still be one which would exclude the present modes of life of our leaders in every field: whether they are business men, public servants, artists, intellectuals or trade-unionists.

We have forbidden ourselves to contemplate any decrease in the activity of anyone, any lowering of production as a whole. But the reallocation of incomes would bring about a great shift in activities. The demand for some goods and services would be increased. The demand for others would drop or disappear. It is not beyond the skill of those economists who have specialized in consumer behaviour to calculate roughly how far the demand of certain items would rise and how far the demand of certain others would drop.

A number of the present activities of our society would fade out for lack of a buyer. Thereby Wicksteed's "misdirection of productive activities" would be redressed. This great economist argued with feeling that inequality of income distorts the allocation of productive resources; [7] efforts in a free market economy being directed to the point at which they will be best remunerated, the rich can draw such efforts away from the satisfaction of poor men's urgent wants to the satisfaction of rich men's whims; the big incomes are, so to speak, magnets attracting efforts away from their best application. In our reformed society this evil would be done away with.

I for one would see without chagrin the disappearance of many activities which serve the richer, but no one surely would gladly accept the disappearance of all the activities which find their market in the classes enjoying more than £500 of net income. The production of all first-quality goods would cease. The skill they demand would be lost and the taste they shape would be coarsened. The production of artistic and intellectual goods would be affected first and foremost. Who could buy paintings? Who even could buy books other than pulp?

Can we reconcile ourselves to the loss suffered by civilization if creative intellectual and artistic activities fail to find a market? We must if we follow the logic of the felicific calculus. If the two thousand guineas heretofore spent by two thousand buyers of an original piece of historical or philosophical research, are henceforth spent by forty-two thousand buyers of shilling books, aggregate satisfaction is very probably enhanced. There is therefore a gain to society, according to this mode of thought which represents society as a collection of independent consumers. Felicific calculus, counting in units of satisfactions afforded to individuals, cannot enter into its accounts the loss involved in the suppression of the piece of research. A fact which, by the way, brings to light the radically individualistic assumptions of a viewpoint usually labelled socialist.

7. P. H. Wicksteed, *Common Sense in Political Economy*, London, 1933, pp.189–91.

In fact, and although this entails an intellectual inconsistency, the most eager champions of income redistribution are highly sensitive to the cultural losses involved. And they press upon us a strong restorative. It is true that individuals will not be able to build up private libraries; but there will be bigger and better and ever more numerous public libraries. It is true that the producer of the book will not be sustained by individual buyers; but the author will be given a public grant, and so forth. All advocates of extreme redistribution couple it with most generous measures of state support for the whole superstructure of cultural activities. This calls for two comments. We shall deal first with the measures of compensation, and then with their significance.

THE MORE REDISTRIBUTION, THE MORE POWER TO THE STATE

Already, when stressing the loss of investment capital which would result from a redistribution of incomes, we found that the necessary counterpart of lopping off the tops of higher incomes was the diversion by the State from these incomes of as much, or almost as much, as they used to pour into investment; the assumption which followed logically was that the State would take care of investment: a great function, a great responsibility, and a great power.

Now we find that by making it impossible for individuals to support cultural activities out of their shrunken incomes, we have devolved upon the State another great function, another great power.

It then follows that the State finances, and therefore chooses, investments; and that it finances cultural activities, and must thenceforth choose which it supports. There being no private buyers left for books or paintings or other creative work, the State must support literature and the arts either as buyer or as provider of *beneficia* to the producers, or in both capacities.

This is a rather disquieting thought. How quickly this State mastery follows upon measures of redistribution we can judge by the enormous progress towards such mastery which has already followed from limited redistribution.

VALUES AND SATISFACTIONS

But the fact that redistributionists are eager to repair by State expenditure the degradation of higher activities which would result from redistribution left to itself is very significant. They want to prevent a loss of values. Does this make sense? In the whole process of reasoning which sought to justify redistribution rationally, it was assumed that the individual's satisfaction was to be maximized and that the maximization of the sum of individual satisfactions was to be sought. It was granted for argument's sake that the sum of individual satisfactions may be maximized when incomes are equalized. But in this condition of income equality, if it be the best, must not market values set by the buyers and the resulting allocation of resources be, *ex hypothesi,* the best and most desirable? Is it not in direct contradiction with this whole line of reasoning to resume production of items that are not now in demand?

Surely, when we achieve the distribution of incomes which, it is claimed, maximizes the sum of satisfactions, we must let this distribution of incomes exert its influence upon the allocation of resources and productive activities, for it is only through this adjustment that the distribution of incomes is made meaningful. And when the resources are so allocated, we must not interfere with their disposition, since by doing so we shall, as a matter of course, decrease the sum of satisfactions. It is then an inconsistency, and a very blatant one, to intervene with state support for such cultural activities as do not find a market. Those who spontaneously correct their schemes of redistribution by schemes for such support are in fact denying that the ideal allocation of resources and activities is that which maximizes the sum of satisfactions.

But it is clear that by this denial the whole process of reasoning by which redistribution is justified falls to the ground. If we say that, although people would be better satisfied to spend a certain sum on needs they are more conscious of, we deprive them of this satisfaction in order to support a painter, we obviously lose the right to argue that James's income must go to the mass of the people because satisfaction will thereby be increased. For all we know, James may be supporting the painter.[8] We cannot accept the criterion of maximizing satisfactions when we are destroying private incomes, and then reject it when we are planning state expenditure.

The recognition that maximizing satisfactions may destroy values which we are all willing to restore at the cost of moving away from the position of maximal satisfaction destroys the criterion of maximizing satisfactions.

8. It is permissible to retort that the rich Jameses put great parts of their incomes to less laudable uses, and to argue that the public powers, taking over the incomes of the Jameses, will do more for culture than the rich had done. There is a strong case here (compare what the princes did for the arts from the Renaissance to the eighteenth century, with the services rendered by the *bourgeois* rich in the eighteenth century); but it is to be noted that what comes into discussion now is redistribution of power from individuals to the State, and not redistribution from the rich to the poor. Whether or not the State is better qualified than the rich to support the arts (and that very much depends on the nature of the government and the nature of the wealthy class), if the State's warrant for taking over the incomes of the rich is its mandate to maximize satisfactions of the national consumers, it is not entitled by that warrant to apply its takings to another object, thus moving away from the position of maximal overall satisfaction.

Inequality and Growth

HENRY C. WALLICH

In this selection from his book, The Cost of Freedom, *first published in 1962, Henry C. Wallich, Professor of Economics at Yale University, emphasizes problems of incentives and the importance of other goals in his discussion of equality. Professor Wallich was a member of the Council of Economic Advisers from 1959 to 1961.*

IN THE United States of America, in the year of prosperity 1957, some 5 per cent of the consumer units collected 20 per cent of total personal income. At the other end of the scale, 20 per cent had to make do with 5 per cent. Per consumer unit, the prosperous 5 per cent at the top had sixteen times more than their less successful countrymen at the bottom. These hard facts call for some hard thinking.

We have made great strides in our country toward political equality, and we have made a good advance also toward a classless society. Practically nobody in the United States thinks of himself as belonging to "the proletariat." It takes a sociologist with a research grant to discover an American aristocrat. How, then, do we reconcile economic inequality with our belief in political equality? If one man rates one soul and one vote, why should he be worth widely varying amounts of dollars?

For a partial answer, we can truthfully say that the real differences are not so big as they look in the *Statistical Abstract of the United States.* Figures don't lie, but they may distort. It can be pointed out, for instance, that the gap in living standards is much smaller than the gap in incomes. It is smaller, too, than the rich-poor gap in most other countries. And the living standards of even the lowest group in the United States are still well above the average standard of most of the people on the globe. The width of the rich-poor gap, moreover, has been shrinking during most of the industrial period, despite what many people seem to believe.

Yet the fact remains that the logic of our economic system demands some degree of economic inequality, even in the face of the egalitarianism of our political system. Economic incentives, if they work, mean that some men will earn more than others. We must now face up to the consequences of those recommendations. What have we let ourselves in for?

THE MORALS OF INEQUALITY

There is probably less to economic inequality than meets the eye. Nevertheless, there is still enough to make one uneasy and to compel one to search for either remedy or justification.

This reaction, which seems to come naturally in an egalitarian country, would not have come at all times and places. History knows many civilizations that were built on an unquestioning acceptance of inequality, political as well as economic. The glory of Greece and the grandeur of Rome were built on slavery. Plato's philosophy of government rejected equality in favor of a rigid hierarchy of classes. The teachings of the Church during the Middle Ages and its contemporary feudal society took inequality on earth as given by God and pleasing to Him. Our sensitivity to the problems of inequality is of surprisingly recent date.

This sensitivity to the injustice of unequal incomes varies not only in time, but also in space. Some European countries today seem to be more "sicklied o'er with the pale cast of thought" than the United States. But wherever the question arises, one observes two extremes between which the great majority find their places: Those who see nothing wrong with the existing distribution of incomes, or one even more unequal, and those who take for granted that the only fair shares are equal shares. Each side has its arguments to demonstrate that its position is "naturally just."

Those who approve of inequality usually point to the obvious facts of life. Human beings are biologically unequal. The equality that the Constitution speaks of is one of rights, not of condition —before God and the law, not in the market place. The basic truth of these propositions is undeniable, even though the readiness of their proponents to bear other people's poverty with fortitude is sometimes a little irritating. Yet perhaps not much is proved by truths such as these. If man is the master of his fate, why should he not correct the consequences of biological inequality if he finds them unattractive? We have gone some way in evening up what nature made uneven—why not go the whole way?

The supporters of inequality are fond also of saying that, after all, anybody can get rich if he tries hard enough. That is true enough in any particular case—leaving aside the question of whether the "case" has the ability to work his way to the top. It is conspicuously fallacious for the people as a whole. Even if the population of the United States consisted exclusively of men with the ability and determination of Rockefeller, Ford and Carnegie, they could not all be presidents of corporations. Circumstances—luck, connections and whatever—must inevitably lead a few to the top and keep the vast majority in the lower echelons. We cannot all get ahead of one another.

Finally, one often hears it said in support of income inequality that, after all, a man has a right to the fruits of his labor. If he is smart enough to make a million, why should he not be entitled to it? This principle carried conviction in the days when craftsmen and farmers really "made" what they lived by. Today it does not speak to us quite so clearly. When a man "makes" a million in business today, what is it he really makes, and how much of it is his own contribution? How much is contributed by his collaborators, his predecessors, by society at large? How much of it depends on the state of competition, the state of business and a host of other factors not demonstrably under his control? Economists believe that, under favorable conditions, they can calculate the contribution that an individual makes to the flow of production with the help of the marginal productivity doctrine. But they rarely have the courage to extract a moral claim from such calculations.

If those who regard economic inequality as "natural" fail to make a convincing case, those who go for equality as "the only just solution" perform no better. Righteous indignation and vicarious anguish at the sight of poverty do not add up to a logical demonstration. Equality of income as a principle of justice runs straight into the fact that men are unequal not only as producers but also as consumers. Some of us want an expensive education, some want to travel, some want great variety in clothes, living habits and entertainment—others may find all of this tiresome. Temperaments, moreover, may vary as well as tastes—we were created equal, but not equally cheerful. To endow everybody with equal income will certainly make for very unequal enjoyment and satisfaction. Perhaps some sort of allowance could be made for this. But in practice it would scarcely be feasible to determine for purposes of compensation how many drinks above or below par each individual happened to be born.

The plea for equality also offends the elementary feeling that there should be some relation between performance and reward. We cannot say, to be sure, that a man has a right to whatever he makes, because today there are few things of which we can say who really "made" them. Yet to say positively that a man has no right to what he makes seems to imply that someone else has a better right, which makes little sense. The right of any member of society to an equal share, moreover, would presumably depend on his having put forth a normal amount of effort. To hand a full share to those who not only do not succeed, but do not even try, will strike most people as perverse. Justice seems to escape the egalitarians as it has evaded those who believe in "natural" differences.

WHAT SORT OF INEQUALITY?

Part of this debate amounts to no more than a conflict between self-interest and sentimentality. But it has an honest core, and the wide differences that it reveals among men of good will point to a conflict deeper than pocketbook interest. This conflict can be pursued all the way up into the family history of our term "equality." Among the three sister virtues "liberty, equality, fraternity" which the French Revolution held before the world, "fraternity" originally possessed much of the emotional content today carried by equality. Equality, in turn, was closer to liberty —freedom from oppression and equal treatment under the law. But fraternity—probably too good for this world—early withdrew from public life. Equality, though a little dowdy and somewhat lacking in generosity, in part took her place. In her new and expanded guise she promptly fell out with her former ally, liberty: The compulsion to conform to uniform standards was discovered to be at odds with the right to be different.

The conflict between freedom and equality has become deeper

as equality increasingly has come to mean economic equality. By the same token, however, equality has lost a good part of its halo and much of the ready support that it formerly commanded. For looked at cold-bloodedly, what sort of an ideal is this economic equality? What claims to a fair-minded man's allegiance does it have, what sense does it make as a goal?

Equality of rights before the law is intuitively appealing as a social goal. Particular individuals might of course want for themselves greater powers and privileges than equality of rights would allow. But it is clear that their desires could be granted only at the expense of someone else. The sum total of rights and powers in a community remains fixed—it adds up to 100 per cent. In such a situation, equal sharing of rights and powers offers the obvious solution.

This obvious solution does not translate smoothly into economics. Here the obvious goal seems to be, not equal welfare, but maximum welfare. A man can have more than others and yet not take anything from them, if he creates his own surplus. Economic equality as such seems to bestow no particular blessings. A community where some were rich and the rest well provided for presumably would be considered better off than one in which all were equally poor. Economic equality, unlike its political counterpart, plainly is not an end in itself. It is only a means, designed to reduce poverty; perhaps it is not the most effective means.

That economic equality does not rank with political equality as a moral ideal is plain on several grounds. To demand that none have privileges I do not enjoy seems fair. To insist that none be richer is merely spiteful. People's behavior, moreover, makes clear that economic equality is rarely their true goal. What they strive for is betterment. Insofar as they compare themselves with others, it seems that emulation, the creation of invidious distinctions, as Thorstein Veblen has so well observed, turns out to be a stronger motive than desire for equality. Equality appears in the main as a steppingstone for the underdog on his way to becoming top dog. Once he is past the halfway mark, his interest in equality usually tends to abate. The successful self-made man characteristically seems to be far less concerned about the injustice of inequality than the man whose inheritance weighs heavily on his conscience. In matters of money, there are few who are prepared to say, as Walt Whitman did about democracy, "I will accept nothing that all cannot have on even terms."

I may have labored unnecessarily the simple conclusion that economic equality or inequality is not primarily a matter of justice. To speak against any form of equality, in our day and age, is uphill work. Yet it seems clear that the debate over justice in distribution largely misses its point. The real issue is not which division, equal or unequal, is the more just. The issue is which of the two leads to higher welfare for all. The functional, rather than the moral, aspects of distribution are what matter, and it is these we will look at now.

INEQUALITY AND PROGRESS

The Welfare Case for Equality · The case for greater equality can be established very simply. A dollar means less to a richer man than to a poorer. Therefore, if we take a dollar from the rich man and give it to the poor man, we hurt the rich man less than we help the poor. The sum total of their happiness rises by virtue of the operation. Happiness can be further increased by additional transfers and will reach its peak when everybody's income is up or down to the average and complete economic equality is achieved.

Scientific economics sees a fly in the egalitarian ointment. All we really know is that the millionth dollar means less than the thousandth *to the same man*. We cannot be sure that the millionth dollar means less to one man than the thousandth means to another. True enough, one of these men is rich, the other is poor. But perhaps the pauper is completely satisfied with what he has, while the millionaire is pressed for cash. Or perhaps the pauper is an insensitive clod, incapable of finer feelings, while the millionaire is a delicate aesthete who can exist only in complete luxury. More realistically, the millionaire is probably accustomed to his standard of living and the pauper to his. Even if they are fairly similar individuals, it may hurt the one more to cut his standard than it will cheer the other to increase his.

Rigorous economic theory, therefore, will not subscribe unqualifiedly to the egalitarians' doctrine that redistribution from rich to poor must increase total satisfaction. Nevertheless, for practical purposes, the case is pretty strong, the objections not very convincing. Individuals differ, but people in the mass fall into fairly stable patterns. I would hate to have to argue that the members of the upper income brackets are on average more sensitive and capable of greater enjoyment than the rest. And the unquestionable hardships that would result from a reduction of the upper living standards could be softened by spreading the process over a generation or two.

Thus put, the case for equality is impressive, simply on functional grounds and aside from questions of justice. It can hardly fail to predispose us in favor of greater rather than lesser equality, whenever this does not interfere with growth, or boomerang in other respects. In fact, however, it is apt to defeat itself in these respects more often than not. That will be the next step of the argument.

Growth vs. Redistribution · Once growth comes to be seen as an alternative to redistribution, its potential superiority in providing welfare becomes quickly apparent. Even those who are at the low end of the income scale stand to gain more, in the not-very-long run, from speedier progress than from redistribution. Redistribution is a one-shot operation. What it can do for the lower income groups amounts to less than its enthusiasts claim. Soaking the rich yields political dividends, but not much consumable revenue. And once it is done, the toll of a lower rate of progress is exacted continually thereafter. If the rate of income growth in an egalitarian economy is 2 per cent per year, and 4 per cent in one allowing itself a higher degree of inequality, it will not be many years before the middle class of the egalitarian economy is outdistanced by the "poor" of the other.

The proposition that rapid progress is worth more than redistribution even to the poor has been challenged occasionally. The critics argue that the standard of poverty rises with the standard of living. Accordingly, if we succeeded in doubling or quadrupling the average standard of living, those who fell below it would feel just as poor as they do today. To redistribute, to raise the poor closer to the average, would thus be a surer road to happiness.

Even on their own gloomy premises, these critics overlook one obvious flaw in their reasoning: What happens to the man above the average? If the poor man feels poor simply because he is below average no matter how well off he really is, the rich man presumably feels rich because he is above average. If some future New Deal averages the poor up, it must average the rich down. The first gain, but the others lose.

What really demands our attention here, however, is the gloomy premise itself, which says that apparently we can never get ahead of our needs. This economic relativity theory is profoundly pessimistic—in fact it seems to put an end to all meaningful economic endeavor. No matter how rich we get, the doctrine says, no matter how equally we split our wealth, as a community we shall never feel any better off.

There is probably more than a grain of truth in this doctrine. Man's capacity for enjoyment is limited, luxuries quickly become necessities, and money, as has been observed on occasion, is no guarantee of happiness. Material progress is just one part of the story. If man is constitutionally unable, as these critics seem to think, to achieve happiness, he can at least do something to reduce the positive ills of this vale of tears. Schopenhauer argued that while pleasure is an illusion, pain is real. With all our high standard of living, we still have enough sources of pain—illness, unprotected old age and, above all, lack of real leisure. So long as these are with us, there is little point in even wondering whether or not we would be made happier by more and more progress.

Those who take the gloomy view of man's capacity for happiness must bear in mind, besides, that one answer to their problem can be found precisely in the rapid progress which they want to sacrifice for the joys of equality. It is true that the satisfactions of having and being pall in time. But getting and becoming are always fresh sensations. Insofar as material welfare and creature comforts can do anything for men at all, it is their increase, more than their level, that brings satisfaction. Here lies such justification as one may find for singing the perhaps debatable praises of progress.

Creative Inequality · Let us put aside now the question of whether economic inequality is inequitable. Instead, let us look more searchingly at its constructive role in the economy.

One important explanation of, and reason for, inequality follows from the need to get the right people into the right jobs. It is wasteful if engineers do work that mechanics can handle, or if executives perform chores that could be done by their secretaries. A market economy avoids this by compelling business to compete for talent and to pay each man what he is worth in the job he can do best. The process admittedly works far from perfectly. Many of our income differentials arise from monopoly power rather than from greater productivity. This is true of some wage rates and salaries higher up the line, as well as of some of the profits of venture capital. The benefits of inequality of this sort—except to the recipients—are questionable. But even in more perfect markets, large differentials would arise.

These differentials could be taxed away, of course, as in part they are today. The effectiveness of the selection process, how- ever, suffers correspondingly. A high salary that one cannot keep is no great attraction. If the selection process results in large bonuses, efficiency demands that, in good part, they be left where they land.

Another instance of creative inequality presents itself when we turn to incentives. Here again, the logic of our system pro- duces inequalities that cannot be removed without slowing down the system itself. If we want good performance, we must hold out rewards. To be effective, rewards must raise one man above the other. Not their absolute level, but their differentiation, is what counts. Inequality once more proves to be the price of progress and efficiency.

It might be possible, of course, to shift the needed inequalities from the economic sphere to that of status, prestige and power. In part—to the extent that economic differentials are taxed away —that shift is likely to come automatically, even though unof- ficially. We should then be moving into the world of George Orwell's *Animal Farm*, where everybody is equal, but some are more equal than others. I see no reason to think that power and prestige differentials are any more "just" than economic ones. Certainly they could be a great deal more unpleasant.

If a thoroughgoing economic egalitarianism were to take hold, its chief victim probably would be the incentive to take risks. Successful risk-taking has built most of the big fortunes. It is here that the egalitarians would find their most inviting targets. It is here, also, that the conjunction between equality and stagnation might make itself felt most strongly.

The incentive to invest, to be sure, is not exclusively wedded to the profit motive. It is related to other motivations—competition, sheer expansionism, prestige. But remove profit and enough of the motive force probably will be gone to slow down the rest.

The ability to save is another important consequence of high incomes that has often been stressed. The rich, as has been correctly observed, can afford to save a good part of their incomes. The poor, unfortunately, save little or nothing. Leveling of incomes, it has therefore been thought, would perforce reduce the rate of saving. This argument was especially popular during the Great Depression, when saving tended to outrun investment opportunities. A cut in saving and a corresponding rise in consumption would then have aided recovery. Redistribution of income would have killed two birds with one tax hike.

To the credit of those who developed this doctrine and derived from it a pleasure perhaps more than intellectual, it must be said that they were also the first to discover that the doctrine may not fit the statistical evidence. What they discovered from income distribution data and personal budget studies was rather surprising. A man with $10,000 a year net may save $1,000 and a man with $4,000 may save nothing. But out of any dollar added to their respective incomes, both may save sums that are not so very different. In other words, it is true that the upper brackets save more of their *total* income; it is somewhat doubtful that they save much more than the poor also out of an *increase* in income. A change in income—up or down—seems to lead to a fairly similar change in saving for upper and lower brackets alike.

If this is so, a redistribution of income from rich to poor would cause the poor to begin saving possibly as much as the rich would cease to save. Redistribution, on these premises, would not greatly change the volume of saving out of current income. It would not help to cure a depression brought on by oversaving. By the same token, it would not greatly cut into the savings needed by a fast-growing, high-employment economy. The statistical facts which deprived the liberals of a favorite argument for redistribution have robbed conservatives of an old war horse in the struggle against the egalitarians.

The statistical findings, however, are not entirely clear cut.

It is not only the quantity but also the quality of savings that counts. Industry needs venture capital, and that is not usually supplied by insurance companies buying bonds nor even by pension funds buying blue chip stocks. Venture capital typically comes from wealthy individuals. To dry up their savings would still create an important gap in our financial structure, even though dollarwise they could be replaced from other sources. This much can fairly be argued by those who see a threat in equalization.

On the firing line against egalitarianism, we find also a belief, sometimes a little camouflaged, in the need for an elite—cultural, intellectual, political, economic. Stated in terms of a need for a privileged aristocracy, the view sounds offensive to American ears. The belief in the virtues of a leisure class, in particular, has taken a bad drubbing at the hands of Thorstein Veblen—in the one country where a leisure class proper has scarcely existed. But when the idea is reformulated in terms of "leadership," many people will probably be inclined to agree that something of this sort, based on merit, is needed. Most of the great achievements that history remembers or contemporaries admire are very clearly connected with the existence of a leadership group.

In a minor key, the need for leadership in consumption is readily arguable. Our own experience shows the advantages, for instance, of consumer pioneering. We are all ready to keep up with the Joneses, provided there are Joneses to keep up with. Anyone will buy something that is a necessity, but someone first has to smooth its transition from luxury to the more humdrum status. Conspicuous consumption, in a country constantly offering new kinds of goods, is creative consumption. An egalitarian society promises to be virtuous, frugal and dull.

These ideas do not lend themselves to quantification. It is impossible to say how concentrated wealth should be to stimulate the creation of luxuries, and how well spread to speed up their conversion to mass necessities. To push the need for consumer pioneering very hard smacks unpleasantly of snobbism. But to reject the notion altogether would be evidence of the very egalitarian conformism against which it protests.

One further point deserves to be made. Economic inequality is not purely an economic affair. It touches also upon political stability and social cohesion. In an extreme case, inequality may lead to revolution. So may overzealous efforts to reduce it. A distribution of income that is widely resented may, even though it is economically efficient, do more political harm than economic good. Slower progress would have to be written off as the cost of political and social betterment.

Added to its probable price in terms of growth, action to alter the distribution of income determined by the market is likely to impose a non-economic cost. Typically, this cost takes the form of lengthening the reach of government. Something, somebody, has to be registered, regulated, controlled. A little freedom always goes by the board. Some economic resources, too, that could perhaps be more productively employed must be shifted to this function. If anyone thinks that this is altogether a negligible matter, let him note the lack of enthusiasm with which taxpayers vote the means for even the most pressing functions of government.

How Much Inequality? · We may safely conclude that progress will come faster if some degree of inequality is tolerated. The right man must be put into the right job and given the right incentives. Savings must be kept flowing, and the taste for risk-taking kept alive. There must be scope for consumer pioneering. In addition, we can save ourselves some added regimentation if we are willing to push less hard for equality. All this supports the case for accepting a certain measure of inequality.

A certain measure—but how much? The range is wide, from literal and absolute equality to the equally implausible state of an Eastern potentate of the old days surrounded by a subsistence population. Neither condition commends itself as a base for progress.

Unfortunately, most of the considerations that argue against complete equality desert us when we want to know about the right degree of inequality. Only the market criterion has an answer. It says, in effect, "Put each man in the job which he does best, and pay him what he is worth in it." If we expand this idea to cover also the employment of peoples' savings—pay each type of capital, venturesome or timid or in between, what it produces in its proper use—we end up with a distribution of income according to the market's valuation.

But the market criterion is only one among several. If we judge the desirable degree of inequality according to the incentives that are needed, we may find that the market criterion overshoots the goal. A man may feel himself driven to do his best in response to a reward that would underpay him according to his market value. Why not tax away the difference?

The savings criterion, too, is tantalizingly unspecific. Would a strong concentration of income, if it tends toward higher saving, mean faster progress? It probably would, if that income is concentrated in the hands of an authoritarian government which channels into investment every cent above a low level of consumption. It would not lead to much progress, however, if the recipient were an old style potentate surrounded by a population without purchasing power, without wants—in short, without a market.

The consumer-pioneering criterion of inequality, finally, is likewise more emphatic than specific in its advice. What sort of inequality does it imply? The sort that enabled the Medicis to subsidize Renaissance art and literature? Or the kind that allows the Joneses to have a new portable grill ahead of the rest of us? In the absence of specific answers to such questions, the optimum inequality remains very much a matter of opinion, no matter how willing one may be to surrender equality as a goal in favor of growth.

Equality

R. H. TAWNEY

Professor R. H. Tawney, the distinguished British economic historian, presents a powerful argument against economic inequality in his book, Equality, *from which the following selection is taken. Delivered as the Halley Stewart Lectures for 1929 and first published in 1931, the book has become a classic.*

[THERE ARE] THOSE who have thought that a society was most likely to enjoy happiness and good will, and to turn both its human and material resources to the best account, if it cultivated as far as possible an equalitarian temper, and sought by its institutions to increase equality. It is obvious that, as things are today, no redistribution of wealth would bring general affluence, and that statisticians are within their rights in making merry with the idea that the equalization of incomes would make everyone rich. But, though riches are a good, they are not, nevertheless, the only good; and because greater production, which is concerned with the commodities to be consumed, is clearly important, it does not follow that greater equality, which is concerned with the relations between the human beings who consume them, is not important also. It is obvious that the word "Equality" possesses more than one meaning, and that the controversies surrounding it arise partly, at least, because the same term is employed with different connotations. Thus it may either purport to state a fact, or convey the expression of an ethical judgment. On the one hand, it may affirm that men are, on the whole, very similar in their natural endowments of character and intelligence. On the other hand, it may assert that, while they differ profoundly as individuals in capacity and character, they are equally entitled as human beings to consideration and respect, and that the well-being of a society is likely to be increased if it so plans its organization that whether their powers are great or small, all its members may be equally enabled to make the best of such powers as they possess.

If made in the first sense, the assertion of human equality is untenable. It is a piece of mythology against which irresistible evidence has been accumulated by biologists and psychologists. In the light of the data presented, the fact that, quite apart from differences of environment and opportunity, individuals differ widely in their natural endowments, and in their capacity to develop them by education, is not open to question.

The acceptance of that conclusion, nevertheless, makes a smaller breach in equalitarian doctrines than is sometimes supposed, for such doctrines have rarely been based on a denial of it. It is true, of course, that the psychological and political theory of the age between 1750 and 1850—the theory, for example, of thinkers so different as Helvétius and Adam Smith at the beginning of the period, and John Stuart Mill and Pierre Proudhon at the end of it—greatly underestimated the significance of inherited qualities, and greatly overestimated the plasticity of human nature. It may be doubted, however, whether it was quite that order of ideas which inspired the historical affirmations of human equality, even in the age when such ideas were still in fashion.

It is difficult for even the most sanguine of assemblies to retain for more than one meeting the belief that Providence has bestowed an equal measure of intelligence upon all its members. When the Americans declared it to be a self-evident truth that all men are created equal, they were thinking less of the admirable racial qualities of the inhabitants of the New World than of their political and economic relations with the Old, and would have remained unconvinced that those relations should continue even in the face of proofs of biological inferiority. When the French, who a century and a half ago preached the equalitarian idea with the same fervent conviction as is shown today by the rulers of Russia in denouncing it, set that idea side by side with liberty and fraternity as the motto of a new world, they did not mean that all men are equally intelligent or equally virtuous, any more than that they are equally tall or equally fat, but that the unity of their national life should no longer be torn to pieces by obsolete property rights and meaningless juristic distinctions.

Few men have been more acutely sensitive than Mill to the importance of encouraging the widest possible diversities of mind and taste. In arguing that "the best state for human nature is that in which, while no one is poor, no one desires to be richer," and urging that social policy should be directed to increasing equality, he did not intend to convey that it should suppress varieties of individual genius and character, but that it was only in a society marked by a large measure of economic equality that such varieties were likely to find their full expression and due meed of appreciation. Theologians have not, as a rule, been disposed to ignore the fact that there are diversities of gifts and degree above degree. When they tell us that all men are equal in the eyes of God, what they mean, it is to be presumed, is the truth expressed in the parable of the prodigal son—the truth that it is absurd and degrading for men to make much of their intellectual and moral superiority to each other, and still more of their superiority in the arts which bring wealth and power, because, judged by their place in any universal scheme, they are all infinitely great or infinitely small. And, when observers from the Dominions, or from foreign countries, are struck by inequality as one of the special and outstanding characteristics of English social life, they do not mean that in other countries differences of personal quality are less important than in England. They mean, on the contrary, that they are more important, and that in England they tend to be obscured or obliterated behind differences of property and income, and the whole elaborate facade of a society that, compared with their own, seems stratified and hierarchical.

The equality which all these thinkers emphasize as desirable is not equality of capacity or attainment, but of circumstances, institutions, and manner of life. The inequality which they deplore is not inequality of personal gifts, but of the social and economic environment. They are concerned, not with a biological phenomenon, but with a spiritual relation and the conduct to be based on it. Their view, in short, is that, because men are men, social institutions—property rights, and the organization of industry, and the system of public health and education—should be planned, as far as is possible, to emphasize and strengthen, not the class differences which divide, but the common humanity which unites, them.

Such a view of the life which is proper to human beings may, of course, be criticized, as it often has been. But to suppose that it can be criticized effectively by pointing to the width of the intellectual and moral differences which distinguish individuals from each other is a solecism, an *ignoratio elenchi*. It is true, of course, that such differences are important, and that the advance of psychology has enabled them to be measured with a new precision, with results which are valuable in making possible both a closer adaptation of educational methods to individual needs and a more intelligent selection of varying aptitudes for different tasks. But to recognize a specific difference is one thing; to pass a general judgment of superiority or inferiority, still more to favour the first and neglect the second, is quite another. The nightingale, it has been remarked, was placed in the fourth class at the fowl show. Which of a number of varying individuals is to be judged superior to the rest depends upon the criterion which is applied, and the criterion is a matter of ethical judgment. That judgment will, if it is prudent, be tentative and provisional, since men's estimates of the relative desirability of initiative, decision, common sense, imagination, humility and sympathy appear, unfortunately, to differ, and the failures and fools—the Socrates and St. Francis—of one age are the sages and saints of another.

It is true, again, that human beings have, except as regards certain elementary, though still sadly neglected, matters of health and development, different requirements, and that these different requirements can be met satisfactorily only by varying forms of provision. But quality of provision is not identity of provision. It is to be achieved, not by treating different needs in the same way, but by devoting equal care to ensuring that they are met in the different ways most appropriate to them, as is done by a doctor who prescribes different regimens for different constitutions, or a teacher who develops different types of intelligence by different curricula. The more anxiously, indeed, a society endeavours to secure equality of consideration for all its members, the greater will be the differentiation of treatment which, when once their common human needs have been met, it accords to the special needs of different groups and individuals among them.

It is true, finally, that some men are inferior to others in respect of their intellectual endowments, and it is possible that the same is true of certain classes. It does not, however, follow from this fact that such individuals or classes should receive less consideration than others, or should be treated as inferior in respect of such matters as legal status, or health, or economic arrangements, which are within the control of the community.

It may, of course, be deemed expedient so to treat them. It may be thought advisable, as is sometimes urged today, to spend less liberally on the education of the slow than on that of the intelligent, or, in accordance with the practice of all ages, to show less respect for the poor than for the rich. But, in order to establish an inference, a major premise is necessary as well as a minor; and, if such discrimination on the part of society is desirable, its desirability must be shown by some other argument than the fact of inequality of intelligence and character. To convert a phenomenon, however interesting, into a principle, however respectable, is an error of logic. It is the confusion of a judgment of fact with a judgment of value—a confusion like that which was satirized by Montesquieu when he wrote, in his ironical defence of slavery: "The creatures in question are black from head to foot, and their noses are so flat that it is almost impossible to pity them. It is not to be supposed that God, an all-wise Being, can have lodged a soul—still less a good soul—in a body completely black."

Everyone recognizes the absurdity of such an argument when it is applied to matters within his personal knowledge and professional competence. Everyone realizes that, in order to justify inequalities of circumstances or opportunity by reference to differences of personal quality, it is necessary to show that the differences in question are relevant to the inequalities. Everyone now sees, for example, that it is not a valid argument against women's suffrage to urge, as used to be urged not so long ago, that women are physically weaker than men, since physical strength is not relevant to the question of the ability to exercise the franchise, or a valid argument in favour of slavery that some men are less intelligent than others, since it is not certain that slavery is the most suitable penalty for lack of intelligence.

Not everyone, however, is so quick to detect the fallacy when it is expressed in general terms. It is still possible, for example, for one eminent statesman to ridicule the demand for a diminution of economic inequalities on the ground that every mother knows that her children are not equal, without reflecting whether it is the habit of mothers to lavish care on the strong and neglect the delicate; and for another to dismiss the suggestion that greater economic equality is desirable, for the reason, apparently, that men are naturally unequal. It is probable, however, that the first does not think that the fact that some children are born with good digestions, and others with bad, is a reason for supplying good food to the former and bad food to the latter, rather than for giving to both food which is equal in quality but different in kind, and that the second does not suppose that the natural inequality of men makes legal equality a contemptible principle. On the contrary, when ministers of the Crown responsible for the administration of justice to the nation, they both took for granted the desirability and existence, at any rate on paper, of legal equality. Yet in the eighteenth century statesmen of equal eminence in France and Germany, and in the nineteenth century influential thinkers in Russia and the United States, and, indeed, the ruling classes of Europe almost everywhere at a not very distant period, all were disposed to think that, since men are naturally unequal, the admission of a general equality of legal status would be the end of civilization.

Our modern statesmen do not agree with that view, for, thanks to the struggles of the past, they have inherited a tradition of legal equality, and, fortified by that tradition, they see that the fact that men are naturally unequal is not relevant to the question whether they should or should not be treated as equal before the law. But they have not inherited a tradition of economic equality, for that tradition has still to be created. Hence they do not see that the existence of differences of personal capacity and attainment is as irrelevant to the question whether it is desirable that the social environment and economic organization should be made more conducive to equality as it is to the question of equality before the law, which itself, as we have said, seemed just as monstrous a doctrine to conservative thinkers in the past as the suggestion of greater economic equality seems to them today.

Perhaps, therefore, the remote Victorian thinkers, like Matthew Arnold and Mill, who commended equality to their fellow-countrymen as one source of peace and happiness, were not speaking so unadvisedly as at first sight might appear. They did not deny that men have unequal gifts, or suggest that all of them are capable of earning £10,000 a year, or of making a brilliant show when their natural endowments are rigorously sifted and appraised with exactitude. What they were concerned to emphasize is something more elementary and commonplace. It is the fact that, in spite of their varying characters and capacities, men possess in their common humanity a quality which is worth cultivating, and that a community is most likely to make the most of that quality if it takes it into account in planning its economic organization and social institutions—if it stresses lightly differences of wealth and birth and social position, and establishes on firm foundations institutions which meet common needs, and are a source of common enlightenment and common enjoyment. The individual differences of which so much is made, they would have said, will always survive, and they are to be welcomed, not regretted. But their existence is no reason for not seeking to establish the largest possible measure of equality of environment, and circumstance, and opportunity. On the contrary, it is a reason for redoubling our efforts to establish it, in order to ensure that these diversities of gifts may come to fruition.

It may well be the case that capricious inequalities are in some measure inevitable, in the sense that, like crime and disease, they are a malady which the most rigorous precautions cannot wholly overcome. But, when crime is known as crime, and disease as disease, the ravages of both are circumscribed by the mere fact that they are recognized for what they are, and described by their proper names, not by flattering euphemisms. And a society which is convinced that inequality is an evil need not be alarmed because the evil is one which cannot wholly be subdued. In recognizing the poison it will have armed itself with an antidote. It will have deprived inequality of its sting by stripping it of its esteem.

Humanism is the antithesis of materialism. Its essence is simple. It is the attitude which judges the externals of life by their effect in assisting or hindering the life of the spirit. It is the belief that the machinery of existence—property and material wealth and industrial organization, and the whole fabric and mechanism of social institutions—is to be regarded as means to an end, and that this end is the growth towards perfection of individual human beings. Its aim is to liberate and cultivate the powers which make for energy and refinement; and it is critical, therefore, of all forms of organization which sacrifice spontaneity to mechanism, or which seek, whether in the name of economic efficiency or of social equality, to reduce the variety of individual character and genius to a drab and monotonous uniformity. But it desires to cultivate these powers in all men, not only in a few. Resting, as it does, on the faith that the differences between men are less important and fundamental than their common humanity, it is the enemy of arbitrary and capricious divisions between different members of the human family, which are based, not upon what men, given suitable conditions, are capable of becoming, but on external distinctions between them, such as those created by birth or wealth.

Sharp contrasts of opportunity and circumstances, which deprive some classes of the means of development deemed essential for others, are sometimes defended on the ground that the result of abolishing them must be to produce, in the conventional phrase, a dead-level of mediocrity. Mediocrity, whether found in the valleys of society or, as not infrequently happens, among the peaks and eminences, is always to be deprecated. But whether a level is regrettable or not depends, after all, upon what is levelled.

Those who dread a dead-level of income or wealth do not dread, it seems, a dead-level of law and order, and of security for life and property. They do not complain that persons endowed by nature with unusual qualities of strength, audacity or cunning are artificially prevented from breaking into houses, or terrorizing their neighbours, or forging cheques. On the contrary, they maintain a system of police in order to ensure that powers of this kind are, as far as may be, reduced to impotence. They insist on establishing a dead-level in these matters, because they know that, by preventing the strong from using their strength to oppress the weak, and the unscrupulous from profiting by their cleverness to cheat the simple, they are not crippling the development of personality, but assisting it. They do not ignore the importance of maintaining a high standard of effort and achievement. On the contrary, they deprive certain kinds of achievement of their fruits, in order to encourage the pursuit of others more compatible with the improvement of individual character, and more conducive to the good of society.

Violence and cunning are not the only forces, however, which hamper the individual in the exercise of his powers, or which cause false standards of achievement to be substituted for true. There are also, in most societies, the special advantages conferred by wealth and property, and by the social institutions which favour them. If men are to respect each other for what they are, they must cease to respect each other for what they own. They must abolish, in short, the reverence for riches. And, human nature being what it is, in order to abolish the reverence for riches, they must make impossible the existence of a class which is important merely because it is rich.

The existence of opportunities to move from point to point on an economic scale, and to mount from humble origins to success and affluence, is a condition both of social well-being and of individual happiness, and impediments which deny them to some, while lavishing them on others, are injurious to both. But opportunities to "rise" are not a substitute for a large measure of practical equality, nor do they make immaterial the existence of sharp disparities of income and social condition. On the contrary, it is only the presence of a high degree of practical equality which can diffuse and generalize opportunities to rise. The existence of such opportunities in fact, and not merely in form, depends, not only upon an open road, but upon an equal start. It is precisely, of course, when capacity is aided by a high level of general well-being in the *milieu* surrounding it, that its ascent is most likely to be regular and rapid, rather than fitful and intermittent.

If a high degree of practical equality is necessary to social well-being, because without it ability cannot find its way to its true vocation, it is necessary also for another and more fundamental reason. It is necessary because a community requires unity as well as diversity, and because, important as it is to discriminate between different powers, it is even more important to provide for common needs. Clever people, who possess exceptional gifts themselves, are naturally impressed by exceptional gifts in others, and desire, when they consider the matter at all, that society should be organized to offer a career to exceptional talent, though they rarely understand the full scope and implications of the revolution they are preaching. But, in the conditions characteristic of large-scale economic organization, in which ninety per cent of the population are wage-earners, and not more than ten per cent employers, farmers, independent workers or engaged in professions, it is obviously, whatever the level of individual intelligence and the degree of social fluidity, a statistical impossibility for more than a small fraction of the former to enter the ranks of the latter; and a community cannot be built upon exceptional talent alone, though it would be a poor thing without it. Social well-being does not only depend upon intelligent leadership; it also depends upon cohesion and solidarity. It implies the existence, not merely of opportunities to ascend, but of a high level of general culture, and a strong sense of common interests, and the diffusion throughout society of a conviction that civilization is not the business of an élite alone, but a common enterprise which is the concern of all. And individual happiness does not only require that men should be free to rise to new positions of comfort and distinction; it also requires that they should be able to lead a life of dignity and culture, whether they rise or not, and that, whatever their position on the economic scale may be, it shall be such as is fit to be occupied by men.

· · · · · ·

If every individual were reared in conditions as favourable to health as science can make them, received an equally thorough and stimulating education up to sixteen, and knew on reaching manhood that, given a reasonable measure of hard work and good fortune, he and his family could face the risks of life without being crushed by them, the most shocking of existing inequalities would be on the way to disappear. Sharp contrasts of pecuniary income might indeed remain, as long as society were too imperfectly civilized to put an end to them. But the range of life corrupted by their influence would be narrower than today. It would cease to be the rule for the rich to be rewarded, not only with riches, but with a preferential share of health and life, and for the penalty of the poor to be not merely poverty, but ignorance, sickness and premature death.

In reality, however, even inequalities of income would not continue in such conditions to be, either in magnitude or kind, what they are at present. They would be diminished both directly and indirectly—as a result of the diminution of large incomes by means of taxation, and through the removal of special advantages and adventitious disabilities arising from the unequal pressure of the social environment. Inherited wealth, in particular, would lose most of the importance which it has today. At present, when—after the payment of death duties—more than £400 millions pass by way of inheritance, its influence as a cause of social stratification remains overwhelming. It results, not merely in capricious disparities of fortune between individuals, but in the "hereditary inequality of economic status" between different classes. If the estate duties were increased, part of them required to be paid in land or securities, and a supplementary duty imposed, increasing with the number of times that a property passed at death, the social poison of inheritance would largely be neutralized. As the privileges conferred by it became a thing of the past, and the surplus elements in incomes were increasingly devoted to public purposes, while the means of health and education were equally diffused throughout the whole community, "the career open to talent," which today is a sham, would become a reality. The element of monopoly, which necessarily exists when certain groups have easier access than others to highly paid occupations, would be weakened, and the horizontal stratification, which is so characteristic a feature of English society, would be undermined. While diversities of income, corresponding to varieties of function and capacity, would survive, they would neither be heightened by capricious inequalities of circumstances and opportunity, nor perpetuated from generation to generation by the institution of inheritance. Differences of remuneration between different individuals might remain; contrasts between the civilization of different classes would vanish.

The Distribution of Income

MILTON FRIEDMAN

A contrasting view of the goal of equality is presented by Milton Friedman, Paul S. Russell Distinguished Service Professor at the University of Chicago. The following passage is from his book, Capitalism and Freedom *(1962).*

A CENTRAL ELEMENT IN the development of a collectivist sentiment in this century, at least in Western countries, has been a belief in equality of income as a social goal and a willingness to use the arm of the state to promote it. Two very different questions must be asked in evaluating this egalitarian sentiment and the egalitarian measures it has produced. The first is normative and ethical: what is the justification for state intervention to promote equality? The second is positive and scientific: what has been the effect of the measures actually taken?

THE ETHICS OF DISTRIBUTION

The ethical principle that would directly justify the distribution of income in a free market society is, "To each according to what he and the instruments he owns produces." The operation of even this principle implicitly depends on state action. Property rights are matters of law and social convention. As we have seen, their definition and enforcement is one of the primary functions of the state. The final distribution of income and wealth under the full operation of this principle may well depend markedly on the rules of property adopted.

What is the relation between this principle and another that seems ethically appealing, namely, equality of treatment? In part, the two principles are not contradictory. Payment in accordance with product may be necessary to achieve true equality of treatment. Given individuals whom we are prepared to regard as alike in ability and initial resources, if some have a greater taste for leisure and others for marketable goods, inequality of return through the market is necessary to achieve equality of total return or equality of treatment. One man may prefer a routine job with much time off for basking in the sun to a more exacting job paying a higher salary; another man may prefer the opposite. If both were paid equally in money, their incomes in a more fundamental sense would be unequal. Similarly, equal treatment requires that an individual be paid more for a dirty, unattractive job than for a pleasant rewarding one. Much observed inequality is of this kind. Differences of money income offset differences in other characteristics of the occupation or trade. In the jargon of economists, they are "equalizing differences" required to make the whole of the "net advantages," pecuniary and nonpecuniary, the same.

Another kind of inequality arises through the operation of the market is also required, in a somewhat more subtle sense, to produce equality of treatment, or to put it differently to satisfy men's tastes. It can be illustrated most simply by a lottery. Consider a group of individuals who initially have equal endowments and who all agree voluntarily to enter a lottery with very unequal prizes. The resultant inequality of income is surely required to permit the individuals in question to make the most of their initial equality. Redistribution of the income after the event is equivalent to denying them the opportunity to enter the lottery. This case is far more important in practice than would appear by taking the notion of a "lottery" literally. Individuals choose occupations, investments, and the like partly in accordance with their taste for uncertainty. The girl who tries to become a movie actress rather than a civil servant is deliberately choosing to enter a lottery; so is the individual who invests in penny uranium stocks rather than government bonds. Insurance is a way of expressing a taste for certainty. Even these examples do not indicate fully the extent to which actual inequality may be the result of arrangements designed to satisfy men's tastes. The very arrangements for paying and hiring people are affected by such preferences. If all potential movie actresses had a great dislike of uncertainty, there would tend to develop "co-operatives" of movie actresses, the members of which agreed in advance to share income receipts more or less evenly, thereby in effect providing themselves insurance through the pooling of risks. If such a preference were widespread, large diversified corporations combining risky and nonrisky ventures would become the rule. The wildcat oil prospector, the private proprietorship, the small partnership, would all become rare.

Indeed, this is one way to interpret governmental measures to redistribute income through progressive taxes and the like. It can be argued that for one reason or another, costs of administration perhaps, the market cannot produce the range of lotteries or the kind of lottery desired by the members of the community, and that progressive taxation is, as it were, a government enterprise to do so. I have no doubt that this view contains an element of truth. At the same time, it can hardly justify present taxation, if only because the taxes are imposed *after* it is already largely known who have drawn the prizes and who the blanks in the lottery of life, and the taxes are voted mostly by those who think they have drawn the blanks. One might, along these lines, justify one generation's voting the tax schedules to be applied to an as yet unborn generation. Any such procedure would, I conjecture, yield income tax schedules much less highly graduated than present schedules are, at least on paper.

Though much of the inequality of income produced by payment in accordance with product reflects "equalizing" differences or the satisfaction of men's tastes for uncertainty, a large part reflects initial differences in endowment, both of human capacities and of property. This is the part that raises the really difficult ethical issue.

It is widely argued that it is essential to distinguish between inequality in personal endowments and in property, and between inequalities arising from inherited wealth and from acquired wealth. Inequality resulting from differences in personal capacities, or from differences in wealth accumulated by the individual in question, are considered appropriate, or at least not so clearly inappropriate as differences resulting from inherited wealth.

This distinction is untenable. Is there any greater ethical justification for the high returns to the individual who inherits from his parents a peculiar voice for which there is a great demand than for the high returns to the individual who inherits property? The sons of Russian commissars surely have a higher expectation of income—perhaps also of liquidation—than the sons of peasants. Is this any more or less justifiable than the higher income expectation of the son of an American millionaire? We can look at this same question in another way. A parent who has wealth that he wishes to pass on to his child can do so in different ways. He can use a given sum of money to finance his child's training as, say, a certified public accountant, or to set him up in business, or to set up a trust fund yielding him a property income. In any of these cases, the child will have a higher income than he otherwise would. But in the first case, his income will be regarded as coming from human capacities; in the second, from profits; in the third, from inherited wealth. Is there any basis for distinguishing among these categories of receipts on ethical grounds? Finally, it seems illogical to say that a man is entitled to what he has produced by personal capacities or to the produce of the wealth he has accumulated, but that he is not entitled to pass any wealth on to his children; to say that a man may use his income for riotous living but may not give it to his heirs. Surely, the latter is one way to use what he has produced.

The fact that these arguments against the so-called capitalist ethic are invalid does not of course demonstrate that the capitalist ethic is an acceptable one. I find it difficult to justify either accepting or rejecting it, or to justify any alternative principle. I am led to the view that it cannot in and of itself be regarded as an ethical principle; that it must be regarded as instrumental or a corollary of some other principle such as freedom.

Some hypothetical examples may illustrate the fundamental difficulty. Suppose there are four Robinson Crusoes, independently marooned on four islands in the same neighborhood. One happened to land on a large and fruitful island which enables him to live easily and well. The others happened to land on tiny and rather barren islands from which they can barely scratch a living. One day, they discover the existence of one another. Of course, it would be generous of the Crusoe on the large island if he invited the others to join him and share its wealth. But suppose he does not. Would the other three be justified in joining forces and compelling him to share his wealth with them? Many a reader will be tempted to say yes. But before yielding to this temptation, consider precisely the same situation in different guise. Suppose you and three friends are walking along the street and you happen to spy and retrieve a $20 bill on the pavement. It would be generous of you, of course, if you were to divide it equally with them, or at least blow them to a drink. But suppose you do not. Would the other three be justified in joining forces and compelling you to share the $20 equally with them? I suspect most readers will be tempted to say no. And on further reflection, they may even conclude that the generous course of action is not itself clearly the "right" one. Are we prepared to urge on ourselves or our fellows that any person whose wealth exceeds the average of all persons in the world should immediately dispose of the excess by distributing it equally to all the rest of the world's inhabitants? We may admire and praise such action when undertaken by a few. But a universal "potlatch" would make a civilized world impossible.

In any event, two wrongs do not make a right. The unwillingness of the rich Robinson Crusoe or the lucky finder of the $20 bill to share his wealth does not justify the use of coercion by the others. Can we justify being judges in our own case, deciding on our own when we are entitled to use force to extract what we regard as our due from others? Or what we regard as not their due? Most differences of status or position or wealth can be regarded as the product of chance at a far enough remove. The man who is hard working and thrifty is to be regarded as "deserving"; yet these qualities owe much to the genes he was fortunate (or unfortunate?) enough to inherit.

Despite the lip service that we all pay to "merit" as compared to "chance," we are generally much readier to accept inequalities arising from chance than those clearly attributable to merit. The college professor whose colleague wins a sweepstake will envy him but is unlikely to bear him any malice or to feel unjustly treated. Let the colleague receive a trivial raise that makes his salary higher than the professor's own, and the professor is far more likely to feel aggrieved. After all, the goddess of chance, as of justice, is blind. The salary raise was a deliberate judgment of relative merit.

THE INSTRUMENTAL ROLE OF DISTRIBUTION ACCORDING TO PRODUCT

The operative function of payment in accordance with product in a market society is not primarily distributive, but allocative. The central principle of a market economy is cooperation through voluntary exchange. Individuals cooperate with others because they can in this way satisfy their own wants more effectively. But unless an individual receives the whole of what he adds to the product, he will enter into exchanges on the basis of what he can receive rather than what he can produce. Exchanges will not take place that would have been mutually beneficial if each party received what he contributed to the aggregate product. Payment in accordance with product is therefore necessary in order that resources be used most effectively, at least under a system depending on voluntary cooperation. Given sufficient knowledge, it might be that compulsion could be substituted for the incentive of reward, though I doubt that it could. One can shuffle inanimate objects around; one can compel individuals to be at certain places at certain times; but one can hardly compel individuals to put forward their best efforts. Put another way, the substitution of compulsion for cooperation changes the amount of resources available.

Though the essential function of payment in accordance with product in a market society is to enable resources to be allocated efficiently without compulsion, it is unlikely to be tolerated unless it is also regarded as yielding distributive justice. No society can be stable unless there is a basic core of value judgments that are unthinkingly accepted by the great bulk of its members. Some key institutions must be accepted as "absolutes," not simply as instrumental. I believe that payment in accordance with product has been, and, in large measure, still is, one of these accepted value judgments or institutions.

One can demonstrate this by examining the grounds on which the internal opponents of the capitalist system have attacked the distribution of income resulting from it. It is a distinguishing feature of the core of central values of a society that it is accepted alike by its members, whether they regard themselves as proponents or as opponents of the system of organization of the society. Even the severest internal critics of capitalism have implicitly accepted payment in accordance with product as ethically fair.

The most far-reaching criticism has come from the Marxists. Marx argued that labor was exploited. Why? Because labor produced the whole of the product but got only part of it; the rest is Marx's "surplus value." Even if the statements of fact implicit in this assertion were accepted, the value judgment follows only if one accepts the capitalist ethic. Labor is "exploited" only if labor is entitled to what it produces. If one accepts instead the Ruskinian premise, "to each according to his need, from each according to his ability"—whatever that may mean—it is necessary to compare what labor produces, not with what it gets but with its "ability", and to compare what labor gets, not with what it produces but with its "need."

The achievement of allocation of resources without compulsion is the major instrumental role in the market place of distribution in accordance with product. But it is not the only instrumental role of the resulting inequality. The role that inequality plays in providing independent foci of power to offset the centralization of political power, as well as the role that it plays in promoting civil freedom by providing "patrons" to finance the dissemination of unpopular or simply novel ideas should also be noted. In addition, in the economic sphere, it provides "patrons" to finance experimentation and the development of new products—to buy the first experimental automobiles and television sets, let alone impressionist paintings. Finally, it enables distribution to occur impersonally without the need for "authority"—a special facet of the general role of the market in effecting co-operation and co-ordination without coercion.

FACTS OF INCOME DISTRIBUTION

A capitalist system involving payment in accordance with product can be, and in practice is, characterized by considerable inequality of income and wealth. This fact is frequently misinterpreted to mean that capitalism and free enterprise produce wider inequality than alternative systems and, as a corollary, that the extension and development of capitalism has meant increased inequality. This misinterpretation is fostered by the misleading character of most published figures on the distribution of income, in particular their failure to distinguish short-run from long-run inequality. Let us look at some of the broader facts about the distribution of income.

One of the most striking facts which runs counter to many people's expectation has to do with the sources of income. The more capitalistic a country is, the smaller the fraction of income paid for the use of what is generally regarded as capital, and the larger the fraction paid for human services. In underdeveloped countries like India, Egypt, and so on, something like half of total income is property income. In the United States, roughly one-fifth is property income. And in other advanced capitalist countries, the proportion is not very different. Of course, these countries have much more capital than the primitive countries but they are even richer in the productive capacity of their residents; hence, the larger income from property is a smaller fraction of the total. The great achievement of capitalism has not been the accumulation of property, it has been the opportunities it has offered to men and women to extend and develop and improve their capacities. Yet the enemies of capitalism are fond of castigating it as materialist, and its friends all too often apologize for capitalism's materialism as a necessary cost of progress.

Another striking fact, contrary to popular conception, is that capitalism leads to less inequality than alternative systems of organization and that the development of capitalism has greatly lessened the extent of inequality. Comparisons over space and time alike confirm this view. There is surely drastically less inequality in Western capitalist societies like the Scandinavian countries, France, Britain, and the United States, than in a status society like India or a backward country like Egypt. Comparison with communist countries like Russia is more difficult because of paucity and unreliability of evidence. But if inequality is measured by differences in levels of living between the privileged and other classes, such inequality may well be decidedly less in capitalist than in communist countries. Among the Western countries alone, inequality appears to be less, in any meaningful sense, the more highly capitalist the country is: less in Britain than in France, less in the United States than in Britain—though these comparisons are rendered difficult by the problem of allowing for the intrinsic heterogeneity of populations; for a fair comparison, for example, one should perhaps compare the United States, not with the United Kingdom alone but with the United Kingdom plus the West Indies plus its African possessions.

With respect to changes over time, the economic progress achieved in the capitalist societies has been accompanied by a drastic diminution in inequality. As late as 1848, John Stuart Mill could write, "Hitherto [1848] it is questionable if all the mechanical inventions yet made have lightened the day's toil of any human being. They have enabled a greater population to live the same life of drudgery and imprisonment, and an increased number of manufacturers and others to make fortunes. They have increased the comforts of the middle classes. But they have not yet begun to effect those great changes in human destiny, which it is in their nature and in their futurity to accomplish." [1] This statement was probably not correct even for Mill's day, but certainly no one could write this today about the advanced capitalist countries. It is still true about the rest of the world.

The chief characteristic of progress and development over the past century is that it has freed the masses from backbreaking toil and has made available to them products and services that were formerly the monopoly of the upper classes, without in any corresponding way expanding the products and services available to the wealthy. Medicine aside, the advances in technology have for the most part simply made available to the masses of

1. *Principles of Political Economy* (Ashley edition; London: Longmans, Green & Co., 1909), p. 751.

the people luxuries that were always available in one form or another to the truly wealthy. Modern plumbing, central heating, automobiles, television, radio, to cite just a few examples, provide conveniences to the masses equivalent to those that the wealthy could always get by the use of servants, entertainers, and so on.

Detailed statistical evidence on these phenomena, in the form of meaningful and comparable distributions of income, is hard to come by, though such studies as have been made confirm the broad conclusions just outlined. Such statistical data, however, can be extremely misleading. They cannot segregate differences in income that are equalizing from those that are not. For example, the short working life of a baseball player means that the annual income during his active years must be much higher than in alternative pursuits open to him to make it equally attractive financially. But such a difference affects the figures in exactly the same way as any other difference in income. The income unit for which the figures are given is also of great importance. A distribution for individual income recipients always shows very much greater apparent inequality than a distribution for family units: many of the individuals are housewives working part-time or receiving a small amount of property income, or other family members in a similar position. Is the distribution that is relevant for families one in which the families are classified by total family income? Or by income per person? Or per equivalent unit? This is no mere quibble. I believe that the changing distribution of families by number of children is the most important single factor that has reduced inequality of levels of living in this country during the past half century. It has been far more important than graduated inheritance and income taxes. The really low levels of living were the joint product of relatively low family incomes and relatively large numbers of children. The average number of children has declined and, even more important, this decline has been accompanied and largely produced by a virtual elimination of the very large family. As a result, families now tend to differ much less with respect to number of children. Yet this change would not be reflected in a distribution of families by the size of total family income.

A major problem in interpreting evidence on the distribution of income is the need to distinguish two basically different kinds of inequality; temporary, short-run differences in income, and differences in long-run income status. Consider two societies that have the same distribution of annual income. In one there is great mobility and change so that the position of particular families in the income hierarchy varies widely from year to year. In the other, there is great rigidity so that each family stays in the same position year after year. Clearly, in any meaningful sense, the second would be the more unequal society. The one kind of inequality is a sign of dynamic change, social mobility, equality of opportunity; the other, of a status society. The confusion of these two kinds of inequality is particularly important, precisely because competitive free-enterprise capitalism tends to substitute the one for the other. Non-capitalist societies tend to have wider inequality than capitalist, even as measured by annual income; in addition, inequality in them tends to be permanent, whereas capitalism undermines status and introduces social mobility.

LIBERALISM AND EGALITARIANISM

The heart of the liberal philosophy is a belief in the dignity of the individual, in his freedom to make the most of his capacities and opportunities according to his own lights, subject only to the proviso that he not interfere with the freedom of other individuals to do the same. This implies a belief in the equality of men in one sense; in their inequality in another. Each man has an equal right to freedom. This is an important and fundamental right precisely because men are different, because one man will want to do different things with his freedom than another, and in the process can contribute more than another to the general culture of the society in which many men live.

The liberal will therefore distinguish sharply between equality of rights and equality of opportunity, on the one hand, and material equality or equality of outcome on the other. He may welcome the fact that a free society in fact tends toward greater material equality than any other yet tried. But he will regard this as a desirable by-product of a free society, not its major justification. He will welcome measures that promote both freedom and equality—such as measures to eliminate monopoly power and to improve the operation of the market. He will regard private charity directed at helping the less fortunate as an example of the proper use of freedom. And he may approve state action toward ameliorating poverty as a more effective way in which the great bulk of the community can achieve a common objective. He will do so with regret, however, at having to substitute compulsory for voluntary action.

The egalitarian will go this far, too. But he will want to go further. He will defend taking from some to give to others, not as a more effective means whereby the "some" can achieve an objective they want to achieve, but on grounds of "justice." At this point, equality comes sharply into conflict with freedom; one must choose. One cannot be both an egalitarian, in this sense, and a liberal.

PART TWO   The Measurement
of Inequality

Income Inequality Since the War

ROBERT M. SOLOW

Robert M. Solow, Professor of Economics at the Massachusetts Institute of Technology, examines changes in inequality from the prewar period through the late nineteen-fifties in this selection from an essay originally appearing in Postwar Economic Trends in the United States *(1960).*

OCCUPATIONAL EARNINGS DIFFERENTIALS

THERE ARE TWO KINDS OF INFORMATION which can be brought to bear on the problem of changes in the economic status of occupations and broader occupational groups. One is the census data on annual earnings by occupation. This is very neatly summarized by Herman P. Miller,[1] and this section is largely taken from there. Since the 1940 census collected income information only with respect to wages and salaries, our comparisons leave out of account any other sources of occupational income, self-employment in particular.

The basic fact is that between 1939 and 1951 wage and salary income became more equally distributed among recipients. The equalization is most noticeable among male workers, presumably because the increase in the proportion of part-time workers among women tends to distort the picture. Table 1 shows the

1. [Herman P. Miller, *Income of the American People* (New York, John Wiley & Sons, Inc., 1955), chs. V, VIII, IX, and Appendix C.—*Editor.*]

percentage of all wage or salary income received by each quintile of wage and salary earners for the years 1939, 1945, and 1951.

It is interesting to observe that most of the equalization process was complete by 1945. The direction of change thereafter was

TABLE 1. *Percentage of All Wage or Salary Income Received by Each Quintile of Wage of Salary Recipients 1939, 1945, 1951*

Wage or Salary Recipients	1939	1945	1951
Both sexes			
Lowest fifth	3.4	2.9	3.0
Second fifth	8.4	10.1	10.6
Third fifth	15.0	17.4	18.9
Fourth fifth	23.9	25.7	25.9
Highest fifth	49.3	43.9	41.6
Male			
Lowest fifth	3.5	3.8	4.9
Second fifth	9.0	12.4	13.1
Third fifth	15.5	18.5	19.3
Fourth fifth	23.3	25.4	24.4
Highest fifth	48.7	39.9	38.3

SOURCE: Herman P. Miller, *op. cit.*, p. 104.

the same, but further movement toward equality was rather slower, which suggests that the main cause of the equalization was the approach to full employment from the relatively depressed conditions before the war. Full employment was achieved during the war; the subsequent prosperity prevented any relapse, but there was less push toward further equalization. Years ago Horst Mendershausen pointed out that, although the wage share of aggregate income tended to rise in depressed times, the distribution of income within the working class tended to become more unequal, largely as a result of the uneven incidence of unemployment. It seems reasonable to attribute some of the change between 1939 and 1945 to the reduction in unemployment from one-sixth to something like 2 per cent of the labor force.

But a relatively tight labor market has still other effects on the structure of occupational earnings. Occupational differentials tend to narrow. (Secular forces seem to be working in this direction too.) Between 1939 and 1951 median wage or salary income of course increased sharply in all occupations. But the increases were relatively greatest among laborers, semiskilled workers, and skilled workers, and relatively less sharp among professional, managerial, clerical, and sales workers. Thus those groups which in 1939 were clustered toward the bottom of the ladder had the largest relative increases to 1951. In 1939 the median salary in the class of "managers, officials, and proprietors, excluding farm" was about three times the median wage of "laborers, except farm and mine." By 1951 it was less than twice as large.

For the decade following 1939, the tendency for the lower ranking occupations to gain relative to the better paid ones is observable even on a much finer occupational classification. For example, Miller gives figures for 118 occupations ranked by the median wage or salary income in 1949 (with only full-year workers included, to eliminate the direct effect of irregular employment). All the 17 occupations in which the median wage or salary income increased by 150 per cent or more were in the lowest paid half of the list; of the 33 occupations whose median income failed to double between 1939 and 1949, 29 were in the upper half of the list.

Two more changes contributing to the equalization need to be mentioned. Even within fairly narrow occupational classes income differentials decreased, at least among men. Whether intra-occupational irregularity is measured by the interquintile range or by the share of total income going to the highest fifth of recipients, there was a decrease in about nine-tenths of the occupations in the census classification.

Lastly, there was a slight shift in the occupational composition of the labor force, indicated in Table 2. The socially and economically lowest ranked occupations declined most in relative numbers, and the middle occupations gained more than the very top ones. These changes might be expected to contribute to both the over-all increase in the level of annual earnings and to their diminished dispersion.

The pattern of changes since 1950 has been slightly different. As Table 2 indicates, 1956 showed a gain in relative numbers for the professional and clerical groups, largely at the expense of the skilled and unskilled manual laborers and occupations connected with sales and agriculture. This probably represents a net upgrading, and probably also a slight further decline in inequality. As between 1940 and 1956, the major changes are the decline in agricultural occupations, the increase in professional, managerial, and clerical employment, and the redistribution within the group of manual workers, with the skilled and semiskilled categories gaining at the expense of unskilled and domestic service workers.

The economic implications of all this are clearer than the sociological ones. In particular, the movement out of agriculture is pretty clearly a response to the growth of better paid job opportunities in the urban-industrial sector; but it is less clear

TABLE 2. *Occupational Distribution of Employed Persons,*
1940, 1950, 1956

Major Occupation	1940	1950	1956 *
Professional, technical, and kindred	8.0	8.9	9.5
Farmers and farm managers	11.5	7.8	5.7
Managers, officials, and proprietors, except farm	8.1	9.1	9.9
Clerical and kindred	9.8	12.4	13.7
Sales	6.9	7.1	6.2
Craftsmen, foremen, and kindred	11.6	14.0	13.3
Operatives and kindred	18.1	20.1	19.8
Private household	4.7	2.5	3.3
Service, except private household	7.2	7.7	8.5
Farm laborers and foremen	7.0	4.3	4.5
Laborers, except farm and mine	7.0	6.2	5.6
Wage and salary workers	75.1	81.0	82.6
Self-employed	21.8	17.1	14.9
Unpaid family workers	3.1	2.0	2.2

* Average of April and October.
SOURCE: *Statistical Abstract of the United States,* 1957, p. 212.

that this is felt by the people involved as an unambiguous upward movement. A more careful analysis of the data would have to consider a more detailed breakdown, at least by sex and color. Otherwise some of the shifts may be misunderstood. For example, the increase in the percentage of clerical workers is for the most part a consequence of the heavier representation of women in the labor force. On the other hand the increase in the percentage of craftsmen and other skilled workers is largely masked by the influx of women. The apparent decrease in the skilled fraction between 1950 and 1956 hides an increase in the percentage of males in this category. The increase in service workers is also a phenomenon of the increasing employment of women.

Altogether, then, we have concluded that there has been in recent years a slight shift in favor of labor incomes and against incomes from property; at the same time, the distribution of people among occupations has changed in such a way as to promote equalization.[2] Similar movements have occurred in the earnings of various broad occupational groups and in the distribution of earnings within even narrow occupational groups. To anticipate another conclusion, the distribution of income by size has also become a bit, but only a bit, more equal in the last decade as compared with earlier periods. In view of the close connection between economic status and social status, all this suggests that postwar full employment has brought with it a consistent but slight narrowing of social-class differences. There has been no revolutionary reversal of traditional differentials, but merely a small equalization, in the economic field at least.

THE SIZE DISTRIBUTION OF INCOME

When all is said and done, one of the reasons we care about the distribution of income is that we care about the distinction between rich and poor. Particularly in a society whose ideology is heavily equalitarian, the existence of large inequalities in income is a source of intellectual puzzlement and emotional strain. The sources of inequality—how much is personal ability, whether genetic or environmental; how much is inherited

2. This trend is not a recent development. It goes back at least to 1910 and perhaps earlier. A recent study of the payrolls of a single factory over the period 1919–1954 confirms these conclusions. See L. Soltow, "Income Equality in a Factory Payroll," *Southern Economic Journal,* Vol. XXV (Jan. 1959), pp. 343–348.

wealth; how much is chance; how much is the tendency of any initial advantage to increase itself; how much is inherent in the social or economic rules of the game—all this is too deep a question to be discussed here. But we can at least sketch the facts of the size distribution of income in the years since the war and compare them with the earlier period and with concurrent developments in Europe.

Table 3 gives the relative distribution of personal income before personal income tax for 1935–1936 and at intervals during and since the war. Certainly, the most striking impression the figures make is to confirm the belief that this is a facet of economic life which changes slowly when it changes at all. Between the beginning and end of the period represented, real GNP

TABLE 3. *Distribution of Pre-Tax Personal Income by Quintiles and Top 5 Per Cent of Consumer Units, Selected Years*

Quintile	1935–1936	1941	1944	1947	1950	1954	1956	% Change 1935–1936 to 1954
Lowest	4.1	4.1	4.9	5.0	4.8	4.9	5.0	20
Second	9.2	9.5	10.9	11.0	11.0	11.4	11.3	24
Third	14.1	15.3	16.2	16.0	16.2	16.6	16.5	18
Fourth	20.9	22.3	22.2	22.0	22.3	22.4	22.3	7
Highest	51.7	48.8	45.8	46.0	45.7	44.7	44.9	− 14
Top 5%	26.5	24.0	20.7	20.9	20.4	20.5	20.1	− 19

SOURCES: S. Goldsmith *et al.*, "Size Distribution of Income since the Mid-Thirties," *Review of Economics and Statistics*, Vol. XXXVI (Feb. 1954), p. 9.

S. Goldsmith, "Income Distribution in the United States, 1952–1955," *Survey of Current Business*, June 1956, p. 12.

S. Goldsmith, "Size Distribution of Personal Income," *Survey of Current Business*, April 1958, p. 10.

[Estimates for 1929, 1959, and 1962, as well as the revised estimates for 1950, 1954, and 1956, may be found in Table 1, p. xii, of the Introduction.—*Editor*.]

increased 2.5 times, prices doubled, the unemployment rate fell from 20 per cent to 2.5 per cent; and against this background the relative distribution of income changed by inches. But change it did, and pretty consistently.

This leads to the second conclusion one can draw from Table 3 —that over two decades there was a distinct movement toward equality. In 1935 the 20 per cent of families with the highest incomes earned more than half of all the income. By 1954 this fraction had fallen by a seventh, and the top 20 per cent of families had a bit less than 45 per cent of the total. For the top 5 per cent of families the decline was even sharper. Their share of the melon diminished by a fifth from 26 per cent to 20 per cent in 1956. Each of the four lower quintiles increased its share of personal income, with the second highest quintile making a relative gain substantially smaller than the others.

A third conclusion is of some importance because it fits in with some observations made earlier. Most of the movement toward equalization was complete by 1947, possibly even by 1944. Since 1947 there has been a slight further tendency for the three middle quintiles to gain at the expense of the top fifth. But this change is small as compared with that distinguishing the prewar period from the postwar period as a whole. Once again the suggestion is that the source of the equalization was the full employment brought about in the first instance by the war and maintained with only minor interruptions since. The steady increase in the labor share of national income since 1950 seems to have made no visible difference to the size distribution of personal income. Quite possibly the position of functional groups within the income distribution has changed, but the over-all degree of inequality has not budged.

It should be remembered that the quintiles of Table 3 are not groups of constant membership. Family incomes rise and fall relative to each other regularly with the life cycle and irregularly with the varying fortunes of individuals, businesses, occupations, and industries. Moreover, the high end of the distribution in any year is likely to contain many families whose incomes are temporarily above their "normal" level, and conversely for the bottom group. Hence the over-all degree of income inequality (though not necessarily its trend over time) is exaggerated by distribution of annual income. A more useful measure of inequality would be provided by distributions of income over longer periods than a year, even up to lifetimes. Such distributions would of course show less inequality than the annual ones. How much less would depend on the degree of income mobility, on the rate and extent to which families circulate through the income pyramid. This is a fascinating and important question on which we have very little information.[3] Some figures are available for a few postwar years from the *Survey of Consumer Finances*,[4] but since I know of nothing comparable for prewar years, they are of little help. Of equal interest would be some light on income mobility between generations. This is where inherited wealth and early environmental advantage would play their parts.

There is some evidence that the rate of intergenerational *occupational* mobility remained roughly constant between 1910 and 1940. This statement is at least partly independent of the long-run changes in the occupational structure itself. The latter effect adds to the total of mobility. That the rate of occupational mobility should not have declined may be found surprising, since it has sometimes been argued that much of the occupational mobility of fifty years ago was attributable to such demographic factors as the flow of immigrants, who provided a pool of unskilled labor, and to the failure of the educated and professional groups to reproduce themselves. The impact of these factors has certainly diminished over the years. Yet there is no strong evidence to support this view. If in fact there was little change in the rate of occupational mobility between 1910 and 1940, there would seem to be even less reason to expect any further rigidity to have appeared since 1940. One would expect the persistent prosperity, together with the continued spread of higher education, to have improved mobility chances, if anything.

Some roughly comparable evidence for 1950 bears out this

3. [Some evidence published since this article was written suggests that this factor is not of major importance in accounting for inequality in any given year. Cf. J. N. Morgan, "The Anatomy of Income Distribution," *Review of Economics and Statistics,* 44 (August 1962), p. 272; I. B. Kravis, *The Structure of Income,* 1960, pp. 268–278.—*Editor.*]

4. [Up to 1959, the *Survey of Consumer Finances* was published in various issues of the *Federal Reserve Bulletin,* e.g., July 1954, August 1957. Since 1959, it has been published as a separate volume by the Survey Research Center, University of Michigan.—*Editor.*]

hypothesis.[5] The extent of self-recruitment in the professional and managerial occupations is no larger and perhaps somewhat smaller. Perhaps more important, the route from sales and clerical jobs for the father to professional and managerial employment for the son was more heavily traveled in 1950 than in 1942 and more heavily traveled in 1940 than in 1910. The extent to which the sons of semiskilled and unskilled laborers remain semiskilled and unskilled laborers also declined slightly between 1940 and 1950, with more of the sons going into skilled, white-collar, and eventually higher occupational positions and a substantially larger percentage of the sons moving directly into professional and managerial jobs. Presumably this is one of the important fruits of the public school system. The fact that median earnings in white-collar occupations are no higher and perhaps lower than those in skilled manual or even in some semiskilled manual jobs is less important than the fact that sales and clerical employment is often a means of entry (either between generations or for the same individual) into the better paid and "higher class" professional and managerial jobs.

So far we have looked at the distribution of income as the market imputes it to individuals and families. The distribution of actual consuming power is of course further modified by taxation before it becomes available to families. It is worth taking a look at the distribution of disposable income by size, since it is perhaps a better measure of the extent to which the differential availability of goods and services has changed over the years. There are two conventional aspects to the distribution of Table 4 which require mention. Capital gains and/or the undistributed net profits of corporations are excluded from the definition of income, with a corresponding apparent worsening of the position of top groups. Secondly, although the effects of personal and corporate income taxes and certain transfer payments are allowed for in the figures, there are other real-income-redistributing activities of governments (such as the provision of recreational facilities and schools) which are excluded.

Table 4 shows about what one would expect. The progressive

5. G. L. Palmer, *Labor Mobility in Six Cities* (New York: Social Science Research Council, 1954); also Herman P. Miller, *op. cit.*, p. 31.

nature of the federal income tax is reflected by the greater
equality of the distribution of post-tax income as against that of
pre-tax income. But the difference is slight. And the trend toward equalization, at least over the period 1941–1954, goes at
about the same rate whether or not one takes account of income
tax. The main difference is that, although on a before-tax basis
the fourth quintile slightly increased its share between 1941 and
1954, on an after-tax basis it suffered a slight decline.[6] It is too

TABLE 4. *Distribution of Family Personal Income after
Federal Individual Income Tax Liability, by Quintiles for
Consumer Units Ranked by Size of After-tax Income, 1941,
1950, 1954, 1956*

Quintiles	1941	1950	1954	1956
Lowest	4.3	5.1	5.3	5.3
Second	9.9	11.4	12.0	11.9
Third	15.9	16.8	17.3	17.1
Fourth	23.0	22.7	22.7	22.7
Highest	46.8	44.0	42.7	43.0
Top 5%	21.7	19.2	18.4	18.0

SOURCE: Same as Table 3, p. 55.
[Estimates for 1929, 1959, and 1962, as well as the revised estimates for
1954 and 1956, may be found in Table 3, p. xvi of the Introduction.—*Editor*.]

bad that the 1935–1936 distribution has not been adjusted for
taxes, but it is unlikely that these conclusions would be significantly altered.

Perhaps a more concrete view of the extent and change of inequality is given by such comparisons as the following. On a
before-tax basis, in 1935–1936 the mean income in the top quintile was about thirteen times the mean income in the bottom
quintile; in 1941, twelve times; in 1947, nine times; in 1950, ten
times; and by 1954 down to nine times again. On an after-tax
basis in 1941 the mean income in the top fifth was about eleven
times that in the bottom fifth; in 1950, a bit over eight times;
and in 1954, exactly eight times.[7]

6. The after-tax distributions are perhaps sufficiently more conjectural
than the before-tax that such minor differences ought to be discounted.
7. [For a similar presentation, see Tables 2 and 4 to Introduction (pp. xiv
and xvii.—*Editor*.]

TABLE 5. *Distribution of Total Income before Tax by Quintiles, Selected Countries, Selected Years*

Quintile	United Kingdom			Germany		Netherlands			Sweden			
	1938	1949	1955	Pre-war 1936	Western 1950	1938	1946	1950	1935	1945	1948	1954*
Lowest		7.2	10.7†	3	4		3.2	4.2		2.4	3.2	5.6
Second	33.2	9.8	22.0‡	8	8.5	28.5	8.4	9.6	22.7	8.6	9.6	11.2
Third		15.0		15.5	16.5		14.4	15.7		15.3	16.3	17.1
Fourth	16.8	20.5	23.6	20.5	23	19.0	21.0	21.5	21.2	23.1	24.3	23.3
Highest	50.0	47.5	43.7	53	48	52.5	53.0	49.0	56.1	50.6	46.6	42.8
Top 5%	29.5	23.7	20.2	27.9	23.6	28.9	27.3	24.6	28.1	23.6	20.1	17.0

* Unadjusted tax records; adjusted figures might give slightly lower shares of upper groups, slightly higher shares of lower groups.

† Lowest three deciles.

‡ Fourth through sixth deciles.

SOURCE: *Economic Survey of Europe, 1956* (Geneva: United Nations, 1957), chap. IX, p. 6.

Table 5 provides some comparisons between developments in this country and in a few of the industrial countries of western Europe. In all cases the movement over time has been toward equality; in all cases (except possibly Sweden) the movement has been slight. One important difference shows up between European and American experience. In the United Kingdom, the Netherlands, and Sweden, where figures are available both for an immediately postwar year and for a still later one, there is some evidence that the process of equalization has continued past the end of the war. In this country, it will be remembered, we found that after 1947 only very small changes took place in the pre-tax distribution of income. But in the United Kingdom the share of the top quintile fell by more between 1949 and 1955 than it had between 1938 and 1949. In the Netherlands the whole process seems to have begun after 1946. Sweden started in 1935 with the most unequal distribution of any we have recorded and wound up in 1954 with one of the least unequal. One is tempted to connect this with the fact that, of all the countries represented, real personal income per head increased fastest (between 1938 and 1954) in Sweden.

Contrasting this country with Europe, we started off in the thirties with a slightly less equal distribution of personal income than the United Kingdom, about the same as the Netherlands, and a rather more equal distribution than in Germany or Sweden. By 1954 we had more equal distribution than the Netherlands and western Germany, about the same as the United Kingdom, and a trifle less than Sweden. It appears that in recent years the lowest quintile has had a noticeably smaller share of total income in the United States than in the United Kingdom or in Sweden. Whether this is a consequence of the extent of social security programs, or of demographic facts, or of still other economic and sociological factors would require detailed investigation.

I think it is a fair summary of Tables 3 and 5 to say that the similarities among the five countries surveyed are considerably more striking than the differences. And this is so whether one looks at the picture statistically or in terms of changes over time.

A few comparisons of the distribution of income after tax can be made from Table 6. About the only new evidence that is revealed is the indication of somewhat heavier progression at the top brackets of the United Kingdom income tax as compared with ours, and this hardly comes as a surprise.

No discussion of income inequality is complete without some mention of the demographic changes which play perhaps the most important role of all in the movement toward equalization. The trends revealed in Table 7 would presumably show up even more strongly if it were possible to carry the data backward in time. While the average number of persons per family declined over-all between 1935 and 1952, the decline was far larger in the lowest quintile of the income distribution than elsewhere, so that even a constant degree of inequality on a family basis would be converted into an equalization on the per capita basis

TABLE 6. *Distribution of Total Income after Tax by Quintiles, Selected Countries, Selected Years*

	United Kingdom			Netherlands		Sweden		
Quintile	1938	1949	1955	1946	1950	1935	1945	1948
Lowest	⎫	8.3	⎫	⎫	4.8	⎫	2.7	3.5
Second	⎬ 35.7	⎫	⎬ 12.0	⎬ 7.3	10.4	⎬ 9.9	8.8	10.5
	⎭	⎬	23.8	20.8		⎭		
Third	⎫	⎬ 51.0			17.0	13.5	16.1	17.7
Fourth	⎬	⎭	24.8	21.9	22.8	22.5	24.0	25.2
	⎫ 64.3							
Highest	⎭	40.7	39.4	50.0	45.0	54.1	48.4	43.1
Top 5%	24.7	17.7	15.5	23.2	19.5	25.6	21.3	16.9

SOURCE: *Economic Survey of Europe, 1956* (Geneva: United Nations, 1957) chap. IX, p. 22.

that is most significant for economic welfare. The rich may be getting richer, but it is no longer so true that the poor have children. In 1935 the average number of minor children in the lowest fifth was a third again as large as in the top fifth; by 1952 it had fallen to approximate equality. Perhaps even more revealing is the extent to which families in the bottom quintile now tend to be headed by old people. In 1935 the median age of the family head was forty-three in the bottom fifth and forty-six in the top fifth. In 1952 that median age was still forty-six at the top, but it had risen to fifty-four at the bottom. In 1952, 52 per cent of the *families* (Table 7 does not include unattached individuals) in the bottom quintile were two-person families, against 24.6 per cent at the top; and 30 per cent of the families

TABLE 7. *Family Composition among Families of Two or More Persons, by Quintiles of Family Money Income before Tax, Selected Years*

Quintile	1935–36	1941	1944	1947	1949	1952	1959 *
Average Number of Persons							
Lowest	3.73	3.55	3.10	3.25	3.26	3.19	3.24
Second	3.93	3.63	3.38	3.50	3.48	3.55	3.64
Third	3.92	3.67	3.64	3.63	3.61	3.63	3.80
Fourth	3.87	3.65	3.74	3.69	3.60	3.63	3.83
Highest	3.98	4.00	3.83	4.13	3.89	3.72	3.89
Average Number of Earners							
Lowest	1.10		.98		1.07	1.02	1.02
Second	1.17		1.18		1.32	1.34	1.38
Third	1.24		1.32		1.39	1.44	1.52
Fourth	1.34		1.53		1.59	1.63	1.72
Highest	1.52		1.83		1.98	1.96	1.99
Average Number of Children under 18							
Lowest	1.40	1.30		1.09	1.18	1.11	1.19
Second	1.51	1.35		1.28	1.25	1.35	1.45
Third	1.42	1.31		1.31	1.34	1.40	1.56
Fourth	1.29	1.10		1.19	1.22	1.31	1.50
Highest	1.07	1.00		1.09	1.01	1.07	1.40
Median Age of Family Head							
Lowest	43					54	53
Second	39					43	43
Third	40					41	43
Fourth	41					42	44
Highest	46					46	48

* [Data for 1959 from S. Goldsmith, *Income and Wealth*, Series X, 1964, Table II, p. 257, added by *Editor*.]

SOURCES: S. Goldsmith *et al., op. cit.,* p. 15.

"*Income Distribution,*" supplement to *Survey of Current Business* (Washington, D.C.: Government Printing Office, 1953), p. 69.

S. Goldsmith, *op. cit.,* p. 20.

at the bottom were headed by persons over sixty-five, against only 8 per cent at the top. Finally, as the second panel of Table 7 shows, the higher families in the distribution have always been characterized by a higher average number of earners; but this tendency has grown much more pronounced over time.

Changes in the Size Distribution
of Income

SELMA F. GOLDSMITH

*Selma F. Goldsmith, who as a staff economist for the Office of
Business Economics pioneered in the development of the size
distribution estimates by that agency, presented this paper at the
meetings of the American Economic Association in December
1956.*

THIS PAPER attempts to summarize some recent findings concerning changes that have taken place in income distribution in
the United States during the past twenty-five years. The discussion is directed primarily at the question of whether or not
there has been a reduction over this period in relative income
differences among families and individuals. If so, how large has
it been, and to what extent are the available figures influenced
by particular concepts and definitions?

The two statistical series on income-size distribution to which
we can turn, present essentially the same pattern for the post-
1929 period; namely, a marked decline in the percentage share
of total income accruing to the top income group.

The first of these series, developed by Professor Simon Kuznets,
presents annual data on relative income shares received by successive top percentiles of the population; e.g., by the 5 per cent of
men, women, and children covered on those individual income
tax returns reporting the largest per capita incomes in each
year.[1] The second series, developed by my colleagues and myself, is on a family rather than a population basis and covers the

1. Simon Kuznets, *Shares of Upper Income Groups in Income and Savings* (National Bureau of Economic Research, 1953).

TABLE 1. *Percentage Shares of Income Received by Top 5 Per Cent, Selected Years* *

| | Top 5 Per Cent of Population (Kuznets) | | | Top 5 Per Cent of Consumer Units | |
| | Economic Income Variant (1) | Disposable Income Variant (2) | Economic Income Variant Plus Realized Net Capital Gains (3) | Family Personal Income (4) | Income after Federal Individual Income Tax Liability (5) |
Year					
1929	32.2	33.8	34.8	30.0	29.5
1935–36	28.8	27.9		26.5	
1939	27.8	26.8	27.8	25.8	24.8
1941	25.7	23.0		24.0	21.5
1944	18.7	15.8		20.7	
1946	20.0	17.7	21.4	21.3	
1947	19.1			20.9	
1948	19.4				
1952				20.5	18.2
1962				19.6	17.7
Per cent decrease:					
1929 to 1946	38	48	38	29	
1939 to 1946	28	34	23	17	
1929 to 1948	40				
1929 to 1952				32	38
1939 to 1952				21	27
1929 to 1962				35	40
1939 to 1962				29	29

* Figures for 1962 added from *Survey of Current Business*, April 1964, p. 8, by *Editor*.

SOURCES: Columns 1 and 2, which represent, respectively, before-tax income exclusive of capital gains, and income after federal individual income taxes but inclusive of realized net capital gains, from Simon Kuznets, *Shares of Upper Income Groups in Income and Savings* (National Bureau of Economic Research, 1953), pages 453, 635, 637 (with 1948 extrapolated by Kuznets' "basic variant" series, page 599). Column 3 derived by adding to column 1 Kuznets' adjustment to include net capital gains (page 599, column 5 minus column 1) and subtracting his adjustment for unwarranted inclusions (page 622, column 4 minus column 1). Column 4, which represents personal income before income taxes flowing to families and unattached individuals and excludes capital gains and losses, for 1952 from "Income Distribution in the United States, by Size, 1952–55," *Survey of Current Business*, June 1956; 1946 and 1947 from "Income Distribution in the

full range of family incomes for selected years.[2] The top 5 per cent in this series refers to families and unattached individuals having the largest family personal incomes in each year.

Starting with Kuznets' series, in 1929 the incomes received by the top 5 per cent of the population amounted to about 32 per cent of the total income receipts of all individuals (measured before income taxes and excluding net capital gains). In 1939, this relative share had dropped to 28 per cent, reflecting mainly a loss in relative share by the topmost percentile of the population. After 1939 declines were registered by all bands within the top 5 per cent. By 1946, the relative share of this top group had fallen to 20 per cent and in 1948 it is estimated at somewhat over 19 per cent (Table 1). For the 1929–48 period as a whole, this represented a decline of 40 per cent in the relative share of before-tax income received by the top 5 per cent of the population.

The family income distributions show a similar though somewhat dampened post-1929 decline for the top income group. The relative share of the top 5 per cent of consumer units is estimated at 30 per cent in 1929 and at under 21 per cent in 1944 and in the postwar period.

Both the Kuznets' and family income series represent before-tax incomes and in deriving both of them data from federal

United States, by Size, 1944–50," a supplement to the *Survey of Current Business* (1953); 1941, 1935–36, and 1929 from Selma Goldsmith, George Jaszi, Hyman Kaitz, and Maurice Liebenberg, "Size Distribution of Income since the Mid-thirties," *Review of Economics and Statistics,* February 1954; 1939 derived by interpolation between 1935–36 and 1941 using column 1 as a basis. Column 5, which represents column 4 minus federal individual income tax liabilities other than those on net capital gains, for 1952 and 1941 derived from sources listed for column 4 for those years; 1929 and 1939 obtained by subtracting from amounts underlying column 4 federal individual income tax liabilities excluding liabilities on net capital gains, estimated from data in *Statistics of Income, Part 1, 1929 and 1939* (U.S. Treasury Department).

2. Office of Business Economics, "Income Distribution in the United States by Size, 1944–50," a Supplement to the *Survey of Current Business* (U.S. Department of Commerce, 1953); "Income Distribution in the United States, 1950–53," and "1952–55," *Survey of Current Business,* March 1955, and June 1956; Selma Goldsmith, George Jaszi, Hyman Kaitz, and Maurice Liebenberg, "Size Distribution of Income since the Mid-thirties," *Review of Economics and Statistics,* February 1954.

individual income tax returns represented the primary source material. The difference between them reflects a number of factors, such as differences in the basic unit of measurement (the family versus the person), in the concept of income, and in the adjustments that were made in the basic tax-return statistics by Kuznets, on the one hand, and by the various sets of persons who initially developed the family distributions for selected prewar and postwar years, on the other.

The family income distributions also tell us how the decrease in relative income share of the top 5 per cent of the consumer units was spread among other income groups. Between 1929 and 1947, for example, the 9 percentage points of decline in the share of the top 5 per cent were offset by the following gains: 3½ percentage points by the lowest 40 per cent of families and unattached individuals, 2¼ points by the middle quintile, 2¾ points by the fourth quintile, and ¾ points by the 15 per cent of consumer units directly below the top 5.

A salient point is that for the lowest 40 per cent of consumer units, the period of greatest relative gains was between 1941 and 1944. Since 1944, there has been little change in the relative distribution of family income according to the available figures.

Kuznets has also developed a series in terms of disposable income (i.e., income after federal individual income taxes and inclusive of capital gains). For the top 5 per cent of the population, the relative share in total disposable income dropped from almost 34 per cent in 1929 to well under 18 per cent in 1946, the last year for which this series is available. This represented a decrease of 48 per cent, 10 points more than the 38 per cent drop in the before-tax income share from 1929 to 1946 (Table 1).

These decreases in relative income shares are reflected strikingly in the average income figures for the top income sector. Kuznets' per capita disposable income of the top 5 per cent is about one-eighth lower in 1946 than in 1929, even in current dollars; i.e., before allowance for the higher prices prevailing in the latter year (Table 2). On a before-tax basis the current-dollar per capita income of the top 5 per cent just about kept up with the rise in the consumer price index for the period

1929–46 but fell behind by 1948.[3] However, attention must be called to the limited applicability of the consumer price index in this context. Not until we are able to develop differential cost-of-living indexes appropriate for the various income groups and can solve the problem of how to deflate the portions of income used for income taxes and saving, will we be in a position to measure with precision changes in the distribution of real income.

TABLE 2. *Average Income of Entire Population and of Top 5 Per Cent, Selected Years*

| | Average Income Per Capita (Kuznets) | | | | |
| | Economic Income Variant | | Disposable Income Variant | | Consumer Price Index |
Year	Total Population	Top 5 Per Cent	Total Population	Top 5 Per Cent	1947–49 = 100
1929	$ 674	$4,339	$ 690	$4,666	73.3
1939	537	2,982	528	2,831	59.4
1941	700	3,594	664	3,052	62.9
1946	1,234	4,926	1,166	4,118	83.4
1948	1,400	5,421			102.8
Per cent increase:					
1929 to 1946	83	14	69	− 12	14
1939 to 1946	130	65	121	45	40
1929 to 1948	108	25			40

SOURCES: *Averages* (see Table 1 for definitions) derived from Simon Kuznets, *Shares*, etc., pp. 635, 637, 639, 641, 644 (with 1948 extrapolated from 1947 by Kuznets' "basic variant" series). Consumer price index from Bureau of Labor Statistics.

Several related statistical series lend support to the finding that there has been a reduction in relative income differences in the post-1929 and particularly in the post-1939 period. Confining our attention to the before-tax income measures, these include:

1. Changes in the relative importance of the various types of income in the personal income total. Since 1929 there has been a

3. Geoffrey Moore showed that this fall took place within the top 1 per cent of the population. See "Secular Changes in the Distribution of Income," American Economic Association *Papers and Proceedings*, May 1952.

striking increase in the percentage that wages and salaries and transfer payments constitute of the personal income total flowing to families and unattached individuals. These payments together accounted for 61 per cent of total personal income in 1929, 67 per cent in 1939, and 73 per cent in 1950–55 (Table 3).

TABLE 3. *Per Cent Distribution of Family Personal Income by Major Types of Income and Relative Importance of Compensation of Employees in National Income, Selected Years* *

	1929	1939	1949	1950–55 Average	1960–65 Average
Family personal income:					
Wages and salaries and other labor income	58.9	62.8	64.7	66.4	66.3
Transfer payments	1.8	4.1	6.8	6.8	9.4
Subtotal	60.7	66.9	71.5	73.2	75.7
Business and professional income:					
Farm	7.3	6.3	6.1	5.1	2.8
Nonfarm	10.4	10.2	11.2	9.9	8.2
Dividends and interest	15.3	12.8	7.4	7.3	9.5
Rental income	6.4	3.8	3.8	4.6	3.8
Total	100.0	100.0	100.0	100.0	100.0
Compensation of employees as a per cent of national income originating in:					
Economy as a whole	58.9	66.3	64.8	66.9	70.7
Ordinary business sector (corporations, partnerships, and proprietorships)	61.1	65.4	63.5	65.9	70.7
All other sectors	49.6	69.6	70.8	70.9	70.8
All nonfarm corporations	74.6	80.5	75.3	76.5	79.9
Manufacturing corporations	74	79	73	74	79

* [The original figures in Table 3 have been extended to 1960–65 by the *Editor* and revised to reflect the most recent (1965) revision of the national income series by the Office of Business Economics.]

SOURCES: Upper bank derived by adjusting U.S. Department of Commerce personal income series from *Survey of Current Business*, July 1956, as described on pp. 17–18 and 67 of "Income Distribution in the United States, by Size 1944–1950," U.S. Department of Commerce, 1953. Lower bank, except last line, derived from Table 12 (and underlying data) of 1954 *National Income* supplement and July 1956, issue of *Survey of Current Business*. Last line derived from *Survey of Current Business*, November 1956, p. 20.

In contrast, there was a marked reduction in the shares of dividends and interest—types of income that are heavily concentrated in the upper end of the family income scale.

2. Changes in the relative distribution of the various types of income. By examining the shares of the top 5 per cent in separate types of income, Kuznets found that the relative shares of this top group, based on data from tax returns, declined from 1929 to 1948 for wages and salaries, dividends, interest, and—to a lesser extent—for rental income. More recently, Herman Miller compared the wage and salary data reported in the last two Decennial Censuses of Population for detailed occupation and industry groups and found three factors making for a narrowing of income differentials within the wage and salary sector between 1939 and 1949: (a) decreases in relative income dispersion for men within practically all of the 118 occupations and 117 industries he studied; (b) relatively greater gains in median wage and salary income for low-paid than for high-paid occupations and industries; and (c) an increase in the proportion of workers classified in occupations with comparatively little income dispersion.[4] Unfortunately similar data are not available from the Census for 1929.

3. A narrowing of relative income differences, as measured by mean incomes, between the farm and nonfarm population. Because average incomes are lower for farm than for nonfarm consumer units—even with allowance for income received in kind —a narrowing in this differential, barring other changes, will work in the direction of reducing relative income differences in the over-all income distribution. Per capita income of persons on farms was 3 times as large in 1949 as in 1939—reflecting in part the relatively low level of farm income in the earlier year— whereas the corresponding ratio was 2½ for persons not living on farms.[5] Despite the fall in farm incomes in the past few years, the ratio of per capita income in 1952–55 to that in 1939 is still

4. Herman P. Miller, *Income of the American People* (New York 1955), and "Changes in the Industrial Distribution of Wages in the United States: 1939–49," to be published in Vol. 23 of *Studies in Income and Wealth* (National Bureau of Economic Research).

5. *Farm Income Situation* (No. 159, Agricultural Marketing Service, U.S. Department of Agriculture), July 17, 1956.

substantially higher for farm residents than for nonfarm.[6]

4. Another recent study that has bearing on the subject under discussion is the analysis of changes since 1929 in income distribution by states that has been made by members of the staff of the Office of Business Economics.[7] As part of this study, per capita incomes in the various states for selected years are expressed as percentages of the national average, and these percentages are compared over time. Two major conclusions emerge.

First, "there has been a significant narrowing over the past quarter of a century in the relative differences in average-income levels among States and regions. . . . As shown by the coefficient of variation, relative dispersion in the State per capita income array was reduced by nearly 40 per cent from 1927–29 to 1953–55."

Second, the period of greatest narrowing of state per capita incomes was that of the war years, 1942–44. Only a small part of the reduction in dispersion occurred in the prewar period, and "the regional differentials obtaining in 1944 were carried over with only moderate alteration into the postwar period and since then have tended to remain relatively stable in most regions."

These findings are remarkably consistent with those for the relative distribution of family income by size. As was noted earlier, the period of greatest gain in relative income share for the two lowest quintiles in the family income size distributions was between 1941 and 1944, and after 1944 the available data show little change in the relative distribution of family personal income by size. Of course, the narrowing of state differentials in average income does not of itself prove that there was a reduction in the relative dispersion of income by size, but it does lend credence to the finding that such a reduction took place.

We turn now to certain limitations in the income statistics. To save time I shall simply list four of the general ones: (a) Income

6. [This statement is still true. Per capita income for farm residents in the years 1960–64 averaged more than 5 times that in 1939; for nonfarm residents, it was somewhat less than 4 times. *Farm Income Situation* (July 1965), p. 54.—*Editor.*]

7. *Personal Income by States Since 1929,* a Supplement to the *Survey of Current Business,* 1957.

for a single year is not a satisfactory measure of income inequality. (b) We do not have differential cost-of-living indexes appropriate for various income groups; so that we cannot measure with precision changes in the distribution of real income. (c) The available statistics on the number and composition of families at the lower end of the income scale are particularly unsatisfactory. (d) When we compare income shares of a given quintile or the top 5 per cent in two periods, we are not comparing what has happened to an identical group of families, because the families comprising the quintile may be quite different in the two periods. For certain purposes, as, for example, in interpreting the change in the income share of the top quintile or top 5 per cent of families over, say, a five- to ten-year time span, it would be extremely helpful to know the extent to which the families comprising the top sector differed in the terminal periods. Unfortunately, such family income data do not exist.

Next are several more specific limitations in the concept or coverage of the income measure that is used in determining relative income shares. In the first place, various types of deferred compensation and a sizable amount of income in kind charged to business expense escape measurement in all of the income-size distribution series. Since these types of income presumably have grown in relative as well as absolute importance in the postwar period and since they accrue to a greater extent to upper than to middle or lower income groups, their exclusion from the basic statistics has the effect of exaggerating the decline in the relative share of total income received by the top income sector. Liberal expense accounts, free vacations, deferred compensation contracts, stock options given to corporate executives, and employer contributions to private pension, health, and welfare funds are the main items that have been listed.

Second, special tax allowances introduced in recent years, such as liberalized depreciation and depletion allowances, operate in the direction of understating the real income shares of top income groups in the postwar period. The splitting of dividend income among the children in the family for the purpose of reducing income tax liabilities would work in the same direction to the extent that the practice has grown in recent years, and full allowance for this factor cannot be made on the basis of the available statistics.

Third, another limitation of the statistics which, in this case, has been addressed only to the Kuznets series relates to understatement of reportable amounts of income by top-sector taxpayers. Kuznets measured top-sector incomes as the amounts reported by taxpayers on unaudited income tax returns (except for adjustments to add tax-exempt interest and imputed rent). It is argued that percentage understatement in reportable amounts of income for upper bracket taxpayers may be larger in recent than in prewar years and that the introduction of an allowance for this factor into the Kuznets series would dampen the post-1929 or post-1939 decline in the relative income share of the top percentiles of the population.

Unlike Kuznets' series, the family income distributions have been adjusted to allow for income understatement on tax returns in all years and, with the possible exception of 1929, this adjustment included at least some of the income brackets in which the top 5 per cent of consumer units resided. However, mainly because a sufficiently detailed description of methodology is not available in the case of the family distribution for 1929, it is not possible to determine the magnitude of the adjustment for understatement of income that was applied in the top sector of tax returns in that year and compare it with the corresponding adjustment for the postwar period. As was noted earlier, the post-1929 decline in the relative income share of the top 5 per cent is smaller in the family distributions than in the Kuznets' series where no adjustment for this factor is made. This suggests that the statistical adjustment for income understatement in the family distributions has been relatively larger in postwar years than in 1929, but until a complete reworking of the 1929 distribution is attempted this cannot be definitely asserted.

Fourth, an important point that has been raised frequently by all of those concerned with the statistics on relative income distribution is the effect of the exclusion of capital gains[8] from the

8. [Capital gains are the excess of the current value or price over acquisi-

income measure. The tax incentive to convert property and even other types of income into capital gains is of course well known, and it is argued that the practice has become increasingly widespread in recent years, particularly within the upper income sector.

By limiting capital gains and losses to the realized amounts reported on individual income tax returns (i.e., before statutory percentage reductions and limitations on losses) and by attributing these amounts to the year in which they were realized—both of these are, of course, debatable procedures—Kuznets measured the effect on upper income shares of adding net capital gains to ordinary income. On the basis of his figures, the percentage decline in the relative before-tax income share of the top 5 per cent is the same for the period 1929 to 1946 whether or not capital gains are included (38 per cent; see Table 1). For 1939–46, the percentage decline is reduced by the inclusion of realized capital gains by about one-sixth (from 28 to 23 per cent), and it appears likely that the reduction for the post-1939 period would be more significant if the series were brought up through 1955.

We cannot assign reliable measures to the other factors that have been listed but there is little doubt that taken together they would serve to reduce the post-1929 decline in upper income shares. How large must they be if they were to eliminate the decline entirely? Using Kuznets' series, rough estimates of these amounts can be derived.

In 1946 the aggregate income of the top 5 per cent of the population was 35 billion dollars exclusive of capital gains and 39 billion with realized net capital gains included—20.0 and 21.4 per cent of the respective income totals for that year (Table 1). In order for the relative share of the top 5 per cent to have been as large as in 1929—32.2 per cent exclusive of capital gains or 34.8 per cent with net capital gains included—a minimum of some 20 to 25 billion dollars would have to be added to the 1946 amounts. It is difficult to imagine that the factors listed above

tion cost to an investor of such physical assets as real estate or such paper claims as stocks and bonds. A gain is said to be realized when the asset in question is actually sold at a price in excess of acquisition cost.—*Editor.*]

can account for magnitudes of anything like this size.

To reach 1939 rather than 1929 levels, the amount which would have to be added to the income of the top 5 per cent in 1946 is in the neighborhood of 18 billion dollars if income is measured exclusive of capital gains, or 15 billion if realized capital gains are included. Again, it seems highly unlikely that the adjustments could be this large.

When we consider the postwar period by itself, the relative magnitudes involved are smaller but nevertheless substantial. The personal income flow to families and unattached individuals in 1955 was at an annual rate of somewhat under 300 billion dollars. Thus if the factors listed above accounted for 3 to 4 billion and accrued entirely to the top 5 per cent of consumer units, the relative income share of this top group would be increased by 1 percentage point; i.e., from the presently estimated 21 per cent to 22 per cent; if they totaled 6 to 8 billion, the increase would be 2 percentage points, etc. In the present state of our statistical knowledge we cannot say which figure would be closest to the actual situation.

Fifth, the points noted thus far lie within the framework of personal income as the basic measure of the income flow to consumers. Of concern to many of us has been the fact that the relative distribution of income as it emerged from production may have changed over time in a different way from the distribution of personal income.[9]

The major differences between the production measure of the income flow—national income—and the personal income measure are that national income includes and personal income excludes elements of production not paid out to persons—undistributed corporate profits, the corporate inventory valuation adjustment, taxes on corporate profits, and contributions for social insurance—whereas the reverse is the case for elements of income received by persons but not accruing in production—

9. The effects on relative income distribution of other modifications in income definition such as adding to family personal income the value of free government services and subtracting excise, sales, property, and other taxes in addition to individual income taxes cannot be covered within the confines of this paper.

transfer payments and government interest.

In particular, the fact that the undistributed earnings of corporations have accounted for a larger relative share of national income in the postwar period than before the war, coupled with the fact that they accrue to a relatively large extent to top-income groups, suggests that the post-1929 or post-1939 decline in the income share of the top sector would be smaller when such earnings are taken into account than when they are excluded from the income base.

Using Kuznets' data, Allan Cartter recently demonstrated that by including undistributed corporate profits and corporate income taxes in the income measure—allocating them between the top 5 per cent and all other income groups combined on the basis of Kuznets' distribution of dividends—the decline in the relative income share of the top 5 per cent of the population from 1937 to 1948 was reduced from the one-fourth shown by Kuznets to only 5 per cent (if corporate income taxes are not shifted; to 13 per cent if part of these taxes are assumed to be shifted).[10] This appears at first glance to be in striking contrast to Kuznets' own calculations which showed that for the period 1939–46 the inclusion of undistributed corporate profits had only a moderate effect on the decline in the relative income share of the top 5 per cent. (The decline shown by Kuznets was 34 per cent for disposable income and 27 per cent for disposable income plus these profits. Kuznets assumed no shifting.)

The difference in these results reflects in part differences in the time period studied. Cartter's take-off point, 1937, was a year with very much smaller undistributed corporate profits than 1939; and in 1948 these retained earnings represented a larger share of the national income total than in 1946. Thus Cartter's choice of the time period 1937–48 would be expected to produce more striking results than 1939–46.

But the main difference is due to the definition of undistributed corporate profits. Kuznets included only undistributed profits per se, whereas Cartter distributed corporate income taxes

10. Allan M. Cartter, "Income Shares of Upper Income Groups in Great Britain and the United States," *American Economic Review*, December 1954.

TABLE 4. *Percentage Shares of Top 5 Per Cent of Consumer Units in Family Personal Income and Rough Estimates of Corresponding Shares Using Various Other Definitions of Income, Selected Years*

	1929	1939	1950–55 Average	1962 *	Per Cent Decrease† 1929 to 1950–55	Per Cent Decrease† 1939 to 1950–55
1. Family personal income (before income taxes)	30.0	25.8	20.7	19.7	31	20
2. Family personal income after federal individual income tax liability	29.5	24.8	18.5	17.7	37	25
Family personal income plus:						
3. Undistributed corporate profits	31	27	22	21	29	16
4. Undistributed corporate profits and corporate income taxes	32	28	26	24	20	7
5. Undistributed corporate profits, corporate income taxes, and inventory valuation adjustment	33	27	25	24	22	6
6. Family personal income minus transfer payments	31	27	22	22	28	19
7. National income (= line 5 minus transfer payments and government interest, plus contributions for social insurance)	33	27	26	24	21	5
8. National income minus corporate and individual income taxes	31	25	20	20	36	20

* [Estimates for 1962 prepared by the *Editor* from sources similar to those cited.]   † Based on unrounded figures.

SOURCES: Lines 1 and 2 from sources cited in Table 1, columns 4 and 5. Lines 3–5 estimated by distributing each of the 3 corporate profits items (*Survey of Current Business*, July 1956, Table 1) between the top 5 and the other 95 per cent of consumer units in proportion to Kuznets' estimates of the distribution of dividend receipts (*Shares*, etc., p. 649). For lines 6 and 7, rough estimates of the corresponding distribution of the other income items listed were derived as explained in *Review of Economics and Statistics*, February 1954, p. 20. Line 8 obtained by subtracting corporate income taxes (see line 4) and federal individual income tax liabilities (see line 2) from amounts underlying line 7.

as well. Since factor incomes measured before rather than after income taxes are more useful for many types of economic analysis, it is preferable to impute these taxes along with undistributed profits to obtain a measure of the share of the upper income group in total national product measured at factor costs.

On the basis of rough allocations between the top 5 per cent and the other 95 per cent of consumer units of undistributed corporate profits, the corporate inventory valuation adjustment, corporate income taxes, and the other items of definitional difference between personal and national income, the following conclusions are reached: From 1929 to the average of 1950–55, converting from a personal income to a national income basis reduces the percentage decline in the relative income share of the top 5 per cent of the population by about one-third (i.e., the decline is reduced from about 30 to about 20 per cent). The exclusion of transfer payments accounts for only a small part of the reduction; the major part is due to adding corporate income taxes along with retained corporate earnings (Table 4).

From 1939 to 1950–55 the corresponding reduction is about three-fourths. In place of a 20 per cent decline in the relative share of the top 5 per cent in personal income, there is a decline of only about 5 per cent on a national income basis (i.e., the relative share of the top 5 per cent in national income is estimated at about 27 per cent in 1939 and about 26 per cent in 1950–55). Again, the major reason for the dampening of the decline is the inclusion of retained corporate earnings and particularly corporate income taxes. The 5 per cent decline is too small to be regarded as statistically significant and in fact may be due entirely to limitations of the statistics such as those listed under the first three points above. In other words, if income is measured in terms of the value of national production at factor costs rather than in terms of personal income flows, there appears to have been no reduction in the relative share of the top 5 per cent of consumer units for the period 1939 to 1950–55. On the other hand, if income is measured after income taxes, the decline since 1939 is sizable (Table 4) but, as is true also for the post-1929 period as a whole, the reduction is overstated to an unknown extent by limitations in our income-share measures.

Changes in the Concentration of Wealth

ROBERT J. LAMPMAN

Robert J. Lampman is Professor of Economics at the University of Wisconsin. His study, based on estate tax data, is one of the few sources of information on the changing share of the very wealthy. This selection is from The Share of Top Wealth-holders in National Wealth *(1962).*

INEQUALITY OF WEALTH DISTRIBUTION

PRESUMABLY, since wealth is a good thing to have, it would be good for all families to have some. Also, it would seem that the wider the distribution of wealth, the broader the political base for capitalism. There is doubtless a maximum degree of concentration of wealth which is tolerable in a democracy and compatible with an ideology of equality of economic opportunity. However, inequality due to differences in wealth-holding by age and family responsibilities may have quite a different political meaning from a similar degree of inequality within either the young or the old age group. Rigid class lines arise from great differences in inherited wealth as well as from different motivation, different opportunity for education, and different choice of occupation. To some extent, the difference between "democratic" and "oligarchic" systems of wealth-holding will be drawn as the body politic considers the individual, on the one hand, or the family of several generations, on the other, as the appropriate wealth-holding unit. To a considerable extent, American social policy has developed out of the belief that each generation of individuals should stand on its own with a minimum "handicapping" by previous generations.

In this connection, it should be emphasized that inequality of wealth-holding is not the only determinant of income inequality.

Indeed, to the extent that wealth is held by low-ranking wage or salary earners, it tends to offset income inequality. While capital and land are basic factors in production, and while total wealth is over three times as large as total annual income, the owners of these factors do not receive in the form of property income the greater part of the product in this or any other country. Only about 25 per cent of all income may be characterized as property income.[1]

The size distribution of income is determined by "(a) the rates of pay received by various agents of production and the extent of their utilization, and (b) the distribution among persons of the ownership of these productive agents. Two classes of productive agents must be distinguished: physical property or non-human capital, and human capital representing the productive capacity of individuals. In turn, the latter is divided into 'natural' endowment or 'abilities,' and productive capacity acquired by investment in training."[2] Thinking in these terms, this study is confined to the distribution of nonhuman capital.

There is no particular degree of concentration of wealth which is required for the working of a capitalist system. However, there may be a minimum degree of inequality consistent with a particular set of capitalist institutions, a particular technology, and a particular level of production. Composition of estate data generally show that nonproprietors place consumer capital and security objectives ahead of high yield at high-risk objectives. Only after the first set of objectives is achieved by accumulating property do most nonproprietors move on to the second. This suggests that, particularly as the proportion of the population who are proprietors falls, the availability of equity capital (at existing yields) is a function of the inequality of wealth distribution. If the inequality of wealth-holding were to be sharply re-

1. The precise percentage which one selects depends upon what part of "proprietors' income" one assigns to property and what part to service income, how one treats undistributed corporate profits, and whether he imputes an income to consumer capital.

2. Jacob Mincer, "A Study of Personal Income Distribution," unpublished Ph.D. dissertation, Columbia University, 1957, p. 136. See also Mincer, "Investment in Human Capital and Personal Income Distribution," *Journal of Political Economy*, August 1958, pp. 281–302.

duced, maintenance of the present flow of equity capital could be accomplished only by raising equity yields or by new institutional arrangements for transmuting security-motivated wealth-holding into high-yield-motivated holding.[3] This transmutation is accomplished by insurance company or pension fund purchase of corporate stock. It could also be accomplished by mutualization or provision of capital by patrons, as is indeed done in some cases of corporations' internal financing.

Role of Government · History suggests that public enterprise often follows where equity needs are not privately met. The American people have shown themselves to be pragmatic on the issue of public versus private ownership of capital. About 20 per cent of all wealth in the United States is publicly owned. A vital belief in the efficacy of private enterprise has not precluded a considerable role for government in property regulation, control, and ownership. Indeed, property is a legal concept, and property rights exist only as defined and enforced by government. The meaning of private property increases as governments protect its owners against loss through thievery and embezzlement, as buyers of securities are protected against fraud or misinformation, as orderly markets for sale of assets are maintained, and as wealth-holders are assured against threats of inflation or financial panic and mass liquidation. Government has also affected property values and the security of property by regulation of financial intermediaries, by insuring and even making direct provision for the extension of credit to individuals. By sale of land, as in the Homestead Act, and by social insurance, as in the case of Old Age, Survivors, and Disability Insurance, the federal government has engineered the widespread ownership of prop-

3. It is worth noting here that there is an important distinction, as emphasized by Veblen, between the equity investor who seeks long-term profit out of self-managed business and the speculator who holds or sells on the basis of anticipated profits with no hope or intention of constructively influencing the policy of the business. Certainly the great majority of stockholders in large corporations belong in the latter category of equity investors and view the highly regulated stock market as an escape route from anticipated falls in value due to poor management. Hence, a wide equity market removes some of the "risk" while diluting control.

erty rights. By influencing the transfer of property through gift or bequest and by affecting the possibility for accumulation of large estates, government fiscal policy plays a part in determining the distribution of wealth among persons and among sectors of the economy.

Composition of Estate · From the facts of estate composition, this picture of changing preference emerges. As people get richer, they shift from purchase of consumer capital, including real estate and life insurance, to U.S. bonds and mortgages and notes. As they get still richer, they shift over to corporate stock and state, local, and "other" bonds. As people get older, they reduce their liabilities, "cash out" of miscellaneous property (which includes interest in unincorporated business) and life insurance, and convert to larger holdings of cash, U.S. bonds, corporate stock, and mortgages and notes. As wealth moves into the hands of women, liabilities are reduced, life insurance falls as a percentage of estate and, consequently, all other types of property rise in relative importance.

The differences in type of property held by the several estate sizes are associated with different degrees of inequality among top wealth-holders for each type of asset. The most unequally distributed type of property is state and local bonds and the least concentrated is real estate.

Size Distribution · Over 30 per cent of the assets and equities of the personal sector of the economy in 1953 are assignable to the top wealth-holders who were 1.6 per cent of the total adult population that year. The top group owned at least 80 per cent of the corporate stock, virtually all of the state and local government bonds, and between 10 and 33 per cent of each other type of property in the personal sector in that year. These percentages are quite close to those found by the Survey of Consumer Finances for the same year.

The top wealth-holder group has varied in number and percentage of the total population over the years. Also, its share of total wealth has varied. It appears, however, that the degree of inequality increased from 1922 to 1929, fell to below the pre-1929 level in the 1930's, fell still more during the war and up to 1949, and increased from 1949 to 1956. However, the degree of inequality was considerably lower in 1953 than in either 1929 or 1922.

To make a comparison of degrees of wealth concentration, it is convenient to consider a constant percentage of the total adult population. The top 1 per cent of adults held 24 per cent of personal sector equity in 1953, 31 per cent in 1939, 36 per cent in 1929, and 32 per cent in 1922. It is probable that the decline thus indicated in inequality among individual wealth-holders is greater than would be found if families were considered as the wealth-holding units, since it is apparent from the data that married women are an increasing part of the top wealth-holder group. Converting to a measure of "adults less married women" suggests that half the percentage decline found for individuals between 1922 and 1953 would disappear on a family basis (Table 1 and Chart 1).

TABLE 1. *Share of Personal Sector Wealth (Equity) Held by Top Wealth-holders, Selected Years, 1922–56*

Year	Top 1 Per Cent of Adults	Top 0.5 Per Cent of All Persons	Top 2 Per Cent of Families *
1922	31.6	29.8	33.0
1929	36.3	32.4	
1933	28.3	25.2	
1939	30.6	28.0	
1945	23.3	20.9	
1949	20.8	19.3	
1953	24.2	22.7	28.5
1956	26.0	25.0	

* Families here defined as all adults less married females.
SOURCE: Lampman, Tables 93 and 94.

The leading exception to the general picture of declining concentration is corporate stock. In the total wealth variant the top 1 per cent of adults' share of each type of property declined between the 1920's and the 1950's, except for stock and state and local bonds. For stock, their share ranged from 60 to over 70 per cent.

Inequality of wealth distribution is considerably greater in Great Britain than in the United States, but a pattern of similar decline in inequality is observable in the two countries.

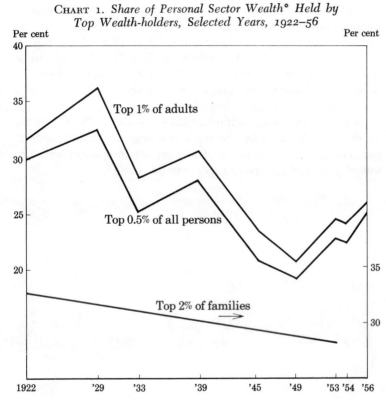

CHART 1. *Share of Personal Sector Wealth* Held by Top Wealth-holders, Selected Years, 1922–56*

* Equity, basic variant.

SOURCE: Table 94, bottom line; Table 93, bottom line; and Table 6 [in original article].

DETERMINANTS OF CHANGES IN INEQUALITY

Three processes may contribute to changes in the degree of inequality of wealth-holding. These are price change, accumulation of wealth out of income, and transfer of wealth. Changes in the relative prices of assets held by rich and poor worked toward increasing the inequality of wealth-holding over the long period 1922–53, but they contributed to lessening inequality during the intervening period of 1929–49. The fall in the share of wealth held by top families is ascribable largely to a failure to maintain a share of saving equal to their share of wealth. The decline of saving inequality is associated in turn with an observed decline in income inequality. The fact that the share of wealth of top individuals fell more than the share of top families is believed to be due to increasing splitting of wealth within families, principally between husbands and wives. One factor which encouraged such splitting was higher rates of income and estate taxation. The main finding about changing inequality—namely, the fall in the share of wealth held by the top 2 per cent of families from 33 per cent in 1922 to 29 per cent in 1953—is compatible with observed price and income changes over this period.

The Distribution of Wealth in 1962

DOROTHY S. PROJECTOR
and GERTRUDE S. WEISS

The results of a recent survey, undertaken cooperatively by the Federal Reserve System and the Bureau of the Census to determine the distribution of wealth and debt among American consumers, have just recently become available. The following summary is from the Survey of Financial Characteristics of Consumers (August 1966). The authors are staff economists in the Division of Research and Statistics, Board of Governors of the Federal Reserve.

THIS REPORT PRESENTS data on the size and composition of wealth of the civilian noninstitutional population of the United States on December 31, 1962. The analyses deal with the determinants of size of wealth, the components of wealth and debt and their diffusion throughout the population, the changes in composition of wealth as wealth increases, and the variation in patterns of ownership among consumer units of differing characteristics.

The Survey differed markedly from other consumer surveys as to sample design in that segments of the population expected to have sizable amounts of wealth were sampled at much higher rates than the remaining population. As a result, the Survey supplies data not hitherto available about the size and composition of wealth of the upper income and wealth groups.

As may be seen from Chart 1, variation among consumer units in the size of their wealth is large. For most consumer units the amount of wealth owned at any point in time is the result of the size and composition of past saving. Only 1 in 20 units in the Survey reported that an inheritance accounted for a substantial portion of its present wealth.

CHART 1. *Distribution of Consumer Units by Amount of Wealth, December 31, 1962*

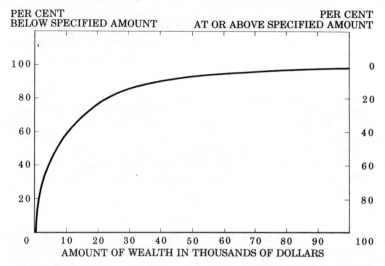

There is a strong positive relation between size of wealth and size of current income. Average wealth is estimated to be about $7,600 for consumer units with incomes less than $3,000 and is larger for each successive income level, reaching well over $1,000,000 for those with incomes of $100,000 and over. The relation between wealth and age is also positive for units with head less than 65 years of age. The wealth of young units—head under 35—for example, was about $6,300 on the average, while that for units in the 55 to 64 age group was more than five times that amount. For units headed by persons 65 and over, the average wealth of about $31,000 was smaller than the average for the 55 to 64 age group, but was still substantially larger than the average of $21,000 for all units.

A major difference among the several forms of consumer wealth—own homes, automobiles, businesses, and the various kinds of liquid and investment assets—is the extent to which ownership is general throughout the population. Some, such as liquid assets, homes, and automobiles, are owned by well over half of all consumer units, whereas others, such as publicly traded stock, investment real estate, and equities in businesses and professions, are owned by fewer than one-fifth. An asset such as a checking account, which is owned by 59 per cent of consumer units, is usually also widely held in each income and age group; for example, ownership ranges from 34 per cent in the lowest income class to 99 per cent in the top income class. Conversely, for an asset such as stock, which is owned by 16 per cent of all units, ownership varies more widely by income groups, from 7 per cent at the lower end of the income range to 97 per cent at the top.

Chart 2 presents measures of the diffusion of wealth, debt, and their components that combine the frequency with the value of each asset or debt. The measure is the share of the aggregate value of each asset or debt held by each segment of the income distribution. The diffusion of total wealth and total debt and of the components of wealth and debt is shown in this chart. The

CHART 2A. *Income Diffusion of Wealth and Debt.*

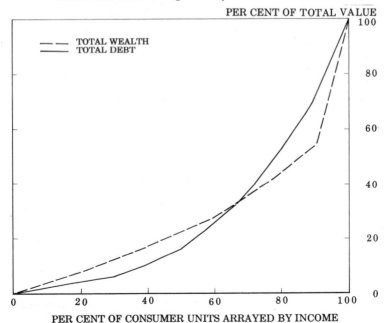

PER CENT OF TOTAL VALUE

TOTAL WEALTH
TOTAL DEBT

PER CENT OF CONSUMER UNITS ARRAYED BY INCOME

lines least bent to the right—for example, home ownership equity —represent those assets that are most widely diffused among income groups. The lines most bent to the right—for example, marketable securities other than stock—represent the assets with ownership least widely diffused among income groups. In general, those assets that are most widely held in the population also tend to show the widest diffusion by this measure.

CHART 2B. *Income Diffusion of the Components of Wealth.*

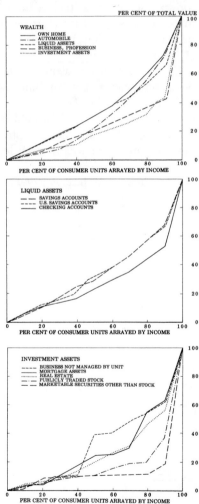

PART THREE   Determinants of Inequality

Determinants of the Distribution of Labor Incomes

GEORGE J. STIGLER

George J. Stigler is Walgreen Professor of American Institutions at the University of Chicago. In his book, The Theory of Price (1966), he examines some of the factors producing inequality in the distribution of labor incomes.

LABOR IS much the most important productive service—it receives four-fifths or more of total income even in an economy as well stocked with capital as the United States. We shall concentrate attention first upon relative wages in various occupations.

COMPETITIVE WAGE STRUCTURE

Competition tends to eliminate differences in rates of wages for similar workers in different occupations and geographical locations, for the worker who is in the job where wages are low will move to the higher paying job. This movement will raise wages in the market the workers are leaving, and lower them in the market the workers are entering.

Equilibrium will be reached in the occupational and geographical wage structure when the net advantages of all occupations open to the worker are equal. "Net advantages" embrace all the factors which attract or repel a worker, and the main content of the theory of competitive wage structure consists of

91

the analysis of these factors. Aside from the wage rate itself, these components of "net advantages" are as follows.

Direct Occupational Expense · If a carpenter must provide his own tools, but an employee in a sash and door plant does not, the former must be compensated for the cost of his tools, in arriving at the comparative net advantages of the two occupations. Few questions are raised by this simple example, but a host of subtle difficulties are raised by other cases—especially since the income tax allows one to deduct occupational expenses. Let us give just one example.

A professor buys books on the subject he teaches. Are they an occupational expense? Yes, since they are necessary to the work he does. Perhaps—but why doesn't he borrow them from the library? No, because he likes the subject and would buy at least some of them even if he were not a professor, say merely a college president. And what if he doesn't get around to reading the book? Should it then be charged to furnishings? These complications can in turn be made more complicated, but they should serve to suggest the shadowy boundaries separating occupational expenses from consumption expenditures.

Costs of Training · Suppose a young man of 17 just finishing high school is attracted by two occupations. In one (A) he will earn $3,000 per year until age 65; in the other (B) he must first go to college for four years. How much should occupation B pay to offset the additional costs of training? These additional costs of training are two: the direct outlays for college (tuition, books, and so on); and the four-year delay before his earnings begin. Living costs during college are not an additional cost because they are already covered by the income which will be earned if he enters A. He should go through the following arithmetic (assuming an interest rate of 8 per cent):

Occupation A

The present value of an annuity of $1 per year for 48 years is $12.1891, so the present value of lifetime earnings in A are $3000 \times \$12.1891 = \$36,567$.

Occupation B

1. The present value of an annuity of $1 per year for 4 years is $3.3121. If direct college costs are $1500 per year, the present value of these costs is $1500 \times \$3.3121 = \$4,968$.

2. The present value of an annuity of $1 per year for 44 years is $12.0771. When he leaves college, his lifetime earnings will have a present value of $\$S_B$ (his annual earnings) $\times 12.0771$. To discount this sum back four years to age 17, it must be multiplied by 0.7350.

The two occupations will therefore have equal present values of lifetime earnings if

$$S_B \times 12.0771 \times 0.7350 - \$4,968 = \$36,567$$
$$S_B = \$4679.$$

It may be noticed that the interest costs of the four-year delay in receiving income in B account for most of the difference; elimination of direct school costs would reduce S_B only to $4,119.[1] Of course a lower interest rate would reduce the equilibrium difference.

To the investment in formal schooling we should also add the investment in acquiring knowledge and skill on the job. If for men of equal age and schooling one job will give experience in one year that increases future income by $20 a year (as compared to experience in the others), clearly it is a more attractive job, and hence in equilibrium earnings must be appropriately lower in this occupation.[2] Even today in most economies the amount invested in acquiring training in the labor force far ex-

---

1. Since the various components of the difference are not additive, there is no simple way of breaking up the difference between the equilibrium earnings in A and B, but
   (1.) The four-year shorter working life in B leads to a present value per dollar of only $\$12.1891 - \$12.0771 = \$0.112$, or about 1 per cent less than in A.
   (2.) The costs of training have a present value of $4,968, or about 14 per cent of the present value of earnings in A.
2. Earnings will be lower by the present value of the future income stream, which depends upon the age of the workers. If the age is 24, and 40 years of the additional earnings will be received after the year, at 8 per cent the present value is $221.

ceeds the amount invested in training through formal education.

The life pattern of earnings in an occupation invariably displays a rising and then falling section. The rising section is due to the increase in ability attributable to experience; the falling section is due to decreased competence and (since earnings depend upon amount of work as well as the wage rate) lesser amount (time or intensity) of work. The lengths of these segments will obviously depend upon the nature of the work, and the 1960 patterns given in Figure 1 display some of the variety we observe.

FIGURE 1. *Life Earning Patterns for White Males in Selected Occupations*

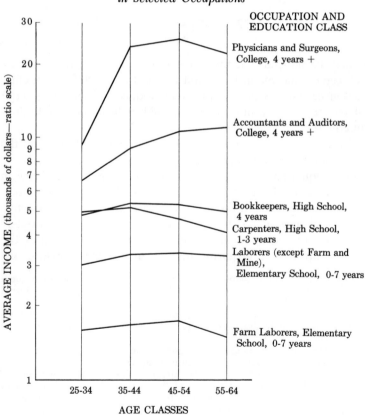

Instability of Employment · An occupation that offers steady employment will yield larger earnings, at the same wage rate, than one in which unemployment is at times substantial. If a postal clerk earns $4,000 a year, a similar occupation in which unemployment averaged 5 per cent would have to pay $4,000/0.95 = $4,211 to yield the same expected return. If the unemployment rate could be estimated accurately, and if men did not tend to stay unemployed longer when they received unemployment insurance, the premium for unemployment insurance would be $211 a year (plus costs of administration). The worker in the occupation with unemployment may be repelled by the uncertainties in employment and income, and demand an extra premium for undertaking them; we now turn to this question.

Uncertainty · Within an occupation there will be dispersion of earnings even for workers of the same age, training, and experience. Much of this difference will be due to differences in personal ability but some will be due to other factors. Variations in unemployment have just been cited as one example, but others can be added: fluctuations in output due to weather (which affects many trades besides farming); fluctuations in amount of work due to business conditions; and so on. These forces will cause fluctuations over time in the average earnings for all members of the occupation.

A second set of truly random forces will also operate. A factory may be closed by fire; only one salesman can get the huge order; personal injuries can hit haphazardly. These random factors have some tendency to cancel out over time, but they do not average out completely in a human lifetime; if the standard deviation of the annual incomes in an occupation is $1,000, the standard deviation of a lifetime average is about $160 [3] so 2.5 per cent of the occupation will have lifetime averages $320 above, and an equal number $320 below, the occupational average.[4]

3. The standard deviation of the mean is $\sigma/\sqrt{n}$, and n is taken here as 40 years. The standard deviation will be larger if, as is likely, there is some correlation of year-to-year fluctuations in earnings.

4. This dispersion of individual earnings is independent of that due to fluctuations in average earnings of the occupation over time, which also may command a risk premium.

Of two occupations with equal averages but unequal dispersions, which will be the more attractive? We may note one certain effect: the occupation with the greater dispersion will pay more in income taxes. A progressive income tax takes more from two incomes of $5,000 and $10,000 than it takes from two incomes of $7,500. This will make the occupation with the more stable incomes more attractive, since it is income after tax that workers will seek to equalize.

Putting this tax effect aside, there is no clear answer to our question. Some people believe in their good luck, and will prefer the occupation with larger prizes; others will take the opposite choice. How the market as a whole behaves is especially difficult to determine, because all observed dispersion is compounded of the effects of uncertainty and of differences in the ability of individuals, and dispersion due to the latter cause is not relevant to the choice. Fortunately our knowledge is incomplete; there is still work for future generations of economists.

Other Factors · The foregoing list of factors which influence the occupational structure of wages is essentially that of Adam Smith. Research since his time has quantified some of these factors, but it has not revealed many others of comparable size.

Differences in living costs have proved to be one substantial factor. Costs are consistently higher the larger the community in which one lives, so occupations which are concentrated in large cities must have higher average earnings than those concentrated in small cities. Thus it has been estimated that average incomes of lawyers would be 20 per cent lower if they were distributed among city sizes in the same proportion as population.[5]

Several other factors have been of comparable importance but of narrower scope. Prestige and social esteem are important in a few occupations, but more often the esteem attaches to those occupations in which earnings are large. Racial discrimination has had an important but declining influence.[6]

5. M. Friedman and Simon Kuznets, *Income from Independent Professional Practice* (New York: National Bureau of Economic Research, 1945), p. 184.

6. See G. Becker, *The Economics of Discrimination* (Chicago: University of Chicago Press, 1957).

EARNINGS OF THE INDIVIDUAL

The labor income of a household consists of the sum of the labor income of its members. Let us begin, however, at a still more basic level, the individual worker.

Suppose all men in an occupation to be strictly homogeneous: they have the same abilities, training, and experience (which is really training in a broad sense), and are therefore of equal age, and when employed work equally long with equal intensity. Their wages would still differ because of chance: luck in an older language, random fluctuation in a newer.

These components of luck are infinitely numerous but we may classify them into roughly three groups:

1. Personal factors—vicissitudes of health and accident.

2. Employer factors—vicissitudes of any one employer, both physical (fire, flood) and economic (bankruptcy).

3. Market factors—vicissitudes in finding new jobs, or getting the best rate of pay for given work.[7]

If we could find a group of identical workers, the differences in their earnings would measure these factors.

Let us now still keep the members of the occupation identical in abilities, and move them back to age 17, when they have just finished high school. Then let each young man be offered the choice of two kinds of future income streams (Figure 2). One stream begins immediately—he enters the labor force and begins to earn. The second stream assumes that he goes on to college: for four years it is negative (by the amount that his tuition, books, and so on, exceed part-time earnings), and then positive. Each stream rises after formal education is completed because men learn also by working, and then eventually declines after some age, as their energies and abilities decline.

These income streams can have the same discounted value on the day of graduation from high school,[8] and in competitive equi-

7. On this last, see my "Information in the Labor Market," *Journal of Political Economy,* Supplement (October 1962).

8. Here we put aside the problem of borrowing to go to school, by assuming that loan funds are available at a given interest rate.

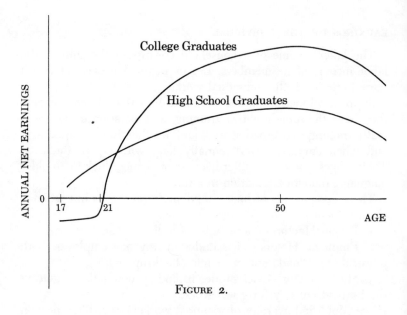

FIGURE 2.

librium the discounted values will indeed be equal. The lifetime earnings, as represented by these present values, are identical. Yet there are now two additional sources of dispersion:

1. The variation in earnings among individuals with given formal education because of age.

2. The variation in earnings among individuals with given age because of formal education.

In fact we should not emphasize *formal* education, because one can learn also at work, and in most societies in the world much more training is obtained at work than in schools, if we measure training by its effect on earnings.

We have reached an interesting conclusion. If the men in an occupation were of identical ability, and worked equal periods and with equal intensity, the present value of their life time earnings would be equal (chance factors aside), but their earnings in any one year or short period of years would display substantial dispersion. Chance factors would also be relatively less important over the entire working life, although there would not be complete cancellation.[9]

There would in fact be a larger dispersion, even under these assumed conditions of identity of workers' competence at age 17, than this analysis suggests. Some dispersion is essentially nominal, and if we could correct earnings for differences in costs of living and costs of working they would vanish. Examples are the higher wage rates in larger cities, where costs of living are higher,[10] and the higher wage rate of employees who use their own cars on company business if they are not compensated directly. These sources of nominal dispersion cannot be wholly eliminated at present (for example, there is no satisfactory index number of the cost of living in communities of different sizes), so they must be kept in mind in interpreting present-day data.

Moreover, we must notice one final source of dispersion of earnings compatible with equal abilities. Men differ in their comparative desires for money and leisure, so one man will work 40 weeks, another 50, or one will work overtime when another does not. These choices will yield different money incomes but may represent equal streams of utility.

When we enlarge our view to compare different occupations—still retaining the assumption of equal abilities—most of the differences will still be of the kinds we have just discussed. For example, a college professor will earn more than a high-school teacher of equal ability because the former has invested for three or four years in getting a Ph.D. Similar remarks can be made

9. Cancellation would be incomplete because of death and serious ailments (which we have put aside) and more generally because fluctuations in earnings in successive years will not be uncorrelated. The law of large numbers would ensure virtual elimination of chance from lifetime earnings if the various events were independent.

10. The higher cost of living in a larger city rests basically on the higher costs of land. Housing costs being higher, wage rates must be higher by compensating amounts (to maintain equality of real earnings with those of workers in smaller cities). Hence all personal services (medical care, haircuts, and the like) will also be more expensive in larger cities. The fact that enterprises in large cities can successfully compete with those in smaller cities despite the higher wage levels is due to the external economies obtainable in large economic centers.

about duration of work, on-job training, and size of community. But in addition we encounter two other sources of dispersion.

Some occupations have incomes which are much more stable over time than those of other occupations. The self-employed worker is much more subject to fluctuations in demand than the salaried worker, so the annual earnings of the former will be higher in good years and lower in poor years. Over a period of, say, five years, of course, most of this difference will be eliminated, but annual data will display large differences. In addition it is generally believed that these occupations with unstable incomes repel workers, so an additional premium must be paid for bearing these fluctuations.

We have not introduced the most obvious of the sources of inequality of earnings; differences in "ability." How much difference there is in abilities of men, no one can say. In fact, ability is not measurable: it consists of more than strength, or I.Q., or creativity, or courage, or tenacity, or a liking for work, or personal charm, or handsome appearance, or unusual vocal cords. The only measure of ability we have, in fact, is the variation in earnings that remains after we have subtracted out the effects of education, age, community size, and other measurable factors.[11] But then we are mixing chance factors with ability, and in plain fact, no one knows how to separate this remaining dispersion into luck and ability. Individuals have the same difficulty: poor bridge players usually say they never get good cards.[12] Since able people congregate in certain occupations—physicists are on average more able than electricians—the aggregate effect of ability (and luck) on income is much greater than the effect within an occupation.

The list of factors making for differences in money income in any year is formidably long, but it is not complete. The differences in ability and luck aside, we have discussed only differences due to voluntary decisions of men, which would exist in

11. Since ability is surely positively correlated with education, and possibly with other factors we have enumerated, some of its effects will be attributed to these other factors.

12. In 1,000 hands, the influence of the cards is negligible. If men lived 1,000 years, we could confidently ascribe their differences in earnings to ability.

fully competitive markets. In addition, any real society will exhibit dispersion because of the workings of several other forces.

First, there will be differences in returns due to monopoly power. If a labor union, or a cartel, succeeds in raising the incomes of its members above the competitive level, an additional source of dispersion will be created. We shall not attempt any direct estimate of the magnitude of such forces, but for select groups earnings can be 20 or 50 per cent higher under favorable conditions than competition would allow.

Second, there are differences in earnings due to market imperfections, quite aside from monopoly. The following are characteristic:

1. It may be that the rate on investment in training is much higher than the going rate of interest for investments of comparable risk, and yet many people may not be able to borrow the funds to make this investment in themselves. We have indicated that this was probably an important source of dispersion at earlier times in the United States, and it is still an important source in many economies. We should also notice, however, that there is substantial overinvestment in the training of many people, provided by parents acting on parental rather than economic motives.[13]

2. Imperfect foresight leads people to acquire training which proves to have a low value, as when a skilled craft is displaced by a technological advance. There are corresponding gains from unexpected increases in demand but they are of shorter duration since one can train additional specialists in a few years.

3. Discrimination against certain groups will lower their incomes—the conspicuous instances in history have of course been racial and religious groups.[14]

We do not add another phenomenon popular with detergent-box orators, nepotism. If an able man bequeaths high office to an incompetent son, this is generally a bequest of property in-

13. A fond parent who invests $10,000 in a child's education with an internal rate of return of 1 per cent, would of course increase that child's money income if instead the $10,000 were invested in bonds and the child were given the income instead of the education.

14. See, for example, the article on Jews in *Palgrave's Dictionary of Political Economy.*

come disguised as wage income, and the son would be richer if the high office were filled with an able appointment and the additional income of the enterprise were paid to the son in dividends. Bequest is an influence on real wage income only when the job, rather than the control of the enterprise, is owned by a person.

FAMILY WAGE INCOME

Families display an astonishing variety of patterns in number of wage earners, but the dominant pattern in multiple earner families is of course for the husband and wife to work.[15] This is the only class of multiple earners we shall discuss.

Leisure is a so-called normal good—people consume more leisure as their income rises, prices remaining constant. We should therefore expect fewer wives to work in the labor force as the incomes of husbands rise. The facts are partially, but only partially, in keeping with this expectation. If we compare different families at a given time, it is generally true that the labor force participation rate—a gracious phrase denoting the fraction of a given class of women who are in the labor force—varies inversely with the husband's earnings. We illustrate this characteristic finding from the 1960 Census (Table 1).

But this is only half the story. Over the last hundred years, the share of women in the labor force has been rising rapidly while average real earnings of both male and female workers

15. The 1960 Census gives the following pattern of families (defined as two or more related persons):

FAMILY EARNER TYPE	NUMBER (1,000's)	1959 MEDIAN INCOME
None	4,840	$1,499
One	23,465	5,179
Husband	19,614	
Wife	1,318	
Single Family Head	2,530	
Multiple	16,825	7,013
Husband-Wife	11,172	
Other	5,653	

In addition 13.2 million unrelated individuals had a median income of $1,596.

TABLE 1. *Labor-Force Participation Rates of Wives in White, Non-farm Families with Husband Present*

Family Type	Earnings of Husband in 1959, 1960, or 1961					
	Under 1,000	$1,000– 2,000	2,000– 3,000	3,000– 5,000	5,000– 7,000	Over 7,000
Children 6–17	53.9	49.2	49.3	47.0	39.2	28.2
Children under 6	32.3	24.6	24.5	21.5	16.0	10.7

have been rising about 2 per cent a year—over time the family appears to have bought less leisure for the wife. The reconciliation with the opposite finding in the cross-sectional data is to be found in the nature of the alternatives to work in the labor force. For a wife, the alternatives are in fact two: leisure; and work within the home. Leisure is undoubtedly a normal good, and if we could put aside work within the home, we would expect a rise in wage rates to lead to a reduction in women's labor force participation (as has in fact taken place with males) because the income effect of higher wage rates would dominate the substitution effect.[16]

The productive work of women within the home has modified this relationship.[17] The increasing labor force participation of wives with secularly rising incomes is due to three main forces:

1. A rise in real wages is a rise in the alternative cost of working within the home, as compared with working in the labor force and buying household services. This secular rise in wage rates therefore leads to a higher labor-force participation.

2. The advances in technology have reduced the costs of purchasing many services previously performed within the household (including preparation of clothing and food, laundry services, cleaning, and so on), and hence increased the comparative efficiency of work for money income.[18]

16. The cost of leisure is foregone earnings, so a rise in wage rates is a rise in the cost of leisure, which would lead to a decline in leisure if real income were held constant.

17. For a fuller analysis, see J. Mincer, "Labor Force Participation of Married Women," in *Aspects of Labor Economics* (New York: National Bureau of Economic Research, 1962).

18. The income tax has been a counter force: if a wife's earnings are taxed at a marginal rate of (say) 30 per cent, a wife must earn $100 in the market to purchase $70 worth of household services.

3. Young children create a major demand for household services not cheaply obtainable in the market. The secular decline in family size has greatly increased the share of time women may serve in the labor force.

The presence of multiple earners affects the distribution of family income in various ways. If the labor force participation rate of wives were independent of that of husbands, the effect of their work would be to increase, and very substantially, the dispersion of family earnings. In fact, two relationships between wives' work and husband's earnings modify this. One force we have already noted: the lower the husband's income, the larger the share of wives who enter the labor force. In addition, when a family has a temporarily low income—perhaps because of ill health or unemployment of the husband—wives enter the labor force to offset this reduction: Mincer's studies indicate that there is a strong negative relationship between wives' labor-force participation and transitory components of income. In fact he finds that the dispersion of earnings of family heads and of entire families are essentially equal.[19] The incomes of families with both husband and wife present had a coefficient of inequality of 0.327 for families with only husbands working in 1959, but there was slightly less inequality (0.309) among families in which both husband and wife worked.[20]

19. See "Labor Supply, Family Income, and Consumption," *Proceedings of American Economic Association* (May 1959), 574–83.
20. These measures, based upon the 1960 Census, unfortunately include also property income. The coefficient for all families, regardless of number of workers, was 0.333.

Determinants of Inequality in a Property-owning Democracy

JAMES E. MEADE

In his recent book, Efficiency, Equality, and the Ownership of Property *(1964), from which this section is taken, Professor Meade analyzes some of the forces determining temporal changes in the distribution of property ownership.*

EXTREME INEQUALITIES in the ownership of property are in my view undesirable quite apart from any inequalities of income which they may imply. A man with much property has great bargaining strength and a great sense of security, independence, and freedom; and he enjoys these things not only *vis-à-vis* his propertyless fellow citizens but also *vis-à-vis* the public authorities. He can snap his fingers at those on whom he must rely for an income; for he can always live for a time on his capital. The propertyless man must continuously and without interruption acquire his income by working for an employer or by qualifying to receive it from a public authority. An unequal distribution of property means an unequal distribution of power and status even if it is prevented from causing too unequal a distribution of income.

Let us turn our attention therefore to the questions why in the sort of free-enterprise or mixed economy with which we are familiar we end up with such startling inequalities in the ownership of property, what changes in our institutional or tax arrangements would be necessary substantially to equalize ownership, and what disadvantages from the point of view of efficiency these reforms could themselves have.

I shall consider these matters in three stages. First, I shall assume that we are dealing simply with a number of adult citizens who have presumably been born in the past but who do not marry or have children or die or even grow old in the sense of experiencing diminished ability or vigour as time passes. I shall at this first stage examine the effects upon property distribution as these citizens work, save, and accumulate property. I shall assume that the State taxes neither income nor property and does not interfere in any way with this process of private capital accumulation.

At a second stage I shall introduce the demographic factors—births, marriages, deaths—and will examine the way in which they are likely to modify the pattern of ownership that would otherwise be developing.

At the third stage I will introduce the State. At this stage we shall be concerned with the ways in which economic and financial policies might be devised to modify the economic and demographic factors in such a way as to lead to a more equal distribution of property.

For the first stage, consider two personal properties: a small one (K_1) and a large one (K_2). Will the small property be growing at a smaller or a larger proportional rate of growth than the large property? If the small property is growing at a greater proportional rate (say, 5 per cent per annum) than the large property (say, 2 per cent per annum), then the ratio of $\dfrac{K_1}{K_2}$ will be becoming more nearly equal to unity. In this case *relative* inequality will be diminishing. We are concerned then at this first stage of our enquiry with the factors which will determine the proportional rate of growth of different properties.

These proportional growth rates (which we will call k_1 and k_2) for our two properties may be expressed as

$$k_1 = \frac{S_1(E_1 + V_1 K_1)}{K_1} \text{ and } k_2 = \frac{S_2(E_2 + V_2 K_2)}{K_2}$$

respectively, where E_1 and E_2 represent the earned incomes or wages of the two property owners and V_1 and V_2 represent the two rates of profit earned by the two owners on their properties K_1 and K_2. Thus $V_1 K_1$ and $V_2 K_2$ represent the unearned incomes of the two property owners and $E_1 + V_1 K_1$ and $E_2 + V_2 K_2$ their earned and unearned incomes. If S_1 and S_2 represent the proportions of these incomes which are saved and added to accumulated property, then $S_1(E_1 + V_1K_1)$ and $S_2(E_2 + V_2K_2)$ are the absolute annual increases in the two properties and these, expressed as a ratio of the two properties, measure their proportionate rates of growth.

In these pages I can do little more than enumerate the various influences at work. Some of them, it will be seen, tend to make $k_1 > k_2$ (these are the equalizing tendencies), and some tend to make $k_2 > k_1$ (these are the disequalizing tendencies). There is undoubtedly at work a large element of these latter disequalizing tendencies—what Professor Myrdal has called the principle of Circular and Cumulative Causation—the "to-him-that-hath-shall-be-given" principle. On the other hand, trees do not grow up to the skies, and there are some systematic equalizing tendencies. It is the balance between these equalizing and disequalizing factors which results in the end in a given unequal, but not indefinitely unequal, distribution of properties. Let us consider in turn the influences of E, V, and S upon the rate of growth of property k.

1. The influence of earned incomes, E, must be an equalizing factor so far as two properties at the extreme ranges of the scale of properties are concerned. We can see the point this way. If K_1 were zero, citizen 1 would have only an earned income E_1. If he saved any part of this, his savings would be S^1E^1 and his proportionate rate of accumulation of property would be $\frac{S_1E_1}{0} = \infty$. Consider at the other extreme a multi-multi-multi-millionaire. Now earning power, E_1 may well be enhanced by the ownership of property, but not without limit. In the case of our multi-multi-multimillionaire, E_2 will be negligible relatively to K_2. If $\frac{E_2}{K_2}$ were for practical purposes zero, k_2 would equal $\frac{S_2V_2K_2}{K_2} = S_2V_2$. As between the extreme ranges then, we have $k_1 > k_2$ and there is bound to be equalization. This is perhaps the basic reason why our measure of relative inequality $\frac{K_1}{K_2}$ can never reach zero or infinity. In the intermediate ranges all we can say is that the higher is $\frac{E}{K}$, the more rapid the rate of growth of

property k, other things being equal. If earning power were equally distributed among our citizens (with $E_1 = E_2$), then this factor would be an equalizing one as between any two properties K_1 and K_2.

2. The factor V, on the other hand, is unquestionably disequalizing—at least in the United Kingdom where there is strong evidence that the rate of return on property is much lower for small properties than for large properties. It is probable that there will be little difference in the V which is relevant for all properties above a certain range. It is doubtful whether the multimillionaire can get any higher yield than the millionaire on his property. But as between the really small properties and the large range of big properties, this influence is likely to be disequalizing and to be a factor enabling the whole range of large properties to grow more rapidly than the small.

3. Finally, what is the influence of S, the proportion of income saved, on k for different sizes of K? Economists have done a great deal of theoretical and statistical work on the factors determining the proportions of income saved and spent. These investigations are of basic importance not only for theories of employment and of growth but also for the determination of the distribution among individuals of the ownership of property.

Let us consider only the implications of two possible features of a probable type of savings function. Let us assume (i) that the proportion of income saved rises with a rise in real income, though not, of course, without limit, since less than 100 per cent of income will be saved however great is income, and (ii) that the proportion of income saved out of any given income falls the larger is the property owned. This second assumption means that a man with £1,000 a year all earned will save more than a man with £1,000 a year which represents the interest on a property of £10,000. For the ability to save will be the same, but the need to accumulate some property will be higher in the first than in the second case.

If the savings function is of this general form, then as between two unequal properties ($K_2 > K_1$) owned by two persons with the same earning power ($E_1 = E_2$), we cannot, without more precise information, say which will be growing the more rapidly.

The fact that a larger total income will be enjoyed by the man with the larger property will tend to raise the proportion of income which he can save; but, on the other hand, the fact that he already has a larger property will tend to reduce the proportion of income which he will save, and, in addition, the fact that $\frac{E}{K}$ is low in his case will keep down the rate of growth of his property.

But with the sort of savings function which we are assuming there are two other kinds of comparison which one can make with more definite results. If one compares two citizens with equal incomes but unequal properties, the small property of the man with the high earning power will be growing the more rapidly; he has the same ability to save but a greater need to accumulate; his savings will be greater and his existing property smaller. If one compares two citizens with the same property, but different incomes, the property of the man with the high income (i.e. the high earning power) will be growing the more rapidly; he has a higher ability to save and the same need to accumulate; his savings will be greater and his existing property the same. The result is, of course, that with our assumed savings function there will be exceptionally strong forces at work associating high properties with high earning power. This combination of forces will exaggerate the inequality in the distribution of total personal incomes.

Let us pass to the second stage of our examination of the factors determining the distribution of property, namely the demographic factors. Consider two citizens, man and wife, each with a property. The rate of growth of their properties is determined by the economic factors we have just considered—S, E, V, and K. They have children. These children grow up and start to earn and to save—they acquire E's and S's of their own. They start to accumulate properties of their own, at first indefinitely high proportional rates of growth, since they start with no property. At some time both parents die and leave their properties to their children. The children at some time—it may be before or after their parents' deaths—choose spouses. And so two citizens and two properties join together in holy matrimony and restart the same process of marriage, birth, and death.

What we want to consider is whether the factors of marriage, birth, and death will lead to a greater or a lesser degree of concentration of property ownership than would have occurred through the processes of capital accumulation which we examined at stage one in the absence of marriage, births, and deaths. The answer depends upon two things: the degree of assortative mating and the degree of differential fertility.

Suppose that any man was equally likely to be married to any woman in our society. Suppose, that is to say, that there were no assortative mating. Then the cycle of birth, marriage, and death would introduce an important equalizing factor into the system. Let us isolate for examination this basic demographic factor by assuming for the moment that every married couple reproduces itself by producing one son and one daughter and then leaves half the joint property of the parents to each child. Consider in this context the wealthiest family in the community, i.e. the family which has the highest joint property of husband and wife; they have a son and a daughter who, if they married each other, would perpetuate the same extreme concentration of wealth which they inherited from their parents; but brother and sister do not marry each other; the rich son must marry a wife with less inherited property than himself and the rich daughter a husband with less inherited property than herself; they in turn have children who are not so much enriched by inheritance as they themselves were. The general reshuffle generation by generation through marriage tends to equalize inherited fortunes. If there were no assortative mating, there would be a strong probability that a citizen whose inheritance was exceptionally high would marry someone with a smaller inheritance and that a citizen whose inheritance was exceptionally low would marry someone with a larger inheritance. But, of course, in fact marriage is strongly assortative. The rich are brought up in the same social milieu as the rich, and the poor in the same social milieu as the poor. The reshufflement of property ownership is very much less marked.

Differential fertility could clearly have an important influence on the distribution of property. If rich parents had fewer children than did poor parents, the large fortunes would become more and more concentrated in fewer and fewer hands. If the rich had more children than the poor, the large properties would fall in relative size as they become more and more widely dispersed and the smaller would grow in relative size as they become more and more concentrated on a smaller number of children. At first sight it might, therefore, appear as if differential fertility might work in either direction—equalizing property ownership if the rich were exceptionally fertile and disequalizing it if the rich were exceptionally infertile. And this would, of course, be so in the short run; and it would be so in the long run as well, if there were some forces at work which caused riches itself to lead to exceptionally high or exceptionally low fertility.

But consider another possible type of cause of differential fertility. Suppose (i) that every couple has at least one child, but (ii) that there is some genetic factor at work which makes some couples more fertile than others and (iii) that this genetic factor is in no way correlated positively or negatively with any other relevant genetic characteristic. We may happen to start with the infertile at the bottom end of the property scale; if so, the immediate effect will be to tend to equalize property ownership. But gradually as time passes the infertile will be found, through the process of concentrated inheritance, further and further up the property scale. In the end it will be the rich who are the infertile and the poor who are the fertile. The permanent influence of such a form of differential fertility will thus ultimately be disequalizing in its effect upon property ownership.

But sons and daughters are endowed not only with inherited property but also with earning power. Here we are confronted with the great problem of nature *versus* nurture. Earning power undoubtedly depends largely upon environmental factors. We have already observed the great importance of investment in education in raising earning power. In a society which left everything including education to private market forces rich fathers could educate their sons much more readily than could poor fathers. The inheritance of a good education would be just like the inheritance of tangible wealth from rich parents.

But high earning power is not wholly due to education and other environmental factors; there can be no doubt that there are also some genetic factors at work in determining a person's ability to earn.

It is possible that by the mechanism of accumulation already described (that is to say, because high earning power makes it easier to accumulate property) there is some positive correlation between large properties and high earning power. But if earning power is to some extent genetically determined, one would expect to find rich parents with high earning power having children with above-average earning power, but not so much above-average as themselves; and one would expect to find the poorest parents with the lowest earning power having children with below-average earning power but not so much below average as themselves. But the association between property ownership and earning power may nevertheless be restored in the next generation by the exceptionally rapid accumulation of property by those children who happen to be born with exceptionally high earning power relatively to their inherited property and by the exceptionally slow rate of accumulation by those children to happen to be born with exceptionally low earning power relatively to their inherited property.

All that one can say in the present unhappy state of almost complete ignorance about this important aspect of society is that in so far as earning power is a factor which leads to the accumulation of property, then any 'regression towards the mean' in the inheritance of earning power would in itself tend to equalize the distribution of the ownership of property.[1]

We have so far considered some of the economic and biological factors which may systematically work towards the equalization or the disequalization of the ownership of property. But

1. The preceding paragraphs suggest that (1) low fertility and (2) high ability to earn may both be factors which tend to raise people upon the social scale and the property ladder. These factors probably both have some genetic elements in their determination. Moreover, it is a well-known fact that men and women are likely to marry within their own class. Thus there may be a continuous process tending to mate the genes for ability with those for infertility and the genes for inability with those for fertility. The dysgenic aspect of such a social arrangement is obvious (cf. Professor R. A. Fisher, *The Social Selection of Human Fertility*, pp. 22–32).

there are, of course, for an individual enormously important elements of pure environmental luck. Was a man lucky or unlucky in the actual school to which he went as a child and in the actual teachers which he there encountered? Was he lucky or unlucky in the actual locality in which he sought work or took his business initiatives? Was he lucky or unlucky in the choice of the subject matter of his education and training? In the choice of industries in which he invested his first savings or initial inheritance? In the bright ideas which he tried to exploit? A lucky combination of an able man with the right idea in the right place at the right time can—as in the case of men such as Henry Ford—lead to an explosive growth of an individual property. We must regard society from the point of view of property ownership as subject to a series of random strokes of good and bad luck, upsetting continuously the existing pattern of ownership. But at the same time there are at work the systematic economic forces of accumulation and the systematic biological and demographic forces of inheritance which are some of them tending to equalize and some of them to disequalize ownership. The striking inequalities which we observe in the real world are the result of the balance of these systematic forces working in a society subject to the random strokes of luck. That is all we can say until this most important field for research and enquiry has been cultivated much more extensively than has been the case up to the present.

PART FOUR   Combatting Inequality

Toward a Property-owning Democracy

JAMES E. MEADE

In this passage from the book, Efficiency, Equality, and the
Ownership of Property, *Professor Meade examines the effectiveness of property and inheritance taxation and educational policy
in reducing inequality in property ownership.*

WE NOW TURN to the last stage of our enquiry into the factors
which affect the distribution of the ownership of property,
namely governmental policy of various kinds. Let us start by
considering the effects of various forms of tax.

We have already considered the possibility of using a progressive income tax as part of the machinery of the Welfare State to
tax the rich in order to raise funds to subsidize the poor, and we
have already noted the fact that progressive income tax of this
kind may have adverse effects upon incentives to work, enterprise, and save. Such taxation will also have some effect as an
equalizer of the distribution of the ownership of property. Since
large properties are an important cause of high incomes, the sub-
jection of high incomes to highly progressive taxation will reduce the ability to save of the owners of large properties more
than it will reduce the ability to save of the owners of small
properties. This will help the small properties to grow at a higher
rate relatively to that of the large properties. This tendency will
be still more marked in so far as the progressive income tax dis-
criminates against unearned incomes and in favour of earned incomes. For a tax on incomes from property as contrasted with a
tax on incomes from work is a more direct imposition on the

owners of large properties as such.

But different properties may earn different incomes according to the form in which they are invested—cash earns nothing; short-dated gilt-edged securities a very small yield; and so on until one comes to the high average yields from risky and enterprising ventures. An annual tax of a progressive character which is based not on the level of total income nor even on the level of unearned income, but upon the value of the total property owned by the taxpayer is the tax which would most directly militate against large properties with the least adverse effects upon incentives to take risks and enterprise with one's capital. This tax like all progressive direct taxes is bound to reduce the level of private savings; it reduces the ability to accumulate capital by the richest citizens who are the most able to save.

Indeed, the essential argument in favour of these taxes which we are at present examining is that they will reduce the net savings and so the net capital accumulation of the largest property owners. If it is desired to maintain the level of total savings and at the same time to discourage the accumulation of the largest properties, it is essential to combine these progressive tax measures with other measures which will stimulate the savings of the small property owners and/or which will raise the public savings (the budget surplus) of the government itself. We shall return to these alternative sources of savings in due course.

But while all forms of progressive taxation are likely to reduce private savings, we may legitimately ask which of these various measures of progressive tax will achieve a given reduction in the rate of growth of the largest properties with the minimum adverse effects on other economic incentives—namely the incentives to work and to take risks. All these forms of progressive taxation may well have some adverse effects upon incentives to work and risk as well as upon the level of savings. For one of the motives to work and risk is to achieve the large income which enables one to accumulate a large property for one's own enjoyment and to bequeath to one's children; and tax arrangements which beyond a point make it very difficult to accumulate property may blunt incentives to make the additional effort to earn the means for further accumulation. But it is probable that a progressive tax on unearned incomes will have less effect in reducing the incentive to earn than will a similar tax on earned incomes; and it is probable that an annual tax assessed on capital wealth (whether it be invested in secure or risky forms) will have less adverse effect upon enterprise than one based on unearned income (which is the fruit of risky rather than of secure investments). The case for an annual tax on capital wealth is thus a strong one. Its disadvantage is the serious extra administrative task of assessing persons' capital wealth as well as their annual income.

There is a second type of fiscal attack on the maldistribution of property—namely death duties. Can one find a system of tax which reduces very little the ability or incentive of the large property owner to work, enterprise, and accumulate during his life time, but which gives him a high incentive to distribute his property widely among those with small properties at his death?

If death duties are to be used seriously as an instrument for the equalization of properties, it is essential that gifts *inter vivos* [1] should be taxed in the same way as bequests at death. Any rich property owner, in the absence of a similar tax on gifts *inter vivos,* can avoid any death-duty obstacle to the concentration of his own wealth into the possession of a single wealthy heir by transferring the greater part of his property as a gift during his lifetime.

Let us consider four possible principles upon which death duties and taxes on gifts *inter vivos* might be assessed.

1. First, there is the principle of the United Kingdom Estate duty according to which a duty is assessed at a progressive rate which rises according to the size of the total estate. A progressive estate duty of this kind (provided that it is accompanied by similar taxation of gifts *inter vivos*) must, of course, exercise a strong equalizing tendency on the distribution of property as it taxes at progressively higher rates the large properties as they pass at death. But it does nothing to induce the rich property owner to distribute his property on his death more widely among a number of beneficiaries.

1. [A gift *inter vivos* is a gift made by one person to another while both are still living.—*Editor.*]

2. The second possible principle would be to tax estates passing at death and gifts *inter vivos* according to the size of the individual bequest. Thus an estate of £1,000,000 bequeathed to a single heir might be taxed at 80 per cent; but if it were left in 100 bequests of £10,000 each, each bequest might be taxed only at 6 per cent. This principle would certainly improve the incentive to split up large properties at death. But it would not encourage the large property owners in choosing his numerous beneficiaries to give preference to those who were not already the owners of large properties. If a large number of rich men split up their estates among a large number of rich children, little is gained as compared with the situation in which each rich man leaves the whole of his estate to one rich child.

3. A third principle would be to tax each individual gift or bequest not solely according to the size of the individual gift or bequest but also according to the existing wealth of the beneficiary. Thus a higher rate of duty would be paid according to the total property which the beneficiary would possess when the gift or legacy was added to his existing wealth. This principle would give a strong incentive to large property owners not only to split their properties into many parts, but also to bequeath these parts to persons who were already the owners of only small properties.

4. With the fourth principle every gift or legacy received by any one individual would be recorded in a register against his name for tax purposes. He would then be taxed when he received any gift or bequest neither according to the size of that gift or bequest nor according to the size of his total property at the time of the receipt of the gift or bequest, but according to the size of the total amount which he had received over the whole of his life by way of gift or inheritance. The rate of tax would be on a progressive scale according to the total of gifts or bequests recorded against his name in the tax register.

The rich property owner would now have every incentive to pass on his property in small parcels to persons who had up to date received little by way of gift or inheritance. This system should serve to diffuse property ownership with the minimum adverse effects upon incentives to earn, enterprise, save, and accumulate property. The testator or donor could avoid tax on handing on his property by leaving a moderate amount to each of a number of persons who had not yet received much by way of gift and inheritance. And, unlike principle (3), no prospective heir would be discouraged from accumulating a property of his own by his own efforts: the duty which he would have to pay on the receipt of any subsequent gift or bequest would not be higher because he had already enriched himself by his own efforts. It would only be higher if he had already been enriched by the receipt of property from someone else.

Principle (4) would thus probably be superior to principle (3) in its effects on incentives to work, risk, and accumulate. Moreover, with principle (4) unlike principle (3) there would be no incentive at all to hand over one's property in small successive doses to any one heir, because the tax payable would be progressive according to the total amount received by gift or inheritance regardless of the timing and size of each individual gift or bequest. On the other hand principle (3) would have a more equalizing effect than principle (4), since it would discourage the passing on of property to rich men whether the source of their riches was their own effort or not.

So much for the progressive taxation of income or wealth. Such fiscal measures are not, however, the only policy measures which may substantially affect the distribution of the ownership of property. Arrangements which encourage the accumulation of property by those with little property are certainly as important as those which discourage further accumulation or encourage dispersal of their fortunes by large property owners. Such arrangements might include: the encouragement of financial intermediaries in which small savings can be pooled for investment in high-earning risk-bearing securities; measures to promote employee share schemes whereby workers can gain a property interest in business firms; and measures whereby municipally built houses can be bought on the installment principle by their occupants.

We have already noted the extreme importance of education as a form of investment which affects earning power. Future developments of educational policy could have a profound effect upon the distribution of earning power and so indirectly, through the power to accumulate, upon the distribution of property. We have already explained how in the past the spread of public elementary education in the developed countries has almost certainly been an important equalizing factor. It has in essence been an investment of capital with a high return, financed out of general taxation for the benefit of every citizen; indeed in countries like the United Kingdom where the rich, in addition to contributing through taxation to the general system of public education, have invested their own funds in their own childrens' education in private schools, public education financed from general taxation has represented an educational investment in the children of the poor.

There is undoubtedly great scope for educational developments which will have further equalizing effects of the same kind. We are becoming aware how greatly within the State system of education itself environmental factors of one kind or another enable the children of the relatively rich to gain more than the children of the poor from such education. It may be that steps can be taken to counteract these forces. Moreover many educational developments, such as the raising of the minimum school-leaving age or the improvement (through the reduction in the size of classes) of the education which is common to all, will expand the equalizing forces which have been so prominent in the past.

But the picture is less certain when one considers possible educational developments in higher education at Universities and similar institutions. There is, of course, one extremely important way in which the expansion of higher education is likely to exercise an equalizing influence. Highly trained persons command a higher wage than do the untrained and the unskilled; the transformation of the relatively untrained into the highly trained through an expanded programme of higher education will decrease the supply of the former and increase the supply of the latter type of worker; the low wages of the unskilled should thus be raised relatively to the high wages of the trained as there are fewer untrained and more trained persons seeking employment in the labour market.

But, on the other hand, there are two reasons for believing that future developments of higher education may be less equalizing than were the earlier educational developments. Indeed they might conceivably in the end turn out to be positively disequalizing in their effects upon ability to earn and to accumulate property.

The first of the marked differences between elementary and higher education is in the division of the costs of such education between the State and the students or their families. None of the cost of elementary education takes the form of earnings foregone; the young boys and girls would not nowadays be in the factories if they were not in the schools. But for higher education earnings foregone make up a very large part, indeed the greater part, of the cost. Though the State provides free of charge the actual educational services and even if it pays in addition some modest maintenance allowances to students, there is a very substantial cost borne by the student or his family in earnings foregone. Such a cost can be more easily met by the rich than by the poor parent. Higher education still involves the investment of private property in the student; and the children of poor parents may be discouraged from it by the desire to start earning at an early date.

But the second difference between elementary and higher education is probably much more important. Even though there is a great expansion in the numbers who receive higher education, it will remain selective; and the basis of selection will be more and more the able boy or girl rather than the son or daughter of wealthy parents. This means increased equality of opportunity. But equality of opportunity is not the same thing as equality of outcome. Indeed, greater equality of opportunity could in the long run mean less, and not greater, equality of wealth. Of course, as between two boys of equal ability, if the son of the poor man is given the same opportunity as the son of the rich man, their ultimate earnings will be equalized. Equality of opportunity does lead to equality of result between those with equal ability. But not all have the same ability and the whole object of selection for higher education will be to select those who are innately able to enjoy the advantages of higher education.

When all have the same access to higher education, it will be the innately able who will succeed. Innate ability will receive the high earnings, accumulate property, and rise in the property scale. This rise of the meritocracy will cause there to be a closer association between ability, earning power, and property at the top of the scale and between lack of ability, low earning power, and small property at the bottom of the scale. The ultimate inequalities in the ownership of property could be greater than before.

The outcome will depend very much upon the educational principle which is adopted. Here there is a possibility of a conflict between "efficiency" and "distributional" considerations in educational policy which is not always fully appreciated. Let us suppose that there is a certain additional amount of money which is going to be spent on education. How should it be spent? On reducing the size of classes in the primary school? On raising the school-leaving age for all children? On increasing the period at the University for the ablest students? On enabling a number of less able students to go to the University?

Now there are many ends to be attained through education other than economic ends. But I want to concentrate attention on the economic effects of educational expenditures. One economic principle for the use of resources in education would be to devote them to those uses which would increase most the productivity and future earning power of the students concerned. I will call this the "efficiency" principle. Another economic principle would be to use the available resources in education in such a way as to equalize the future earning power of different students. I will call this the "distributional" principle. Taken to its logical extreme the "distributional" principle would mean concentrating educational effort and training facilities on the dullards to the neglect of the bright students until the educational advantages of the former just made up for the greater inborn abilities of the latter in the future competition for jobs.

But what would the "efficiency" principle involve? It is very probable that in the past there was little or no conflict between the "efficiency" and the "distributional" principle—universal elementary education was needed on both tickets. But now that this stage in education is virtually complete, will such harmony reign in the future? I do not know; but it would be of great importance if it could be discovered whether, given the present stage of educational development, further expenditure on simple improvements in the basic education of all (for example, smaller classes in primary schools, a higher minimum school-leaving age), or a concentration of expenditure on a few able men and women (for example, more expensive laboratory facilities in the Universities and longer periods of postgraduate work for the ablest technicians) would in fact increase the national product most. It is possible that automation itself may mean that production would be most effectively promoted by the most profound training of a few technicians rather than by the general training of the many. There is a crying need for yet more research into these matters. It may be that the most efficient educational developments will also tend to equalize earning ability and so indirectly property ownership. But one would be betraying one's calling to hold this view without enquiry simply because it is a comfortable view to hold.

Government Measures to Alter the Distribution of Income

Professor Friedman criticizes the progressive income tax as a redistributive device in this passage from his Capitalism and Freedom.

THE METHODS that governments have used most widely to alter the distribution of income have been graduated income and inheritance taxation. Before considering their desirability, it is worth asking whether they have succeeded in their aim.

No conclusive answer can be given to this question with our present knowledge. The judgment that follows is a personal, though I hope not utterly uninformed, opinion, stated, for sake of brevity, more dogmatically than the nature of the evidence justifies. My impression is that these tax measures have had a relatively minor, though not negligible, effect in the direction of narrowing the differences between the average position of groups of families classified by some statistical measures of income. However, they have also introduced essentially arbitrary inequalities of comparable magnitude between persons within such income classes. As a result, it is by no means clear whether the net effect in terms of the basic objective of equality of treatment or equality of outcome has been to increase or decrease equality.

The tax rates are on paper both high and highly graduated. But their effect has been dissipated in two different ways. First, part of their effect has been simply to make the pre-tax distribution more unequal. This is the usual incidence effect of taxation. By discouraging entry into activities highly taxed—in this case activities with large risk and non-pecuniary disadvantages—

they raise returns in those activities. Second, they have stimulated both legislative and other provisions to evade the tax— so-called "loopholes" in the law such as percentage depletion, exemption of interest on state and municipal bonds, specially favorable treatment of capital gains, expense accounts, other indirect ways of payment, conversion of ordinary income to capital gains, and so on in bewildering number and kind. The effect has been to make the actual rates imposed far lower than the nominal rates and, perhaps more important, to make the incidence of the taxes capricious and unequal. People at the same economic level pay very different taxes depending on the accident of the source of their income and the opportunities they have to evade the tax. If present rates were made fully effective, the effect on incentives and the like might well be so serious as to cause a radical loss in the productivity of the society. Tax avoidance may therefore have been essential for economic wellbeing. If so, the gain has been bought at the cost of a great waste of resources, and of the introduction of widespread inequity. A much lower set of nominal rates, plus a more comprehensive base through more equal taxation of all sources of income could be both more progressive in average incidence, more equitable in detail, and less wasteful of resources.

This judgment that the personal income tax has been arbitrary in its impact and of limited effectiveness in reducing inequality is widely shared by students of the subject, including many who strongly favor the use of graduated taxation to reduce inequality. They too urge that the top bracket rates be drastically reduced and the base broadened.

A further factor that has reduced the impact of the graduated tax structure on inequality of income and wealth is that these taxes are much less taxes on being wealthy than on becoming wealthy. While they limit the use of the income from existing wealth, they impede even more strikingly—so far as they are effective—the accumulation of wealth. The taxation of the income from the wealth does nothing to reduce the wealth itself, it simply reduces the level of consumption and additions to wealth that the owners can support. The tax measures give an incentive to avoid risk and to embody existing wealth in relatively stable forms, which reduces the likelihood that existing accumulations of wealth will be dissipated. On the other side, the major route to new accumulations is through large current incomes of which a large fraction is saved and invested in risky activities, some of which will yield high returns. If the income tax were effective, it would close this route. In consequence, its effect would be to protect existing holders of wealth from the competition of newcomers. In practice, this effect is largely dissipated by the avoidance devices already referred to. It is notable how large a fraction of the new accumulations have been in oil, where the percentage depletion allowances provide a particularly easy route to the receipt of tax-free income.

In judging the desirability of graduated income taxation it seems to me important to distinguish two problems, even though the distinction cannot be precise in application: first, the raising of funds to finance the expenses of those governmental activities it is decided to undertake; second, the imposition of taxes for redistributive purposes alone. The former might well call for some measure of graduation, both on grounds of assessing costs in accordance with benefits and on grounds of social standards of equity. But the present high nominal rates on top brackets of income and inheritance can hardly be justified on this ground—if only because their yield is so low.

I find it hard, as a liberal, to see any justification for graduated taxation solely to redistribute income. This seems a clear case of using coercion to take from some in order to give to others and thus to conflict head-on with individual freedom.

All things considered, the personal income tax structure that seems to me best is a flat-rate tax on income above an exemption, with income defined very broadly and deductions allowed only for strictly defined expenses of earning income. I would combine this program with the abolition of the corporate income tax, and with the requirement that corporations be required to attribute their income to stockholders, and that stockholders be required to include such sums on their tax returns. The most important other desirable changes are the elimination of percentage depletion on oil and other raw materials, the elimination of tax exemption of interest on state and local securities, the elimination of special treatment of capital gains, the coordination of income, estate, and gift taxes, and the elimination of numerous deductions now allowed.

An exemption, it seems to me, can be a justified degree of graduation. It is very different for 90 per cent of the population to vote taxes on themselves and an exemption for 10 per cent than for 90 per cent to vote punitive taxes on the other 10 per cent— which is in effect what has been done in the United States. A proportional flat-rate tax would involve higher absolute payments by persons with higher incomes for governmental services, which is not clearly inappropriate on grounds of benefits conferred. Yet it would avoid a situation where any large numbers could vote to impose on others taxes that did not also affect their own tax burden.

The proposal to substitute a flat-rate income tax for the present graduated rate structure will strike many a reader as a radical proposal. And so it is in terms of concept. For this very reason, it cannot be too strongly emphasized that it is not radical in terms of revenue yield, redistribution of income, or any other relevant criterion. Our present income tax rates range from 20 per cent to 91 per cent, with the rate reaching 50 per cent on the excess of taxable incomes over $18,000 for single taxpayers or $36,000 for married taxpayers filing joint returns. Yet a flat rate of 23½ per cent on taxable income as presently reported and presently defined, that is, above present exemptions and after all presently allowable deductions, would yield as much revenue as the present highly graduated rate.[1] In fact, such a flat rate, even with no change whatsoever in other features of the law, would yield a higher revenue because a larger amount of taxable income would be reported for three reasons: there would be less incentive than now to adopt legal but costly schemes that reduce the amount of taxable income reported (so-called tax

1. This point is so important that it may be worth giving the figures and calculations. The latest year for which figures are available as this is written is the taxable year 1959 in U.S. Internal Revenue Service, *Statistics of Income for 1959.* For that year: Aggregate taxable income reported on

Individual tax returns	$166,540 million
Income tax before tax credit	39,092 million
Income tax after tax credit	38,645 million

A flat rate tax of 23½ per cent on the aggregate taxable income would have yielded (.235) × $166,540 million = $39,137 million.

If we assume the same tax credit, the final yield would have been about the same as that actually attained.

avoidance); there would be less incentive to fail to report income that legally should be reported (tax evasion); the removal of the disincentive effects of the present structure of rates would produce a more efficient use of present resources and a higher income.

If the yield of the present highly graduated rates is so low, so also must be their redistributive effects. This does not mean that they do no harm. On the contrary. The yield is so low partly because some of the most competent men in the country devote their energies to devising ways to keep it so low; and because many other men shape their activities with one eye on tax effects. All this is sheer waste. And what do we get for it? At most, a feeling of satisfaction on the part of some that the state is redistributing income. And even this feeling is founded on ignorance of the actual effects of the graduated tax structure, and would surely evaporate if the facts were known.

To return to the distribution of income, there is a clear justification for social action of a very different kind than taxation to affect the distribution of income. Much of the actual inequality derives from imperfections of the market. Many of these have themselves been created by government action or could be removed by government action. There is every reason to adjust the rules of the game so as to eliminate these sources of inequality. For example, special monopoly privileges granted by government, tariffs, and other legal enactments benefiting particular groups, are a source of inequality. The removal of these, the liberal will welcome. The extension and widening of educational opportunities has been a major factor tending to reduce inequalities. Measures such as these have the operational virtue that they strike at the sources of inequality rather than simply alleviating the symptoms.

The distribution of income is still another area in which government has been doing more harm by one set of measures than it has been able to undo by others. It is another example of the justification of government intervention in terms of alleged defects of the private enterprise system when many of the phenomena of which champions of big government complain are themselves the creation of government, big and small.

Progressive Taxation and the Accumulation of Wealth

HENRY SIMONS

Henry C. Simons, Professor of Economics at the University of Chicago, was an ardent supporter of the progressive income tax as a redistributive device. This selection, from his Personal Income Taxation *(1938), examines some of the problems posed by the use of such a tax and possible solutions to them.*

ONE MAY BEGIN by saying what one thinks about inequality. Indeed, one may assert a substantially equalitarian position; or, at least, that there is presumption in favor of equality and that the burden of proof rests with him who would depart from it. With such a start, one may hold that every increase in the degree of progression is, *with reference merely to distributional effects,* a desirable change, and without limit short of substantial equality among those taxed. The same position may be acceptable even to persons not sympathetic toward a thoroughgoing equalitarianism, for the existing distribution may bear no trace of the *kind* of inequality which they approve. And all the practical implications may commend themselves to cautious critics committed only to the view that inequality is sadly excessive here and now.

The case for drastic progression in taxation must be rested on the case against inequality on the ethical or aesthetic judgment that the prevailing distribution of wealth and income reveals a degree (and/or kind) of inequality which is distinctly evil or unlovely.

Such a view obviously takes account merely of the distributional effects of progression. Yet this is obviously but one side of the problem. The degree of progression in a tax system may also affect production and the size of the national income available for distribution. In fact, it is reasonable to expect that every gain, through taxation, in better distribution will be accompanied by some loss in production. The real problem of policy, thus, is that of weighing the one set of effects against the other.

Two simple points should be noted at the outset. First, the effect of a higher degree of progression in taxation upon the distribution of income is certain; the effect upon production, problematical. One is a matter of arithmetic; the other, largely, of social psychology. Second, if reduction in the degree of inequality is a good, then the optimum degree of progression must involve a distinctly adverse effect upon the size of the national income. It is only an inadequate degree of progression which has no effect upon production and economic progress.

But what are these sources of loss, these costs of improved distribution? There are possible effects (a) upon the supplies of highly productive, or at least handsomely rewarded, personal services, (b) upon the use of available physical resources, (c) upon the efficiency of enterpriser activity, and (d) upon the accumulation and growth of resources through saving. Of these effects, all but the last may be regarded as negligible, under any degree of progression which is at all likely to obtain.

The attractiveness of jobs surely varies with the remunerations which they carry. What competing firms must pay to get experts away from one another is vastly different from what society would be obliged to pay in order to keep the experts from being ditch-diggers. Physical resources it will always be more profitable to employ than to leave idle, so long as progression falls short of 100 per cent or does not rise precipitously to that level. Our captains of industry (enterprisers) are mainly engaged not in making a living but in playing a great game; and it *need* make little difference whether the evidence of having played well be diamonds and sables on one's wife or a prominent place in the list of contributors under the income tax. Besides the mere privilege of exercising power is no mean prize for the successful enterpriser.

These remarks define, of course, an extreme and not wholly tenable position. But the adverse effects of increasing progression may be estimated only in terms of predictions of human behavior; and one may well doubt that most of them would be important, at least under any degree of progression which is politically pos-

sible or administratively practicable for the significant future.
With respect to capital accumulation, however, the consequences
are certain to be significantly adverse. How increased progression
would affect the *incentive* to accumulation or saving, it would be
rash to predict. Here the ultimate question is essentially that of
the probable effect of small changes in the rate of interest upon
the rate of saving. That the incentive would be unaffected, is as
reasonable as any other position, many economists to the contrary
notwithstanding.

Nevertheless, it is hardly questionable that increasing progression is inimical to saving and accumulation. Under an individualistic system, great inequality is necessary to rapidly increasing
indirectness in the productive process—necessary to the increasing use of resources in the production of more (and different)
resources. The cost of our present stock of productive instruments was, in a significant sense, decades and centuries of terrible
poverty for the masses. Conversely, the cost of justice will be a
slowing-up in our material advance (though this effect may be
modified if and as governments assume the role of savers).

Increasing progression means augmenting incomes where saving is impossible and diminishing incomes too large to be used
entirely for consumption. Thus, it means diversion of resources
from capital-creation to consumption uses. The classes subject to
the highest rates will not greatly curtail consumption; and persons at the bottom of the income scale, paying smaller taxes, will
use their additional income largely to improve their standard of
life. Some curtailment of consumption at the upper end of the
scale may be expected, as may some increase of saving at the
lower end. That the net effect will be increased consumption,
however, hardly admits of doubt.

Here perhaps is a real cost, a limitation, for one who would
lead us away from extreme inequality via taxation. Increased
saving is a true blessing, other things being equal; its curtailment,
undeniably a loss. Nevertheless, the position that progression
should be applied only moderately, because of its effect upon accumulation, is by no means inviting when one considers precisely
what it means.

There is, first of all, a question as to whether society should make large sacrifices to further accumulation. To stress obligations to our children's children is often a means of diverting attention from patent obligations to our contemporaries. Of course progress should be encouraged; but its costs should give us pause, in a society mature enough to exercise some deliberate control. Both progress and justice are costly luxuries—costly, above all, in terms of each other. Let us raise the question, in passing, as to whether we have been quite safely removed from the predicament of that hypothetical society which employed every increase in its income for the purposes of further increase, and so on until the end of time.

There is also a difficult question, from the point of view of the economics of welfare, as to the relative importance of productional and distributional considerations. There is real point, if not truth, in the suggestion that, within wide limits, the quality of human experience would be about the same at one income level as at another if the *relative* position of persons and classes remained unchanged. Poverty, want, and privation are in large measure merely relative. Thus, something can be said for mitigation of inequality, even at the cost of reduction in the modal real income.

It is important to recognize that each generation inherits a system of property rights, as well as a stock of means of production— that it receives its resources with mortgages attached. If we deliberately limit the degree of progression, out of regard for effects on accumulation, we are in effect removing taxes from those who consume too much and transferring them to classes which admittedly consume too little; and against the additional capital resources thus painfully acquired are mortgages, property rights, in the hands of those freed from tax. While the saving will really have been done by those at the bottom of the income scale, those free from tax and their assigns will enjoy the reward. This method of fostering increase in productive capacity thus increases the concentration of property and aggravates inequality.

If the productivity of capital were highly inelastic the phenomenon of diminishing returns might be relied upon to mitigate the distributional effects. The masses would surely participate to some extent in the blessings of greater productive capacity. In fact, however, the scheme looks a bit like taxing small incomes to reduce consumption in the hope that those relieved of tax will save more after consuming all they can, and then allowing 1 per cent to those who have really done the saving and 4 per cent to those who have served merely by paying smaller taxes. We are thus placed under the strange necessity of lamenting the flatness of the productivity curve—of lamenting the otherwise glorious prospect of using additional capital goods very productively. The anomaly arises, of course, merely from the institution of property, which largely sets the distributional problem of taxation.

A possible solution of this difficulty is budgetary provision for capital accumulation on the part of governments. In this way, fiscal policy might promote or sustain accumulation without incurring the doubly unfavorable terms involved in restricting progression to that end. Whether and how far this is really feasible are questions of political morality and administrative efficiency. The same questions arise when one asks how large government expenditures should be and, indeed, are at the heart of the problem of social control through fiscal devices. If governments can administer and effectively direct the production and distribution of certain classes of goods and services, expenditures and taxation may properly be high. If governments could handle effectively the business of investment, more drastic measures for modifying the degree of inequality would be desirable and expedient.

Opportunities for extending the scope of socialized consumption are clearly numerous. Many goods and services, of great importance for general welfare, might be distributed freely or with substantial relaxing of prevailing price controls. The prospect for public administration of saving is much less promising. For the immediate future, however, the retirement of public debts will provide an adequate offset to the adverse effects of progression on saving; and, after debts were entirely retired, governments might still contribute somewhat to the volume of savings available for private investment by adhering to a pay-as-you-go policy. Moreover, they might proceed gradually with investment in private industry. The techniques of a conservative investment business are fairly well established; and governmental bodies might, on a moderate scale, function quite as well as the investment depart-ments of the better banks and insurance companies. Considerable investment might be made without involving the government in the management of private business—just as governments may distribute all sorts of consumption services while leaving many steps in their production in the hands of private enterprise. Indeed, governments might well remain in a quite passive, creditor role, merely dispensing investment funds according to interest return and security.

To the inevitable protest that this means socialism, one may reply that the program is properly part of a promising scheme for saving the free-enterprise system and the institution of political freedom.[1] The contention here is not that there should be correction of the effects of extreme progression upon saving but that government saving, rather than modification of the progression, is the appropriate method for effecting that correction, if such correction is to be made.

1. These paragraphs were written years ago, at a time when the writer was less sensitive to the difficulty or impossibility of maintaining representative government in the face of increasing centralization and collectivism. Complete revision has not seemed necessary, however, for, although the shades of emphasis are sometimes unfortunate, the central position seems sound. The direct provision by governments of capital funds for private industry is something which can be viewed only with grave misgivings. However, if we were faced with a dangerous tendency toward capital consumption and disaccumulation, such a policy would seem preferable to that of making taxes less progressive (or more regressive) than otherwise would have been expedient. Actually, it is altogether academic to consider how the government might find adequate outlets for its own saving, with our present debt, and with great industries which can never be effectively competitive still under private ownership. To suggest that the government might protect our capital resources by assuming the role of saver is not to suggest that it become even a passive investor in competitive, private industries during the next century!

Capitalism, Socialism, and the Distribution of Wealth and Income

A. C. PIGOU

Alternative redistributive policies under capitalism and socialism are examined by one of Britain's most distinguished economists, Professor A. C. Pigou, in his Socialism versus Capitalism, *first published in 1937.*

THE UNEVEN DISTRIBUTION of post-tax available income brings it about that large masses of productive resources are devoted to satisfying the whims of the rich—providing them with expensive motor cars, fine houses, fashionable dresses and so on—while large numbers of people are inadequately fed, clothed, housed and educated. The maldistribution of productive resources as between essential and superfluous *things* is not, of course, as is sometimes loosely supposed, a *further* evil, superimposed upon and additional to the evil of unequal distribution of incomes among persons. It is the same evil viewed from a different angle. But it is, none the less, real and exceedingly important. The reason why widely unequal distribution of income is an evil is that it entails resources being wasted, in the sense that they are used to satisfy less urgent needs while more urgent needs are neglected. Obviously the evil is a very grave one. It is particularly grave in its effects on the young; for, in so far as poverty deprives the children of the poor of proper nutrition and of educational opportunities, it weakens their earning power later on, and so tends to perpetuate itself. Inequality of income in one generation is thus not merely an evil in itself, it is also a cause of inequality in the next generation. These considerations constitute a powerful case for *some sort* of change making for increased equality; provided always that such a change can be accomplished without entailing new evils as serious as those that are attacked.

What sorts of change then suggest themselves? First, of course, death duties might be graduated still more steeply than they are against large estates. There are also available plans of the type suggested by the Italian economist Rignano for taxing estates that are inherited more severely at the second and later transfers than at the first. An ingenious modification of this plan has been proposed by Dr. Hugh Dalton. His scheme is that, when an estate is inherited, there should be levied, besides estate duty in its present form, a second duty, against which the inheritor is given an annuity, to be paid during his life and to lapse at his death, roughly equal to the income that would have been yielded by the sum taken under the duty. Measures like these, by reducing inequalities in property ownership, would indirectly reduce inequalities in pre-tax incomes; and this, of course, implies that post-tax incomes also would be rendered less unequal. Secondly, income tax might be graduated more steeply. This would obviously diminish the inequality of post-tax incomes, even though it had no direct effect on pre-tax incomes. But, in so far as large post-tax income facilitates the accumulation of property, which yields further income, the imposition of heavy taxes on rich people would probably also render pre-tax incomes less unequal, and so would affect post-tax incomes in a double way. Thirdly, subsidies, provided out of taxes on better-to-do persons, might be paid to encourage the production of things that enter predominantly into the purchases of the poor. This device for transferring income is an indirect one; but, for some things, such as housing and milk, which are, perhaps, *needed* even more than they are *wanted*, it is effective. Finally, State-provided social services might be greatly extended and improved, with particular regard to the physical and mental development of the young. If policies on these lines were pressed further and, of course, there is nothing in the technical structure of capitalism to prevent their being pressed—post-tax incomes would be made more equal by a double process. On the one hand, the benefit received by poor persons under the head of social services would, in effect, represent transfers of available income to them: on the other hand, the improvement in their capacities, to which the social services led, would enable them presently to earn for themselves larger pre-tax and pre-benefit incomes.

In this list of possible remedies for inequality of incomes I have not mentioned socialism; elimination of profit, public ownership of the means of production, all-round central planning. Ought I to have done so? Since advocates of socialism base themselves largely on the evils of inequality, it would seem that I ought; it would seem that socialism must constitute an obvious and direct means of attacking inequality. But here we encounter a paradox. If socialism were introduced by the confiscation from private owners of the means of production, the State would secure at a blow something like a third of the total income of the country, a third which is now, as we have seen, mainly held by rich people; and, whether it decided to retain this income for itself or to re-distribute it among the poor, the existing inequality among personal incomes would be greatly reduced. But the official advo-cates of socialism, at least in this country, do not propose to introduce it by way of confiscation. They propose to purchase the means of production from their present holders at a fair valu-ation; that is, they propose to hand over to them government scrip, the interest on which, when allowance has been made for diminished risk of loss, will be roughly equivalent to what the private holders are now receiving as income from their prop-erty. In other words, apart from minor adjustments, the distribu-tion of income among persons will be exactly the same after the introduction of socialism as it was before. Dr. Dalton, in his book *Practical Socialism for Britain*, tells us this without any am-biguity. "The initial act," he writes, "not being accompanied by any act of confiscation of private property rights, but only by a change in their form, makes no direct contribution to equality." Of course, he does not stop here. He goes on to propose that, after the initial act has been accomplished, vigorous use should be made of fiscal weapons—a steeper graduation of income tax and a reform of the death duties. But these measures, though they are part of the programme of the Labour Party, are cer-tainly not a part of socialism, as it has been defined here. For our immediate purpose, therefore, they are beside the point. The question for us is, not how far would the programme advocated by the Labour Party make incomes less unequal, but how far would the introduction of socialism do this. *Prima facie* the answer is that socialism, introduced as the Labour Party propose to introduce it, would have no effect whatever on the distribution of income. That is our paradox.

But, of course, this impression is only true in part. The act of introducing socialism in the way proposed would not *directly* affect distribution then and there. But the fact of socialism having been *established* would affect it indirectly and later on. If the compensation paid to expropriated owners was given in the form of terminable annuities, it would clearly do this when the time came for the annuities to lapse. Apart from that, the most obvious way in which it would do it would be through the substitution of salaried managers for private entrepreneurs and of rentiers at fixed interest for ordinary shareholders. For this would mean that henceforward the risks of industry, the chances of loss, with their counterpart, chances of gain, would be shifted from private persons to the general body of the community acting through the State. Under the present organisation of industry unsuccessful venturers lose their money, while successful ones, sometimes through skill at outbargaining other people, sometimes through sheer luck, make large gains. Under a socialised form of industry there would be no scope for these gains. The large, occasionally the enormous, incomes, to which they give rise, would no longer be made. To that extent the distribution of wealth and income would be made noticeably less unequal. This is not a small matter. For, as Foxwell once wrote: "It is far more important and far more practicable to take care that the acquisition of new wealth proceeds justly than to redistribute wealth already acquired." [1]

Nor is this all. At first sight it seems that the direct attacks on inequality by highly graduated income tax and death duties, to which I referred just now, are entirely independent of socialism, and could be carried through equally well under the present economic system. But that, socialists rightly claim, is not so. I do not mean that to carry these measures far under the present

1. Introduction to Menger's *Right to the Whole Produce of Labour,* p. cx.

system would be *politically* impracticable. That contention is not open to socialists, at least to socialists who intend to seek their own ideal by peaceful means. For the vested interests and the inertia arrayed against the reform of capitalism are certainly no stronger than those arrayed against the supplanting of capitalism by socialism. What I mean is something subtler than that. Under the present system a limit is set to the use of these fiscal weapons by the fear that, if they are wielded too strenuously, the accumulation of capital in the country for home use will be checked; since the ability and the willingness of those who now provide a large part of it will both be weakened. As a consequence of this, it is often argued, though, indeed, the rich would be made poorer, total income would be reduced in still larger measure, so that the poor, instead of being better off, would in the end themselves be losers. This argument, despite the fact that it is more popular among the rich than among the poor, nevertheless has *some* cogency. Heavy taxes on large incomes *may* to some extent check the accumulation of capital for home use. Even if the proceeds of these taxes are invested by the State and not transferred to the poor, they may indirectly and ultimately do that. Moreover, cogent or not, the argument certainly persuades. It constitutes a real force, under the existing economic organisation, to hold back attacks on inequality of wealth and income by means of fiscal weapons. But, once establish socialism, and the whole argument disappears. The accumulation of capital is cared for directly by the State. There is no longer need to rely on the ability and the willingness of private persons to provide it. The State has the power to take whatever it pleases for capital development before any income at all is distributed to individuals. The establishment of general socialism, therefore, both mitigates inequalities of pre-tax incomes to some extent, and also enables measures for equalising post-tax incomes, when pre-tax incomes are given, to be pressed more strongly than is at present practicable. This is so even though the socialist planning authority allows its citizens free choice of occupation, relying on the persuasion of divergent rates of remuneration to secure the numbers that it needs for various kinds of work. If it has recourse to coercion, it has still greater freedom.

Without any fear about indirect effects on capital accumulation, it can make, at choice, equal payments to everybody or payments adjusted to family needs. Thus the paradox previously described is whittled away, and the case for socialism as a remedy for inequalities of distribution among persons is much stronger than, at one stage of our discussion, it seemed to be.

PART FIVE   Poverty

The Invisible Poor

MICHAEL HARRINGTON

Michael Harrington, a free-lance writer, was perhaps the first to focus nationwide attention on the poverty issue in his book, The Other America, *first published in 1962. The following selection is from chapter one, "The Invisible Land."*

THERE IS a familiar America. It is celebrated in speeches and advertised on television and in the magazines. It has the highest mass standard of living the world has ever known.

In the 1950's this America worried about itself, yet even its anxieties were products of abundance. The title of a brilliant book was widely misinterpreted, and the familiar America began to call itself "the affluent society." There was introspection about Madison Avenue and tail fins; there was discussion of the emotional suffering taking place in the suburbs. In all this, there was an implicit assumption that the basic grinding economic problems had been solved in the United States.

While this discussion was carried on, there existed another America. In it dwelt somewhere between 40,000,000 and 50,000,000 citizens of this land. They were poor. They still are. Tens of millions of Americans are, at this very moment, maimed in body and spirit, existing at levels beneath those necessary for human decency. If these people are not starving, they are hungry, and sometimes fat with hunger, for that is what cheap foods do. They are without adequate housing and education and medical care.

The Government has documented what this means to the bodies of the poor. But even more basic, this poverty twists and deforms the spirit. The American poor are pessimistic and defeated, and they are victimized by mental suffering to a degree unknown in Suburbia.

The millions who are poor in the United States tend to become increasingly invisible. Here is a great mass of people, yet it takes an effort of the intellect and will even to see them. The other America, the America of poverty, is hidden today in a way that it never was before. Its millions are socially invisible to the rest of us. No wonder that so many misinterpreted John Kenneth Galbraith's title and assumed that "the affluent society" meant that everyone had a decent standard of life. The misinterpretation was true as far as the actual day-to-day lives of two-thirds of the nation were concerned. Thus, one must begin a description of the other America by understanding why we do not see it.

There are perennial reasons that make the other America an invisible land.

Poverty is often off the beaten track. It always has been. The ordinary tourist never left the main highway, and today he rides interstate turnpikes. He does not go into the valleys of Pennsylvania where the towns look like movie sets of Wales in the thirties. He does not see the company houses in rows, the rutted roads (the poor always have bad roads whether they live in the city, in towns, or on farms), and everything is black and dirty. And even if he were to pass through such a place by accident, the tourist would not meet the unemployed men in the bar or the women coming home from a runaway sweatshop.

Then, too, beauty and myths are perennial masks of poverty. The traveler comes to the Appalachians in the lovely season. He sees the hills, the streams, the foliage—but not the poor. Or perhaps he looks at a run-down mountain house and, remembering Rousseau rather than seeing with his eyes, decides that "those people" are truly fortunate to be living the way they are and that they are lucky to be exempt from the strains and tensions of the middle class. The only problem is that "those people," the quaint inhabitants of those hills, are undereducated, underprivileged, lack medical care, and are in the process of being forced from the land into a life in the cities, where they are misfits.

These are normal and obvious cases of the invisibility of the poor. They operated a generation ago; they will be functioning a generation hence. It is more important to understand that the very development of American society is creating a new kind of blindness about poverty. The poor are increasingly slipping out of the very experience and consciousness of the nation.

If the middle class never did like ugliness and poverty, it was at least aware of them. "Across the tracks" was not a very long way to go. There were forays into the slums at Christmas time; there were charitable organizations that brought contact with the poor. Occasionally, almost everyone passed through the Negro ghetto or the blocks of tenements, if only to get downtown to work or to entertainment.

Now the American city has been transformed. The poor still inhabit the miserable housing in the central area, but they are increasingly isolated from contact with, or sight of, anybody else. Middle-class women coming in from Suburbia on a rare trip may catch the merest glimpse of the other America on the way to an evening at the theater, but their children are segregated in suburban schools. The business or professional man may drive along the fringes of slums in a car or bus, but it is not an important experience to him. The failures, the unskilled, the disabled, the aged, and the minorities are right there, across the tracks, where they have always been. But hardly anyone else is.

In short, the very development of the American city has removed poverty from the living, emotional experience of millions upon millions of middle-class Americans. Living out in the suburbs, it is easy to assume that ours is, indeed, an affluent society.

This new segregation of poverty is compounded by a well-meaning ignorance. A good many concerned and sympathetic Americans are aware that there is much discussion of urban renewal. Suddenly, driving through the city, they notice that a familiar slum has been torn down and that there are towering, modern buildings where once there had been tenements or hovels. There is a warm feeling of satisfaction, of pride in the way things are working out: the poor, it is obvious, are being taken care of.

The irony in this is that the truth is nearly the exact opposite to the impression. The total impact of the various housing programs in postwar America has been to squeeze more and more people into existing slums. More often than not, the modern apartment in a towering building rents at $40 a room or more. For, during the past decade and a half, there has been more subsidization of middle- and upper-income housing than there has been of housing for the poor.

Clothes make the poor invisible too: America has the best-dressed poverty the world has ever known. For a variety of reasons, the benefits of mass production have been spread much more evenly in this area than in many others. It is much easier in the United States to be decently dressed than it is to be decently housed, fed, or doctored. Even people with terribly depressed incomes can look prosperous. There are tens of thousands of Americans in the big cities who are wearing shoes, perhaps even a stylishly cut suit or dress, and yet are hungry. It is not a matter of planning, though it almost seems as if the affluent society had given out costumes to the poor so that they would not offend the rest of society with the sight of rags.

Then, many of the poor are the wrong age to be seen. A good number of them (over 8,000,000) are sixty-five years of age or better; an even larger number are under eighteen. The aged members of the other America are often sick, and they cannot move. Another group of them live out their lives in loneliness and frustration: they sit in rented rooms, or else they stay close to a house in a neighborhood that has completely changed from the old days. Indeed, one of the worst aspects of poverty among the aged is that these people are out of sight and out of mind, and alone.

The young are somewhat more visible, yet they too stay close to their neighborhoods. Sometimes they advertise their poverty through a lurid tabloid story about a gang killing. But generally they do not disturb the quiet streets of the middle class.

And finally, the poor are politically invisible. It is one of the cruelest ironies of social life in advanced countries that the dispossessed at the bottom of society are unable to speak for themselves. The people of the other America do not, by far and large, belong to unions, to fraternal organizations, or to political parties. They are without lobbies of their own; they put forward no legislative program. As a group, they are atomized. They have no face; they have no voice.

Thus, there is not even a cynical political motive for caring about the poor, as in the old days. Because the slums are no longer centers of powerful political organizations, the politicians need not really care about their inhabitants. The slums are no longer visible to the middle class, so much of the idealistic urge to fight for those who need help is gone. Only the social agencies have a really direct involvement with the other America, and they are without any great political power.

Forty to 50,000,000 people are becoming increasingly invisible. That is a shocking fact. But there is a second basic irony of poverty that is equally important: if one is to make the mistake of being born poor, he should choose a time when the majority of the people are miserable too.

John Kenneth Galbraith develops this idea in *The Affluent Society*, and in doing so defines the "newness" of the kind of poverty in contemporary America. The old poverty, Galbraith notes, was general. It was the condition of life of an entire society, or at least of that huge majority who were without special skills or the luck of birth. When the entire economy advanced, a good many of these people gained higher standards of living. Unlike the poor today, the majority poor of a generation ago were an immediate (if cynical) concern of political leaders. The old slums of the immigrants had the votes; they provided the basis for labor organizations; their very numbers could be a powerful force in political conflict. At the same time the new technology required higher skills, more education, and stimulated an upward movement for millions.

Perhaps the most dramatic case of the power of the majority poor took place in the 1930's. The Congress of Industrial Organizations literally organized millions in a matter of years. A labor movement that had been declining and confined to a thin stratum of the highly skilled suddenly embraced masses of men and women in basic industry. At the same time this acted as a pressure upon the Government, and the New Deal codified some of the social gains in laws like the Wagner Act. The result was not a basic transformation of the American system, but it did transform the lives of an entire section of the population.

In the thirties one of the reasons for these advances was that misery was general. There was no need then to write books about unemployment and poverty. That was the decisive social experience of the entire society, and the apple sellers even invaded Wall Street. There was political sympathy from middle-class reformers; there were an elan and spirit that grew out of a deep crisis.

Some of those who advanced in the thirties did so because they had unique and individual personal talents. But for the great mass, it was a question of being at the right point in the economy at the right time in history, and utilizing that position for common struggle. Some of those who failed did so because they did not have the will to take advantage of new opportunities. But for the most part the poor who were left behind had been at the wrong place in the economy at the wrong moment in history.

These were the people in the unorganizable jobs, in the South, in the minority groups, in the fly-by-night factories that were low on capital and high on labor. When some of them did break into the economic mainstream—when, for instance, the CIO opened up the way for some Negroes to find good industrial jobs—they proved to be as resourceful as anyone else. As a group, the other Americans who stayed behind were not originally composed primarily of individual failures. Rather, they were victims of an impersonal process that selected some for progress and discriminated against others.

Out of the thirties came the welfare state. Its creation had been stimulated by mass impoverishment and misery, yet it helped the poor least of all. Laws like unemployment compensation, the Wagner Act, the various farm programs, all these were designed for the middle third in the cities, for the organized workers, and for the upper third in the country, for the big market farmers. If a man works in an extremely low-paying job, he may not even be covered by social security or other welfare programs. If he receives unemployment compensation, the payment is scaled down according to his low earnings.

One of the major laws that was designed to cover everyone, rich and poor, was social security. But even here the other Americans suffered discrimination. Over the years social security payments have not even provided a subsistence level of life. The middle third have been able to supplement the Federal pension through private plans negotiated by unions, through joining medical insurance schemes like Blue Cross, and so on. The poor have not been able to do so. They lead a bitter life, and then have to pay for that fact in old age.

Indeed, the paradox that the welfare state benefits those least who need help most is but a single instance of a persistent irony in the other America. Even when the money finally trickles down, even when a school is built in a poor neighborhood, for instance, the poor are still deprived. Their entire environment, their life, their values, do not prepare them to take advantage of the new opportunity. The parents are anxious for the children to go to work; the pupils are pent up, waiting for the moment when their education has complied with the law.

Today's poor, in short, missed the political and social gains of the thirties. They are, as Galbraith rightly points out, the first minority poor in history, the first poor not to be seen, the first poor whom the politicians could leave alone.

The first step toward the new poverty was taken when millions of people proved immune to progress. When that happened, the failure was not individual and personal, but a social product. But once the historic accident takes place, it begins to become a personal fate.

The new poor of the other America saw the rest of society move ahead. They went on living in depressed areas, and often they tended to become depressed human beings. In some of the West Virginia towns, for instance, an entire community will become shabby and defeated. The young and the adventurous go to the city, leaving behind those who cannot move and those who lack the will to do so. The entire area becomes permeated with failure, and that is one more reason the big corporations shy away.

Indeed, one of the most important things about the new poverty is that it cannot be defined in simple, statistical terms. If a group has internal vitality, a will—if it has aspiration—it may live in dilapidated housing, it may eat an inadequate diet, and it may suffer poverty, but it is not impoverished. So it was in those ethnic slums of the immigrants that played such a dramatic role in the unfolding of the American dream. The people found themselves in slums, but they were not slum dwellers.

But the new poverty is constructed so as to destroy aspiration; it is a system designed to be impervious to hope. The other America does not contain the adventurous seeking a new life and land. It is populated by the failures, by those driven from the land and bewildered by the city, by old people suddenly confronted with the torments of loneliness and poverty, and by minorities facing a wall of prejudice.

In the past, when poverty was general in the unskilled and semi-skilled work force, the poor were all mixed together. The bright and the dull, those who were going to escape into the great society and those who were to stay behind, all of them lived on the same street. When the middle third rose, this community was destroyed. And the entire invisible land of the other Americans became a ghetto, a modern poor farm for the rejects of society and of the economy.

It is a blow to reform and the political hopes of the poor that the middle class no longer understands that poverty exists. But, perhaps more important, the poor are losing their links with the great world. If statistics and sociology can measure a feeling as delicate as loneliness, the other America is becoming increasingly populated by those who do not belong to anybody or anything. They are no longer participants in an ethnic culture from the old country; they are less and less religious; they do not belong to unions or clubs. They are not seen, and because of that they themselves cannot see. Their horizon has become more and more restricted; they see one another, and that means they see little reason to hope.

Galbraith was one of the first writers to begin to describe the newness of contemporary poverty, and that is to his credit. Yet because even he underestimates the problem, it is important to put his definition into perspective.

For Galbraith, there are two main components of the new poverty: case poverty and insular poverty. Case poverty is the plight of those who suffer from some physical or mental disability that is personal and individual and excludes them from the general advance. Insular poverty exists in areas like the Appalachians or the West Virginia coal fields, where an entire section of the country becomes economically obsolete.

Physical and mental disabilities are, to be sure, an important part of poverty in America. The poor are sick in body and in spirit. But this is not an isolated fact about them, an individual "case," a stroke of bad luck. Disease, alcoholism, low IQ's, these express a whole way of life. They are, in the main, the effects of an environment, not the biographies of unlucky individuals. Because of this, the new poverty is something that cannot be dealt with by first aid. If there is to be a lasting assault on the shame of the other America, it must seek to root out of this society an entire environment, and not just the relief of individuals.

But perhaps the idea of "insular" poverty is even more dangerous. To speak of "islands" of the poor (or, in the more popular term, of "pockets of poverty") is to imply that one is confronted by a serious, but relatively minor, problem. This is hardly a description of a misery that extends to 40,000,000 or 50,000,000 people in the United States. They have remained impoverished in spite of increasing productivity and the creation of a welfare state. That fact alone should suggest the dimensions of a serious and basic situation.

Finally, one might summarize the newness of contemporary poverty by saying: These are the people who are immune to progress. But then the facts are even more cruel. The other Americans are the victims of the very inventions and machines that have provided a higher living standard for the rest of the society. They are upside-down in the economy, and for them greater productivity often means worse jobs; agricultural advance becomes hunger.

In the optimistic theory, technology is an undisguised blessing. A general increase in productivity, the argument goes, generates a higher standard of living for the whole people. And indeed, this has been true for the middle and upper thirds of American society, the people who made such striking gains in the last two decades. But the poor, if they were given to theory, might argue the exact opposite. They might say: Progress is misery.

As the society became more technological, more skilled, those who learn to work the machines, who get the expanding education, move up. Those who miss out at the very start find themselves at a new disadvantage. A generation ago in American life, the majority of the working people did not have high-school educations. But at that time industry was organized on a lower level of skill and competence. And there was a sort of continuum in the shop: the youth who left school at sixteen could begin as a laborer, and gradually pick up skill as he went along.

Today the situation is quite different. The good jobs require much more academic preparation, much more skill from the very outset. Those who lack a high-school education tend to be condemned to the economic underworld—to low-paying service industries, to backward factories, to sweeping and janitorial duties. If the fathers and mothers of the contemporary poor were penalized a generation ago for their lack of schooling, their children will suffer all the more. The very rise in productivity that created more money and better working conditions for the rest of the society can be a menace to the poor.

But then this technological revolution might have an even more disastrous consequence: it could increase the ranks of the poor as well as intensify the disabilities of poverty. At this point it is too early to make any final judgment, yet there are obvious danger signals. There are millions of Americans who live just the other side of poverty. When a recession comes, they are pushed onto the relief rolls. If automation continues to inflict more and more penalties on the unskilled and the semiskilled, it could have the impact of permanently increasing the population of the other America.

Even more explosive is the possibility that people who participated in the gains of the thirties and the forties will be pulled back down into poverty. Today the mass-production industries where unionization made such a difference are contracting. Jobs are being destroyed. In the process, workers who had achieved a certain level of wages, who had won working conditions in the shop, are suddenly confronted with impoverishment. This is particularly true for anyone over forty years of age and for members of minority groups. Once their job is abolished, their chances of ever getting similar work are very slim.

It is too early to say whether or not this phenomenon is temporary, or whether it represents a massive retrogression that will swell the numbers of the poor. To a large extent, the answer to this question will be determined by the political response of the United States in the sixties. If serious and massive action is not undertaken, it may be necessary for statisticians to add some old-fashioned, pre-welfare-state poverty to the misery of the other America.

Poverty in the 1960's is invisible and it is new, and both these factors make it more tenacious. It is more isolated and politically powerless than ever before. It is laced with ironies, not the least of which is that many of the poor view progress upside-down, as a menace and a threat to their lives. And if the nation does not measure up to the challenge of automation, poverty in the 1960's might be on the increase.

There are mighty historical and economic forces that keep the poor down; and there are human beings who help out in this grim business, many of them unwittingly. There are sociological and political reasons why poverty is not seen; and there are misconceptions and prejudices that literally blind the eyes. The latter must be understood if anyone is to make the necessary act of intellect and will so that the poor can be noticed.

Here is the most familiar version of social blindness: "The poor are that way because they are afraid of work. And anyway they all have big cars. If they were like me (or my father or my grandfather), they could pay their own way. But they prefer to live on the dole and cheat the taxpayers."

This theory, usually thought of as a virtuous and moral statement, is one of the means of making it impossible for the poor ever to pay their way. There are, one must assume, citizens of the other America who choose impoverishment out of fear of work. But the real explanation of why the poor are where they are is that they made the mistake of being born to the wrong parents, in the wrong section of the country, in the wrong industry, or in the wrong racial or ethnic group. Once that mistake has been made, they could have been paragons of will and morality, but most of them would never even have had a chance to get out of the other America.

There are two important ways of saying this: The poor are caught in a vicious circle; or, The poor live in a culture of poverty.

In a sense, one might define the contemporary poor in the United States as those who, for reasons beyond their control, cannot help themselves. All the most decisive factors making for opportunity and advance are against them. They are born going downward, and most of them stay down. They are victims whose lives are endlessly blown round and round the other America.

Here is one of the most familiar forms of the vicious circle of poverty. The poor get sick more than anyone else in the society. That is because they live in slums, jammed together under unhygienic conditions; they have inadequate diets, and cannot get decent medical care. When they become sick, they are sick longer than any other group in the society. Because they are sick more often and longer than anyone else, they lose wages and work, and find it difficult to hold a steady job. And because of this, they cannot pay for good housing, for a nutritious diet, for doctors. At any given point in the circle, particularly when there is a major illness, their prospect is to move to an even lower level and to begin the cycle, round and round, toward even more suffering.

This is only one example of the vicious circle. Each group in the other America has its own particular version of the experience. But the pattern, whatever its variations, is basic to the other America.

The individual cannot usually break out of this vicious circle. Neither can the group, for it lacks the social energy and political strength to turn its misery into a cause. Only the larger society, with its help and resources, can really make it possible for these people to help themselves. Yet those who could make the difference too often refuse to act because of their ignorant, smug moralisms. They view the effects of poverty—above all, the warping of the will and spirit that is a consequence of being poor—as choices. Understanding the vicious circle is an important step in breaking down this prejudice.

What shall we tell the American poor, once we have seen them? Shall we say to them that they are better off than the Indian poor, the Italian poor, the Russian poor? That is one answer, but it is heartless. I should put it another way. I want to tell every well-fed and optimistic American that it is intolerable that so many millions should be maimed in body and in spirit when it is not necessary that they should be. My standard of comparison is not how much worse things used to be. It is how much better they could be if only we were stirred.

Changes in the Number and Composition of the Poor

HERMAN P. MILLER

Herman P. Miller, Chief of the Population Division, U. S. Bureau of the Census, reviewed some of the findings on the number of poor for a Conference on Poverty in America at the University of California at Berkeley in February 1965.

REVISED ESTIMATES OF POVERTY

Figures recently published by the federal government provide the best measure of the number and characteristics of the poor that has been available since the onset of the current debate on poverty. When the Council of Economic Advisers made its study of poverty several years ago, it used a cash income of less than $3,000 in 1962 as the poverty line for families of two or more persons and income of less than $1,500 for unrelated individuals (persons living alone or with nonrelatives). The failure to take various factors like size of family, the age of family head, and farm residence into account was recognized as a serious shortcoming that had to be tolerated because of the lack of more refined estimates. Early this year, however, the Department of Health, Education, and Welfare retabulated the Census Bureau's sample statistics for 1963, using a flexible poverty line which eliminates many of the shortcomings cited above.

The basic procedure employed in preparing the revised estimates involves the use of an economy budget, developed by the Department of Agriculture, which specifies in great detail the weekly quantities of foods needed by men, women, and children in various age groups in order to maintain nutritional adequacy. According to the HEW report, this budget, which is "adapted to the food patterns of families in the lowest third of

152

the income range, has for many years been used by welfare agencies as a basis for food allotments for needy families."[1] Using the quantities specified in the budget and food prices published by the Department of Agriculture, annual estimates of food costs needed to maintain nutritional adequacy were prepared for 124 different types of families classified by farm and nonfarm residence, age and sex of head, and number of children. These annual food costs were converted to incomes on the basis of assumed relationships between food expenditures and total income.

Families of three or more persons were assumed to be in poverty if their income was less than 33 per cent of the cost of the economy food budget. The poverty line for these families was obtained by multiplying the cost of the food budget by a factor of three. Data recently available from the 1960 Survey of Consumer Expenditures suggest that this is a reasonable relationship between income and food expenditures for low-income families.[2] A ratio of 27 per cent was used for two-person families, while unrelated individuals were assumed to need 80 per cent of the requirement for a couple, "on the premise that the lower the income the more difficult it would be for one person to cut expenses such as housing and utilities below the minimum for a couple."[3] The estimates for farm families are based on the assumption that they would need 40 per cent less cash income than nonfarm families of the same size and type, since many farmers receive part of their food and most of their housing without cash payment.

A summary of the dollar values used as the poverty line for selected types of families is shown in Table 1. The poverty line of $3,130 for a nonfarm family of four assumes that a daily expenditure of 70 cents per person will provide an adequate diet and that an additional $1.40 per person will provide for all other needs—housing, clothing, medical care, transportation, etc. The

1. Mollie Orshansky, "Counting the Poor: Another Look at the Poverty Profile," *Social Security Bulletin*, XXVIII (January 1965), pp. 3–29.

2. Helen H. Lamale, "Expenditure Patterns of Low Consumption Families," paper presented at the December 1964 meeting of the American Statistical Association.

3. Orshansky, *op. cit.*

TABLE 1. *Selected Poverty Income Criteria for Families,
by Size, Sex of Head, and Residence, United States, 1963*

Number of persons in family	Income on nonfarm residence		Income on farm residence	
	Male head	Female head	Male head	Female head
1 (under age 65)	$1,650	$1,525	$ 990	$ 920
1 (aged 65 and over)	1,480	1,465	890	880
2 (under age 65)	2,065	1,875	1,240	1,180
2 (aged 65 and over)	1,855	1,845	1,110	1,120
3	2,455	2,350	1,410	1,395
4	3,130	3,115	1,925	1,865
5	3,685	3,660	2,210	2,220
6	4,135	4,110	2,495	2,530
7 or more	5,100	5,000	3,065	2,985

SOURCE: Mollie Orshansky, "Counting the Poor: Another Look at the
Poverty Profile," *Social Security Bulletin*, XXVIII (January 1965), Table E.

poverty lines for other family types are designed to provide
equivalent levels of living. Using these dollar values, retabula-
tions were made of the income data from the March 1964 Current Population Survey, comparing the income reported for each
family with the income "required" by that family. If the reported
income was below the required amount for that family type, the
family was classified as poor. Families identified as poor on this
basis were then retabulated according to various characteristics.

An examination of the revised estimates of poverty shows that,
in 1963, about 34.5 million persons were in families with incomes
insufficient to purchase an adequate budget. They constituted
slightly less than one-fifth (18 per cent) of all persons in the
United States. About 5 million lived alone or with nonrelatives
and 30 million were members of family groups. One-half of the
30 million were children, the great majority of whom were living
with both parents (Table 2).

A comparison of the economy budget estimates with those that
would have been obtained by the application of the cruder
standards used by the Council of Economic Advisers shows a
remarkable similarity in the overall totals. The CEA standards
would have produced about 33.5 million persons in poverty, or
approximately one million less than the number based on the

TABLE 2. *Persons in Poverty Status in 1963, by Alternative Definitions (Number in Millions)*

Type of unit	Total of U.S. population	Below the economy budget [a]		Below the CEA definition [b]		Below income tax level [c]	
		Number	Per cent of total	Number	Per cent of total	Number	Per cent of total
All persons	187.2	34.6	18	33.4	18	34.0	18
Farm	12.6	3.2	25	4.9	39	6.4	51
Nonfarm	174.6	31.4	18	28.5	16	27.6	16
Unrelated individuals	11.2	4.9	44	4.9	44	4.0[d]	36
Members of families	176.0	29.7	17	28.5	16	30.0	17
Children under 18	68.8	15.0	22	10.8	16	15.7	23

[a] Economy level of the poverty index developed by the Social Security Administration by family size and farm-nonfarm residence, centering around $3,100 for four persons.

[b] Interim measure used by Council of Economic Advisers—under $3,000 for families and under $1,500 for unrelated individuals.

[c] Level below which no income tax is required, beginning in 1965.

[d] Estimated: income-tax cutoff is $900; census 1963 income data available only for total less than $1,000; this figure has been broken down into less than $500 and $500-$999 on basis of 1962 proportions.

SOURCE: Mollie Orshansky, "Counting the Poor: Another Look at the Poverty Profile," *Social Security Bulletin,* XXVIII (January 1965), Table 1.

economy budget. The CEA standard would also have produced an additional 1.5 million impoverished farm residents (because of the failure to take noncash income into account), and, most significantly, 4 million fewer impoverished children (because no adjustment was made for size of family).

Leading characteristics of families with incomes below the economy budget are shown in Table 3. Attention is called here to some of the more significant highlights:

(a) About 7 million families and 5 million unrelated individuals were in poverty in 1963. Their aggregate income was $11.5 billion below their estimated minimum requirements.[4] This amount might be regarded as a rough estimate of the cost of raising the incomes of all families and individuals above the poverty line as that term is now defined.[5]

(b) Although the 2 million families with a female head accounted for about one-fourth of the poor families, they accounted for nearly one-half of the income gap between actual receipts and minimum requirements. At a cost of about $5 billion all families with a female head could be provided with incomes sufficient to meet minimum requirements as that term is currently defined.

(c) About 2 million families (about a fourth of all the poor families) were headed by a person who worked full-time throughout the year. Increases in aggregate demand and a full-employment economy probably would not benefit these families, except perhaps by providing work for wives and children.[6] Although the heads of this large segment of poor families were fully employed, their incomes were insufficient to raise their families

4. *Ibid.*, Table 4.

5. [In Robert Lampman's terminology, this is called the "poverty income gap."—*Editor*.]

6. If aggregate demand were increased to the point at which there was an extreme shortage of unskilled labor, there might be a tendency for the wages of the unskilled to rise more rapidly than the wages of skilled workers, as was the case during World War II. Such a situation is highly unlikely today, and, even if it existed, it would be accompanied by severe inflationary pressures. [On this point, see James Tobin, "On Improving the Economic Status of the Negro," below, pp.196–204.—*Editor*]

above the poverty line. As an incidental fact, it may be noted that, if the families with a female or a nonwhite head are sub-

TABLE 3. *Selected Characteristics of Families in Poverty Status in 1963, by Alternative Definitions (Number in Millions)*

Selected characteristics	Total number of families	Families below economy budget Number	Per cent of total	Families with incomes under $3,000 Number	Per cent of total
All families	47.4	7.2	15	8.8	19
Residence					
Farm	3.1	0.7	23	1.3	43
Nonfarm	44.3	6.5	15	7.5	17
Color					
White	42.7	5.2	12	6.8	16
Nonwhite	4.7	2.0	42	2.0	43
Age of Head					
14 to 24 years	2.7	0.7	26	0.8	30
25 to 64 years	38.0	5.0	13	4.9	13
65 years and over	6.7	1.5	24	3.1	45
Type of Family					
Male head	42.5	5.2	12	6.5	15
Female head	4.9	2.0	40	2.3	47
Size of Family					
2 persons	15.3	2.5	16	4.6	30
3–5 persons	25.5	2.9	11	3.2	13
6 or more persons	6.6	1.8	27	1.0	15
Employment Status of Head					
Not in labor force	8.8	3.0	34	4.3	49
Unemployed	1.4	0.4	28	0.4	28
Employed	37.2	3.7	10	4.1	11
Work Experience of Heads in 1963					
Worked in 1963	40.7	4.6	11	5.1	13
Worked at full-time jobs	37.9	3.6	10	3.8	10
50–52 weeks	30.7	2.0	7	2.1	7
Worked at part-time jobs	2.8	1.0	36	1.4	50
Did not work	6.7	2.6	38	3.7	55

SOURCE: Mollie Orshansky, "Counting the Poor: Another Look at the Poverty Profile," *Social Security Bulletin*, XXVIII (January 1965), Table 2.

tracted from the total, we find 1.3 million poor families (about 20 per cent of the total) headed by a white man who was fully employed throughout the year.[7] These figures dramatize the fact that low wages are still a major cause of poverty in the United States.

(d) About 1.5 million family heads worked at full-time jobs, but did not work throughout the year. The poverty of these families was attributable to a combination of low wage rates and periods of idleness associated largely with unemployment or illness. Although today's poor are frequently presented as psychologically or spiritually handicapped, the fact is that about 50 per cent of them are headed by a full-time worker whose wages are simply too low to support a family.

(e) The 2 million nonwhite families constituted about one-fourth of the poor families. About 40 per cent of these families were headed by women, few of whom had year-round full-time employment. A very large proportion of nonwhite poor live in the South; only about one-fourth live in large metropolitan areas in the North or West.

(f) The 1.5 million families with an aged head constitute about one-fifth of the poor families. The aged are a far smaller fraction of the poor when the economy budget rather than a flat $3,000 is used as the poverty line.

IS POVERTY BEING REDUCED FAST ENOUGH?

The chapter on poverty in the *Economic Report of the President* for 1964 begins with a call to action. It states that we have "been erasing mass poverty in America. But the process is far too slow. It is high time to redouble and to concentrate our efforts to eliminate poverty." [8] The reason for haste, presumably, is that poverty, in the eyes of the Council of Economic Advisers, has become an anachronism in our society. We tolerated it in an earlier era because we had no choice. Now, however, we have it within our means to raise the floor below which we will not let

7. Orshansky, *op. cit.*

8. *Economic Report of the President*, January 1964, p. 55.

people fall. Since poverty can now be eliminated, the report argues, it should be.

There is an implication in the Economic Report that there has been a slowdown in recent years in the rate at which poverty is being reduced. The report states that "from 1957 through 1962, when total growth was slower and unemployment substantially higher (than in 1947–1956) the number of families in poverty fell less rapidly." [9] The statement is carefully phrased in terms of the *number* rather than the *proportion* of families below the poverty line. The latter, however, is the more critical relationship since the number of families is constantly rising over time.

An examination of the basic figures used by the CEA shows that between 1947 and 1963 the proportion of families with incomes below $3,000 (in terms of 1962 purchasing power) dropped from 32 per cent to 19 per cent (Table 4). In other

TABLE 4. *Per Cent of Families with Money Income Less than $3,000, 1947–1963 (1962 Dollars)*

Year	Per cent of families
1947	32
1950	32
1951	29
1952	28
1953	26
1954	28
1955	25
1956	23
1957	23
1958	23
1959	22
1960	21
1961	21
1962	20
1963	19

SOURCE: Figures for 1947 to 1962 from *Economic Report of the President,* 1964, p. 57; estimate for 1963 derived from U.S. Bureau of the Census, *Current Population Reports—Consumer Income,* Series P-60, No. 43.

9. *Ibid,* p. 60.

words, during this 16-year period we moved 40 per cent of the way toward the complete eradication of poverty as that term is now defined. Between 1947 and 1956 the proportion of families with incomes under $3,000 dropped from 32 per cent to 23 per cent or at the rate of one percentage point per year. There was no change between 1956 and 1958. Since that time the proportion of families below the $3,000 poverty line dropped once again from 23 per cent to 19 per cent or just under one percentage point per year.

In other words, the experience in the reduction of poverty from 1958 to 1963 was not appreciably different from the experience during the decade immediately following the Second World War. Even if the reduction in the incidence of poverty during recent years had been less rapid, the slower progress would not necessarily have been attributable to a slowdown in the rate of economic growth as alleged by the Council. In the first place, as the numerical base diminishes it becomes increasingly difficult to achieve the same absolute rate of reduction in the incidence of poverty. It was much easier to reduce the incidence of poverty by one percentage point when one-third of the families were below the poverty line than it is at present when fewer than one-fifth are at that level. Moreover, we must remember that, as we get closer to the very bottom of the income distribution, we are dealing increasingly with the hard-core poor whose incomes in a large proportion of the cases arise outside of the labor market and are not necessarily responsive to economic growth.

Although economic growth tends to reduce poverty by pushing families above the poverty line, it also tends to increase poverty in a statistical sense by making it possible for the young and the old to maintain their own residences, thereby creating large numbers of low-income families that might not otherwise exist as independent units. The available statistics suggest that the observed reductions in poverty during the 1950's were not appreciably affected by these kinds of statistical aberrations. If we examine, for example, changes in the incidence of poverty among urban families headed by a person 35 to 44 years of age (Table 5), we find trends that closely parallel those noted for the

TABLE 5. *Per Cent of Urban Families with Head 35–44
Years of Age with Income under $3,000, 1947–1960
(1959 Dollars)*

Year	Per cent of urban families
1947	20
1948	20
1949	21
1951	17
1952	16
1953	15
1954	14
1955	11
1956	10
1957	12
1958	11
1959	11
1960	11

SOURCE: Data for 1947–1960 from Herman P. Miller, *Trends in the Income of Families and Persons in the United States: 1947 to 1960*, U.S. Bureau of the Census, Technical Paper No. 8, Table 3.

entire population. Since this group of families is not likely to be affected by the process of fractionalization described above, it can be inferred that the change in the incidence of poverty among them reflects the impact of economic forces.

In general, it appears that the conclusions based on data for all families do not require significant alteration when changes in the living arrangements and in the urban-rural distribution of the population are taken into account. A more sensitive test of this thesis can be made by the application of a standardization procedure to the data. The actual percentage distributions for families by residence and age of head are available for each year since 1947. If a constant set of population weights is applied to these data, estimates can be made of the change in the proportion of families below the poverty line, independent of changes in the residence or age distribution of the population. The application of this standardization procedure to the data produced results that did not differ appreciably from the unadjusted data shown in Table 4.

IS THE COMPOSITION OF THE POOR CHANGING?

This is an important question, and it is one that we should be able to answer on the basis of available data; yet it turns out to be quite complex. If $3,000 (in terms of 1962 purchasing power) is used as the poverty line, we can agree unequivocally with the Council of Economic Advisers that "certain handicapping characteristics, notably old age, or absence of an earner or of a male head, have become increasingly prominent in the poor population." [10] We find that in 1963, 35 per cent of the families with incomes under $3,000 were aged as compared with only 26 per cent in 1951 (Table 6). Similarly the proportion of broken fam-

TABLE 6. *Selected Characteristics of "Poor" Families, 1951 and 1963*

Family income for selected year	Per cent of families with family head characteristics		
	65 years and over	Female	Nonwhite
1951			
Under $2,000 (current dollars)	32	23	21
Under $3,000 (1962 dollars)	26	19	20
1963			
Under $3,000 (1962 dollars)	35	26	23

SOURCE: Derived from U.S. Bureau of the Census, *Current Population Reports—Consumer Income,* Series P-60, Nos. 12 and 43.

ilies among the poor increased from 19 per cent to 26 per cent, and the proportion of nonwhite families increased from 20 per cent to 23 per cent. All of these changes support the conclusion of the Council.

However, is $3,000 the appropriate poverty line for 1951? The congressional study of low-income families that was conducted in 1949 used $2,000 as the poverty line for that year. Evidently the contemporary conception of poverty that prevailed in the United States shortly after the Second World War called for a poverty

10. *Ibid.*, p. 72.

line of about $2,000. Are we justified in changing our conception of poverty for this earlier period and imposing a new and higher poverty line merely because our current standards have changed? I think not. If we examine the composition of the poor using a $2,000 poverty line for 1951 (in current dollars) and a $3,000 poverty line for 1963 (also in current dollars) we find very much smaller changes in the composition of the poor than those cited above. The aged, for example, represented 32 per cent of the poor in 1951, using the $2,000 poverty line for that year, and 35 per cent of the poor in 1963, using the $3,000 poverty line. Similarly, broken families constituted 23 per cent of the poor in 1951 and 26 per cent in 1963.

Thus, the use of contemporary definitions of poverty suggests that there has been very little change in the composition of the poor, whereas the use of a fixed poverty line suggests that there has been a great deal of change. The reason for the difference is obvious when the underlying statistics are considered. The magnitude of poverty and the characteristics of the poor depend to a large extent on the location of the poverty line. The aged, broken families and similar disadvantaged groups will be prominent among the poor if a low poverty line is used. As the poverty line is moved closer to the middle of the distribution there is a greater tendency to include average families rather than those with special characteristics. In 1951, an income of $3,000 (in 1962 purchasing power) represented the lowest third of the income distribution, whereas in 1963 the same income represented the lowest fifth. Since the $3,000 poverty line in 1951 was much closer to the middle of the distribution, the aged and broken families represented far smaller fractions of the poor.

The question of the appropriate poverty line that should be used for historical analysis is only now receiving mature consideration. The historical analysis of the change in the number and composition of the poor in the *Economic Report of the President* for 1964 is in terms of a fixed poverty line of $3,000. All references in that report to the elimination of poverty must be construed as the elevation of families above the $3,000 mark measured in terms of 1962 purchasing power.

This static view of the poverty line was more specifically stated in a recent article by Robert Lampman in which he said, "the precise income level selected to mark off poverty from nonpoverty is not critical, *so long as it is unchanged over time,* except for necessary adjustments relative to the prevailing price level." [11] This position may represent sound strategy for a short-term viewpoint; however, it is fraught with peril for historical analysis. Moreover, it represents economically unsound thinking for a dynamic society and is at variance with the way in which we have actually gone about measuring poverty at different points in time.

The essential weakness of this position can perhaps best be seen by re-examining some of the observations made about the poverty line in 1904 by Robert Hunter, who made one of the first quantitative studies of poverty in the United States. In this study, which is most sympathetic to the plight of the poor, Hunter states, "However desirable and socially valuable an income of $754 a year for each family would be, it is unquestionably too high for a fair estimate of the minimum necessary one. . . . To estimate in the most conservative way possible, let us take more or less arbitrarily $460 a year as essential to defray the expenses of an average family—a father, a mother, and three children—in the cities and industrial communities. . . . In the South, about $300 a year would probably cover the cost of like necessities." [12] Even if we allow for a tripling of prices since 1900, it is apparent that at the turn of the century Hunter could not conceive of a poverty line as high as $2,000 (in current dollars) for a family of five living in a metropolitan area.

We can see what a disservice Hunter would have done to the cause of the poor if he had been willing to settle for a fixed poverty line based on the experience of his time.

There is ample evidence of a relatively sharp upward movement in the poverty line even during the short period since the end of World War II. As previously noted, when the Joint Economic Committee made the first congressional investigation of low-income families in 1949 the poverty line was set at $2,000

11. Robert J. Lampman, "One-fifth of a Nation," *Challenge,* XII (April 1964), p. 12.

12. Robert Hunter, *Poverty* (New York: Macmillan, 1907), p. 52.

for a family of two or more persons. Price increases since that time should have raised the level to about $2,500 in 1962; but the poverty line actually used in 1962 was $3,000, an increase of about 20 per cent in 13 years, or roughly 1.5 per cent per year. Further evidence of this tendency is provided by Bureau of Labor Statistics data which show that the cost of a "modest but adequate" level of living (excluding taxes) for a working-class family of four persons in New York City was about $4,000 in 1947 and about $5,200 in 1959 (both figures in terms of 1961 purchasing power). In other words, the modest but adequate level of living rose by 28 per cent in New York City in this 12-year period—a growth rate of about 2 per cent per year.

The essential fallacy of a fixed poverty line is that it fails to recognize the relative nature of "needs." The poor will not be satisfied with a given level of living year after year when the levels of those around them are going up at the rate of about 2.5 per cent per year. Old-timers may harken back to the "good old days" when people were happy without electricity, flush toilets, automobiles, and television sets; but they must also realize that, once it becomes possible for all to have these "luxuries," they will be demanded and will quickly assume the status of "needs." For these reasons, it is unrealistic in an expanding economy to think in terms of a fixed poverty line.

Recently, Theodore W. Schultz has attempted to use the elasticity concept borrowed from the theory of demand to explain the relationship between the rise in per capita income and the rise in the poverty line. He notes that the rise in the poverty line over time "represents an increase in the demand for welfare services for the poor, that this increase in demand as it is revealed by the social-political process is a function of the rise in per capita income which can be treated as income elasticity." [13] Schultz goes on to state that "the underlying behavior here is consistent with an income elasticity somewhat less than unity. During the period since the mid-thirties real income per family virtually doubled and the poverty line, measured in constant dollars, appears to

13. Theodore W. Schultz, "Investing in Poor People: An Economist's View," *American Economic Review,* Papers & Proceedings, May 1965, pp. 511–512.

have risen by 75 per cent." [14] If it is true, as Schultz alleges, that the percentage change in the poverty line is not as great as the percentage change in income, then we might expect on that account alone to find a decrease in the incidence of poverty over time in a growing society.

14. This estimate is based on an unpublished study by Eugene Smolensky, "The Past and Present Poor," prepared by the U.S. Chamber of Commerce, quoted in Schultz, cited above.

The Poverty Band and the Count of the Poor

OSCAR ORNATI

Oscar Ornati, Professor of Economics at the New School for Social Research, presented the findings of a research program at that institution, sponsored by the Twentieth Century Fund, in Poverty Amid Affluence, *from which the following selection is taken.*

POVERTY IN THIS STUDY is defined as the lack of command over goods and services sufficient to meet minimum needs.

Objectively, poverty can be measured in terms of the proportion of currently agreed-upon basic "necessities" that income can buy. Most necessary to human health and well-being, everybody will agree, are basic food, shelter, and clothing. Those who measure poverty quantitatively will concentrate their attention on these necessities. Those concerned with more than bare subsistence will ask another question—are all Americans sharing reasonably well in the current United States affluence? Such critics will be interested in income inequality as well as insufficiency. In addition to lacking the barest necessities of life, being "poor" in the United States in the 1960's may also mean that one belongs to the bottom 20 per cent of the population that receives less than 5 per cent of total family personal income. One can be poor, then, from an insufficiency of food, clothing, and housing. Or one can be poor from having a much less than proportionate share in available goods and services.

The staff of the New School poverty study developed a three-level "band" concept to synthesize definitions of poverty in the United States in the twentieth century. The sources used were some sixty budgets for workers' families prepared over the years by governmental and private agencies. These budgets are operational definitions of poverty, for various administrative purposes such as the payment of money for relief. They provide a reliable index of contemporary practice and a rough social consensus about who is "poor." Starting from such budgets, it is possible to arrive at the dollar amounts required, year by year, to maintain a four-member family, consisting of an employed father, an unemployed mother, and two minor children, at levels of "minimum subsistence," "minimum adequacy," and "minimum comfort." The accompanying chart (Figure 1) portrays the three-level "poverty band" so constructed for the years 1905 to 1960.

FIGURE 1. *The Poverty Band, 1905–1960 (constant 1960 dollars)*

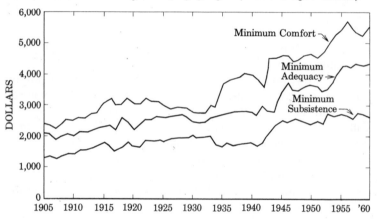

SOURCE: Appendix 2, Table B [in original article].

The titles "minimum subsistence," "minimum adequacy," and "minimum comfort" have actually been applied to some of the budgets by their makers . . . Budgets to determine needs at the "subsistence" level were constructed mainly to establish eligibility for public assistance. The mid-level standards, those termed "fair," were constructed primarily to determine a "living wage" and, more recently, are used by community service societies to decide whether families needing and requesting counseling and guidance should pay for it or not. The higher level budgets, generally termed "minimum comfort," on the other hand have in common only the fact that none was constructed for relief purposes. Of this latter group, many were used in settling wage disputes—mostly of skilled workers or civil service workers—or were constructed to measure costs and changes in costs of maintaining a commonly accepted standard of living without reference to a particular wage or relief action.

The life styles so set, and the derived notion of poverty or deprivation—in the apparent objectivity of a package of specific needs—reflects society's judgments of differences in social function and status. In practice the minimum which a family needs to maintain physical efficiency is ascertained by surveying what families actually buy. The separating of minimum needs of those on relief from those who use the community agencies for non-money services is done by asking what the latter have and what they spend it on . . .

At all times, as Figure 1 demonstrates, there have persisted differences in what society considers sufficient. Moreover, definitions of poverty constantly change. As the general United States income level has risen, living standards have risen. Expectations have risen. Concepts of who is poor have risen. Thus, through the years, standards of sufficiency, however defined, have generally risen. The topmost, or "minimum comfort," standard has risen rapidly—from $2,437 in 1905 to $5,609 in 1960 when valued in constant dollars of 1960 purchasing power—as the average American's definition of comfort has risen. Similarly, the intermediate level of the poverty band, that of "minimum adequacy" standards, rose from $2,098 to $4,348 in this period when measured in constant 1960 dollars. The "minimum subsistence" level has remained less affected by the general increase in the economy's output and productivity. Governed mainly by the minimum amount society wishes to provide the destitute, it advanced in the same period, and again in constant dollars, from $1,386 to $2,662.

Using the three income levels charted in Figure 1 and relating them to studies on income distribution, the New School poverty study staff arrived at estimates of the number of poor in the United States since 1929 *by contemporary standards.* In making this count, the dollar equivalents of the "subsistence," "adequacy," and "comfort" standards were adjusted to allow for variations through time in average family size and for the needs of unattached individuals.

In 1960, our figures show, almost 20 million persons lived in conditions at least as bad as those described by reference to the "minimum subsistence" budgets; 46 million lived under conditions below those described in terms of the "minimum adequacy"

FIGURE 2. *Number of Persons Below Three Budget Levels in Selected Years, by Contemporary Standards and by 1960 Standards*
I. *By Contemporary Standards in Current Dollars*
II. *By 1960 Standards in Constant Dollars*

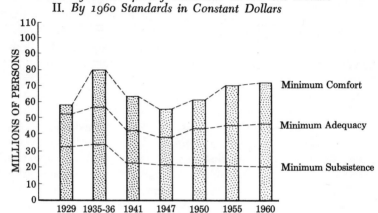

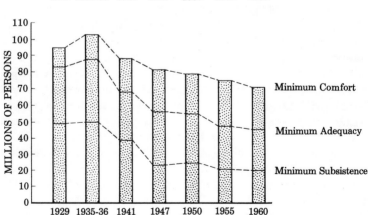

SOURCE: Appendix 5, Table B [in original article].

budgets; and 71 million lived at a standard described as being less than that of "minimum comfort." Of all households (consumer units) in the United States, by this count, 11 per cent fell below the "subsistence" budget standard in 1960, 26 per cent below the "adequacy" standard, and 40 per cent below the "comfort" standard.

How has the number of poor changed since prewar years? The change can be measured, first of all, by taking a count for a series of years of the number who failed to meet the standards of sufficiency prevailing at the time, with these standards expressed in then current dollar values. Such a count, made in the New School poverty study, is illustrated in the first part of Figure 2. Here we trace, through three decades, the numbers of persons falling below the three levels used in this study, according to the then existing standards evaluated in current dollars. We see that, by this measure, there were fewer poor in 1960 than in 1929 by low- and middle-level budget definitions but more when the "minimum comfort" definition is used. In three decades, 12 million people—though, of course, not necessarily the same people—were lifted out of the worst poverty. But there were in 1960, by the same measure, 71 million people below the currently defined "comfort" level, compared with 58 million in 1929. Evidently many of those who, so to speak, rose out of yesterday's stark poverty entered the areas above subsistence but below present-day standards of healthful, decent living.

A simple count does not, however, take into consideration the growth of population through the years. In order to relate the trends to population size, the New School poverty study staff made similar measurements in terms of percentages, in this case of households or "consumer units." As Figure 3 shows, the percentage of households living at each of the three budget levels used in this study has decreased somewhat since 1929. Although many people still live below "subsistence," the decrease in the proportion of households below that standard has been particularly steady and striking, despite the increased cost of living. This is partly because there has been less growth in administratively determined "subsistence" budgets than in the "minimum" comfort budgets. Also involved is the fact that prior to the mid-forties

FIGURE 3. *Per Cent of Households Below Three Budget Levels in Selected Years, by Contemporary Standards in Current Dollars*

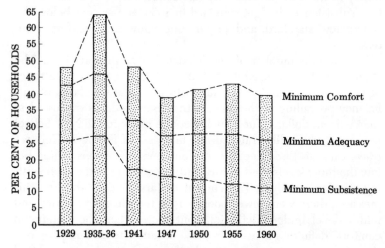

SOURCE: Appendix 5, Table A [in original article].

most families were dependent upon one breadwinner only. It is estimated that in 1929, for instance, 62 per cent of American families had only one source of income. By 1960 this proportion of families had fallen to 46 per cent.[1] In the 1960's, women's participation in the labor force generally means two pay checks per family. The probability of extreme poverty is thus somewhat less among low-paid workers' families.

The changes over the years in the incidence of poverty can be measured in another way—by projecting present standards back to earlier years. This the New School poverty study staff also did, using a simple monetary deflation of 1960 standards in order to rule out changes in the value of the dollar. The results of these computations are shown graphically in the second part of Figure 2. In each of the years shown on the chart (except 1955, and then

1. Data for 1929 from Maurice Leven, Harold Moulton and Clark Warburton, *America's Capacity to Consume*, The Brookings Institution, Washington, 1934, p. 236; data for 1960 from *Current Population Reports*, Bureau of the Census, Series P60-6 and P60-37.

only at the level of "subsistence"), there were more persons living below today's standard than below the contemporary historical standard.

Thus, if we project today's operational definitions of poverty back to an earlier period, it appears that more people three decades ago were "poor" than were considered to be poor at the time. And, quite evidently, if we were to use the standards of thirty years ago and project them forward to today, we would find that "poverty" had decidedly dwindled. Either exercise tells us more about changing standards than about those judged to be poor by their fellow citizens.

It is in this context that the notion of relativity as applied to poverty over time shows all its shortcomings. To say that poverty is relative is not helpful to society. If comparisons from one period to another are to be made, the New School study staff feels they should be made in terms of *contemporary* standards.

Approaches to the Reduction of Poverty: I

ROBERT J. LAMPMAN

Professor Lampman presented this paper at a session of the American Economic Association meetings in December 1964 on "The Economics of Poverty."

THE GREATEST ACCOMPLISHMENT of modern economies has been the raising of living standards of the common man and the reduction of the share of the population in poverty. Contrary to the gloomy predictions of Malthus, production has increased faster than population and, unlike the expectations of Marx, inequality of income has not steadily increased. The growth in value of product per person is generally understood to arise out of more capital, economies of scale and specialization, better management and organization, innovation with regard both to end products and techniques of production, greater mobility of factors, and improved quality of labor. All of these in turn yield additional income which, in a benign spiral, makes possible more and higher quality inputs for further growth.

The process of growth has not meant simply higher property incomes. As a matter of fact, income from property has fallen as a share of national income. Neither has growth meant a widening of differential for skill in labor incomes. Rates of pay for the most menial of tasks have tended to rise with average productivity. Social policies in fields such as labor and education aimed at assuring opportunities for all have narrowed initial advantages of the more fortunate. Such policies, along with taxation, social insurance, and public assistance measures which redistribute income toward the poor have tended to stabilize if not reduce the degree of the income inequality.

A growth in productivity of 2 percent per person per year and a relatively fixed pattern of income inequality probably have combined to yield a net reduction in poverty in most decades of American history. However, the rate of reduction has undoubtedly varied with changes in the growth rate, shifts from prosperity to depression, changes in immigration, in age composition, and in differential family size by income level.

The Poverty Rate and the Poverty Income Gap · Using a present-day standard for poverty and even without recognizing the relativity of poverty over long periods, we would estimate that poverty had become a condition that afflicted only a minority of Americans by the second decade of this century. This situation was upset by the Great Depression of the 1930's but later restored by the booming economy of World War II. The postwar period has yielded a somewhat above average rate of growth in productivity and a reduction in poverty which probably is at least average for recent decades. The number of families in poverty (as marked off from nonpoverty by a $3,000 income at 1962 prices) fell from 12 million in 1947 to 9 million in 1963. This was a drop from 32 percent to 19 percent of families.

The rate of reduction one records or predicts will vary somewhat with the definition of poverty which he adopts. The Council of Economic Advisers adopted an income cut-off of $3,000 of total money income for families and $1,500 for unrelated individuals.[1] It is not inconsistent with those guidelines to make further modification for family size, using $3,000 as the mark for an urban family of four persons with variations of $500 per person and to set a lower mark for rural families. Such a procedure yields a slightly lower rate of reduction in the percentage of all persons in poverty than is suggested by the 32- to 19-percent drop shown above. This discrepancy is due to a shift in family size and the rural to urban migration during the postwar years.

It is possible that consideration of personal income as opposed to total money income, of average rather than one year's income, of assets and extraordinary needs as well as income, and of related matters would alter our understanding of how poverty has been reduced. It is clear that some of these considerations affect the number and the composition of the population counted as poor; and it is obvious that the rate of reduction would vary if we varied the poverty line over time.

These matters of definition are important to a refinement of the generalized goal of elimination of poverty to which President

1. *Annual Report* (1964), Chap. 2.

Johnson has called us. Economists can assist in reaching a national consensus on the specific nature of the goal, of ways to measure the distance from and rate of movement toward the goal.

At this point in time, poverty is clearly a condition which afflicts only a minority—a dwindling minority—of Americans. The recent average rate of change, namely, a fall in the percentage of families in poverty by one percentage point per year, suggests that the poverty problem is about twenty years from solution. This rate of reduction may be difficult to maintain as we get down to a hard core of poverty and a situation in which further growth will not contribute to the reduction of the poverty rate. My own view is that this rate is still highly responsive to changes in the growth rate and that it will continue to be so for some time ahead. The relationship between the two rates is a complex one and is influenced by such things as demographic change, changes in labor force participation, occupational shifts in demands for labor, and derived changes in property incomes and social security benefits. Some groups—notably the aged, the disabled, and the broken families—have poverty rates that appear to be relatively immune to growth in average income. One powerful drag on the responsiveness of the poverty rate to growth, which has now about run its course and will shortly reverse, is the aging and reduction in labor force participation of family heads.

While the size of the poverty population is dwindling, the size of what can be called the "poverty income gap" is diminishing. This gap—the aggregate amount by which the present poor population's income falls short of $3,000 per family or $1,500 per unrelated individual—is now about $12 billion, or 2 percent of GNP. As time goes on this gap will assuredly be less, both because of economic growth and because of scheduled increases in social insurance benefits. (Transfers now make up about $10 billion of the $25 billion income of the poor.) Projecting recent rates of change suggests that by 1975 the poor will be no more than 12 percent of the population and the poverty income gap will be as little as 1 percent of that year's GNP.

As I see it, the goal of eliminating poverty needs to have a time dimension and intermediate targets. I assume we want a rate of progress at least as fast as that of recent years. Further, it helps to think of the goal in two parts: the reduction of the poverty rate and the reduction of the poverty income gap. This means we want to work from the top down and from the bottom up, so to speak. The aim of policy should be to do each type of reduction without slowing the other and to do both with the least possible sacrifice of and the greatest possible contribution to other important goals.

Why Poverty Persists · As background to such strategic decisions, it is useful to categorize the causes of poverty in today's economy. But perhaps it is necessary first to brush aside the idea that there has to be some given amount of poverty. Most economists have long since given up the idea that a progressive society needs the threat of poverty to induce work and sobriety in the lower classes. Similarly, one can consign to folklore the ideas that some are rich only because others are poor and exploited, that if none were poor then necessary but unpleasant jobs would go undone, that the middle class has a psychological need to exclude a minority from above-poverty living standards, and that poverty is a necessary concomitant of the unemployment which necessarily accompanies economic growth.

Why, then, is it that there remains a minority of persons who are involuntarily poor in this affluent society? How does our system select the particular members for this minority? To the latter question we offer a three-part answer: (1) Events external to individuals select a number to be poor. (2) Social barriers of caste, class, and custom denominate persons with certain characteristics to run a high risk of being poor. (3) The market assigns a high risk of being poor to those with limited ability or motivations.

One cannot look at the data on who are the poor without sensing that many are poor because of events beyond their control. Over a third of the 35 million poor are children whose misfortune arises out of the chance assignment to poor parents. In some cases this poverty comes out of being members of unusually large families. Among the poor adults, about a third have either suffered a disability, premature death of the family breadwinner, or family dissolution. A considerable number have confronted a declining demand for services in their chosen occupation, industry, or place of residence. Some have outlived their savings or have lost them due to inflation or bank failure. For many persons who are otherwise "normal" poverty may be said to arise out of one or a combination of such happenings.

A second factor that operates in the selection of persons to be poor is the maintenance of social barriers in the form of caste, class, and custom. The clearest example of this, of course, is racial discrimination with regard to opportunities to qualify for and to obtain work. (It is perhaps worth emphasizing here that only a fifth of the present poor are nonwhite, and that only a minority of the nonwhites are presently poor.) Similar types of arbitrary barriers or market imperfections are observable in the case of sex, age, residence, religion, education, and seniority. They are formalized in employer hiring procedures, in the rules of unions and professional and trade associations, in governmental regulations concerning housing and welfare and other programs, and are informally expressed in customer preferences. Barriers, once established, tend to be reinforced from the poverty side by the alienated themselves. The poor tend to be cut off from not only opportunity but even from information about opportunity. A poverty subculture develops which sustains attitudes and values that are hostile to escape from poverty. These barriers combine to make events nonrandom; e.g., unemployment is slanted away from those inside the feudalistic walls of collective bargaining, disability more commonly occurs in jobs reserved for those outside the barriers, the subculture of poverty invites or is prone to self-realizing forecasts of disaster.

The third factor involved in selecting persons out of the affluent society to be poor is limited ability or motivation of persons to earn and to protect themselves against events and to fight their way over the barriers.[2] To the extent that the market is perfect one can rationalize the selection for poverty (insofar as earnings alone are considered) on the basis of the abilities and skills needed by the market and the distribution of those abilities and skills in the population. But we note that ability is to some extent acquired or environmentally determined and that poverty tends to create personalities who will be de-selected by the market as inadequate on the basis of ability or motivation.

2. For an insight into the relative importance of this factor see James N. Morgan, Martin H. David, Wilbur J. Cohen, and Harvey E. Brazer, *Income and Welfare in the U.S.* (1962), pp. 196–98.

Countering "Events" · Approaches to the reduction of poverty can be seen as parallel to the causes or bases for selection recounted above. The first approach, then, is to prevent or counter the events or happenings which select some persons for poverty status. The poverty rate could be lessened by any reduction in early death, disability, family desertion, what John Kenneth Galbraith referred to as excessive procreation by the poor, or by containment of inflation and other hazards to financial security. Among the important events in this context the one most relevant to public policy consideration at this time is excessive unemployment. It would appear that if the recent level of over 5 percent unemployment could be reduced to 4 percent, the poverty rate would drop by about one percentage point.[3] Further fall in the poverty rate would follow if—by retaining and relocation of some workers—long-term unemployment could be cut or if unemployment could be more widely shared with the nonpoor.

To the extent that events are beyond prevention, some, e.g., disability, can be countered by remedial measures. Where neither the preventive nor the remedial approach is suitable, only the alleviative measures of social insurance and public assistance remain. And the sufficiency of these measures will help determine the poverty rate and the size of the poverty income gap. It is interesting to note that our system of public income maintenance, which now pays out $35 billion in benefits per year, is aimed more at the problem of income insecurity of the middle class and at blocking returns to poverty than in facilitating exits from poverty for those who have never been out of poverty. The nonpoor have the major claim to social insurance benefits, the levels of which in most cases are not adequate in themselves to keep a family out of poverty. Assistance payments of $4 billion now go to 8 million persons, all of whom are in the ranks of the poor, but

3. Unemployment is not strikingly different among the poor than the nonpoor. Nonparticipation in the labor force is more markedly associated with poverty than is unemployment. However, it seems that about 1 million poor family heads experience unemployment during the year. (*Census Population Reports*, P-60, No. 39, Feb. 28, 1963, Tables 15 and 16.) If half of this group were moved out of poverty by more nearly full employment, then the poverty rate would be one percentage point lower. Another way to estimate this is as follows. The national income would be $30 billion higher than it is if we had full employment. And a $30 billion increase in recent years has generally meant a full percentage point drop in the percent of families in poverty.

about half of the 35 million poor receive neither assistance nor social insurance payments. One important step in the campaign against poverty would be to reexamine our insurance and assistance programs to discover ways in which they could be more effective in helping people to get out of poverty. Among the ideas to be considered along this line are easier eligibility for benefits, higher minimum benefits, incentives to earn while receiving benefits, ways to combine work-relief, retraining, rehabilitation, and relocation with receipt of benefits.

Among the several events that select people for poverty, the ones about which we have done the least by social policy are family breakup by other than death and the event of being born poor. Both of these could be alleviated by a family allowance system, which the United States, almost alone among Western nations, lacks. We do, of course, have arrangements in the Federal individual income tax for personal deductions and exemptions whereby families of different size and composition are ranked for the imposition of progressive rates. However, it is a major irony of this system that it does not extend the full force of its allowances for children to the really poor. In order to do so, the tax system could be converted to have negative as well as positive rates, paying out grants as well as forgiving taxes on the basis of already adopted exemptions and rates. At present there are almost $20 billion of unused exemptions and deductions, most of which relate to families with children. Restricting the plan to such families and applying a negative tax rate of, say, 20 percent, to this amount would "yield" an allowance total of almost $4 billion. This would not in itself take many people out of poverty, but it would go a considerable distance toward closing the poverty income gap, which now aggregates about $12 billion.

It would, of course, be possible to go considerably further by this device without significantly impairing incentives to work and save. First, however, let me reject as unworkable any simple plan to assure a minimum income of $3,000. To make such an assurance would induce many now earning less than and even some earning slightly more than $3,000 to forego earnings opportunities and to accept the grant. Hence the poverty income gap of $12 billion would far understate the cost of such a minimum income plan. However, it would be practicable to enact a system of progressive rates articulated with the present income tax schedule.[4] The present rates fall from 70 percent at the top to 14 percent at income just above $3,700 for a family of five, to zero percent for income below $3,700. The average negative tax rates could move, then, from zero percent to minus 14 percent for, say, the unused exemptions that total $500, to 20 percent for those that total $1,000 and 40 percent for those that total $3,700. This would amount to a minimum income of $1,480 for a family of five; it would retain positive incentives through a set of grants that would gradually diminish as earned income rose.

The total amount to be paid out (interestingly, this would be shown in the federal budget as a net reduction in tax collections) under such a program would obviously depend upon the particular rates selected, the definition of income used, the types of income-receiving units declared eligible, and the offsets made in public assistance payments. But it clearly could be more than the $4 billion mentioned in connection with the more limited plan of a standard 20 percent negative tax rate. At the outset it might involve half the poverty income gap and total about $6 billion. This amount is approximately equal to the total federal, state, and local taxes now paid by the poor. Hence it would amount to a remission of taxes paid. As the number in poverty fell, the amount paid out under this plan would in turn diminish.

Breaking Down Barriers · The approaches discussed thus far are consistent with the view that poverty is the result of events which happen to people. But there are other approaches, including those aimed at removing barriers which keep people in poverty. Legislation and private, volunteer efforts to assure equal educational and employment opportunities can make a contribution in this direction. Efforts to randomize unemployment by area redevelopment and relocation can in some cases work to break down "islands of poverty." Public policy can prevent or modify the forming of a poverty subculture by city zoning laws, by public housing and by regulations of private housing, by school redistricting, by recreational, cultural, and public health programs. It is curious that medieval cities built walls to keep poverty outside. Present arrangements often work to bottle it up inside cities or parts of cities and thereby encourage poverty to function as its own cause.

4. Cf. Milton Friedman, *Capitalism and Freedom* (1962), pp. 192–93.

Improving Abilities and Motivations • The third broad approach to accelerated reduction of poverty relates to the basis for selection referred to above as limited ability or motivation. The process of economic growth works the poverty line progressively deeper into the ranks of people who are below average in ability or motivation, but meantime it should be possible to raise the ability and motivation levels of the lowest. It is interesting that few children, even those of below average ability, who are not born and raised in poverty, actually end up in poverty as adults. This suggests that poverty is to some extent an inherited disease. But it also suggests that if poor children had the same opportunities, including preschool training and remedial health care, as the nonpoor (even assuming no great breakthroughs of scientific understanding), the rate of escape from poverty would be higher. Even more fundamentally, we know that mental retardation as well as infant mortality and morbidity have an important causal connection with inadequate prenatal care, which in turn relates to low income of parents.

A belief in the economic responsiveness of poor youngsters to improved educational opportunities underlies policies advocated by many educational theorists from Jeremy Bentham to James B. Conant. And this widely shared belief no doubt explains the emphasis which the Economic Opportunity Act places upon education and training. The appropriation under that Act, while it seems small relative to the poverty income gap, is large relative to present outlays for education of the poor. I would estimate that the half-billion dollars or so thereby added increases the national expenditure for this purpose by about one-seventh. To raise the level of educational expenditure for poor children—who are one-fifth of the nation's children but who consume about a tenth of educational outlay—to equal that of the average would cost in the neighborhood of $3 billion. Such an emphasis upon education and training is justified by the fact that families headed by young adults will tend, in a few years, to be the most rapidly increasing group of poor families.

Approaches to the Reduction of Poverty: II

Harry G. Johnson, Professor of Economics at the University of Chicago, was a discussant of the foregoing paper delivered by Professor Lampman at the American Economic Asociation meetings in December 1964.

I WOULD LIKE to begin by suggesting that two other approaches [beside the economic]—those of the economic historian and of the social philosopher—might be useful in placing the current concern about poverty in perspective. From the point of view of economic history, it is, I think, significant that this is the second instance of presidential concern about poverty in this century, and that in both cases the economic conjuncture has been one of unusually high and prolonged unemployment, suggesting that poverty is a stagnation-correlated fashion. It is also worth noting that the maximum income required to be considered poor has been rising over the long run, which implies that poverty is a socially relative category and that it may be naïve to expect to make substantial permanent inroads on it. From the point of view of social philosophy, the poverty problem is largely a middle-class moral concern, and correspondingly programs for attacking poverty are conceived in middle-class terms and to a significant degree self-frustrating through concern for the preservation of middle-class values. Professor Robert Lampman has made the point that existing social security serves more to block regression into poverty than to open escape routes from it; I would add the observation that contemporary thinking about poverty is dominated by the notion of elevating the poor into the middle class— hence the stress now laid on education as the key to the poverty problem—and is both seriously handicapped and forced into deviousness by the requirement that this elevation be accomplished in ways consistent with middle-class morality.

To be specific, poverty is invariably defined in terms of inadequacy of income to support a minimum standard of decent living. One might therefore naïvely suppose that the solution to the poverty problem would be simply to arrange income transfers to the poor on an appropriate scale. Such payments of social conscience money would not seriously strain the resources of an economy as affluent as this one, and they would have the advantage of eliminating a large part of the administrative overhead required by existing and proposed assistance and welfare programs. It is true that they would generate some waste, by making poverty more eligible than work to some people and by encouraging various kinds of fraud; but waste is one of the main uses of resources that an affluent society can and does afford, and given our society's tolerance of organized crime and of sharp business practices, the anxiety to prevent or punish fraudulent poverty is something of an eccentricity. It is also arguable that the experience of a decent income would itself have a powerful educative influence in inculcating middle-class habits and ambitions. Yet the simple solution of arranging adequate transfer payments is universally rejected out of hand, on the grounds that it would "impair incentives to work and save."

I am not arguing that poverty should necessarily be tackled exclusively by income transfers, but only that income transfers are dismissed summarily by arguments that either rely on a mythology of free enterprise that is inconsistent with concern about poverty, or depend implicity on assertions about economic behavior that require more empirical investigation than they have been accorded as yet. This is my main quarrel with Professor Lampman's paper, which is on the whole a very useful, compact, and well-organized treatment of the subject. Lampman brushes aside "the idea that there has to be some given amount of poverty," and consigns to folklore a number of rationalizations of this notion. But in his own discussion of the approach of countering "events" that cause poverty—and specifically of the problem of childhood poverty—he is led by the same folklore to produce a compromise negative tax rate plan that would preserve poverty though ameliorating it by reducing the poverty income gap. Lampman rejects "as unworkable any simple plan to assure a minimum income of $3,000." The term "unworkable" is a vague, practical-sounding adjective, commonly employed to close off dangerous thought. What Lampman means by it is the testable but untested empirical proposition that $3,000 would cause many people to cease work, combined with the personal judgment that the resulting cost would be politically unacceptable. I am skeptical about the empirical proposition; but even if it were true, a rough calculation from Lampman's figures, made by assuming that all the present private income of the poor would have to be replaced by public transfers, produces a total bill of $27 billion, or 4½ percent of GNP, as compared with the poverty income gap of $12 billion or 2 percent of GNP. Four and a half percent of GNP may well be politically unacceptable; but it is really small potatoes as war finance goes, if war on poverty is really what has been declared. Lampman's alternative negative tax scheme is equally dependent on an untested proposition about incentives to work. It also ignores the strong possibility that the preoccupation of parents with the earning of money—especially in broken homes —is an important factor in the perpetuation of poverty among the children of the poor. I would myself prefer to recommend an explicit system of family allowances. More generally, I believe that in many cases of poverty income transfers would be the most efficient solution.

In conclusion, I offer a few brief comments. First, I suspect that if poverty specialists referred to modern growth models rather than the classical models based on the iron law of wages, they might be surprised by the slowness rather than the speed of progress in overcoming poverty. Second, it would seem to me desirable to work out what the prevalence of poverty would be exclusive of the effects of existing programs, to determine how far progress in reducing poverty has been automatic and how far it has been due to social policy intervention in the economy. Third, I would place more emphasis than Lampman does on the factor of discrimination—against Negroes, against women, against the aged, and against the uneducated—as a cause of poverty. Fourth, I concur in Lampman's emphasis on the interaction of causal factors in poverty; but this leads me to place much greater emphasis on the importance of maintaining full employment for the reduction of poverty, on the grounds that a tight labor market is a powerful long-run solvent of discriminatory barriers to participation in the labor market at nonpoverty wages.

A Proposal for a Minimum Guaranteed Income

THE AD HOC COMMITTEE
ON THE TRIPLE REVOLUTION

The Ad Hoc Committee on The Triple Revolution, composed of a number of prominent writers, educators, and other citizens, prepared a statement in 1964 entitled "The Triple Revolution," [1] which was given wide circulation. Those sections of the Committee's statement bearing on its proposal for a minimum guaranteed income for all are given below.

THE UNITED STATES operates on the thesis, set out in the Employment Act of 1946, that every person will be able to obtain a job if he wishes to do so and that this job will provide him with resources adequate to live and maintain a family decently. Thus job-holding is the general mechanism through which economic resources are distributed. Those without work have access only to a minimal income, hardly sufficient to provide the necessities of life and enabling those receiving it to function as only "minimum consumers."

The fundamental problem posed by the cybernation revolution in the United States is that it invalidates the general mechanism so far employed to undergird people's rights as consumers. Up to this time economic resources have been distributed on the basis

1. The three revolutions are described in the statement as follows: "The Cybernation Revolution: The cybernation revolution has been brought about by the combination of the computer and the automated self-regulating machine. This results in a system of almost unlimited productive capacity which requires progressively less human labor.

"The Weaponry Revolution: New forms of weaponry have been developed which cannot win wars but which can obliterate civilization. We are recognizing only now that the great weapons have eliminated war as a method for resolving international conflicts.

"The Human Rights Revolution: A universal demand for full human rights is now clearly evident . . . The civil rights movement within the United States . . . is only the local manifestation of a worldwide movement toward the establishment of social and political regimes in which every individual will feel valued and none will feel rejected on account of his race."

of contributions to production, with machines and men competing for employment on somewhat equal terms. In the developing cybernated system, potentially unlimited output can be achieved by systems of machines which will require little cooperation from human beings. As machines take over production from men, they absorb an increasing proportion of resources while the men who are displaced become dependent on minimal and unrelated government measures—unemployment insurance, social security, welfare payments. These measures are less and less able to disguise a historic paradox: that a growing proportion of the population is subsisting on minimal incomes, often below the poverty line, at a time when sufficient productive potential is available to supply the needs of everyone in the United States.

The existence of this paradox is denied or ignored by conventional economic analysis. The general economic approach argues that potential demand, which if filled would raise the number of jobs and provide incomes to those holding them, is under-estimated. Most contemporary economic analysis states that all of the available labor force and industrial capacity is required to meet the needs of consumers and industry and to provide adequate public services: schools, parks, roads, homes, decent cities, and clean water and air. It is further argued that demand could be increased, by a variety of standard techniques, to any desired extent by providing money and machines to improve the conditions of the billions of impoverished people elsewhere in the world, who need food and shelter, clothes and machinery and everything else the industrial nations take for granted.

There is no question that cybernation does increase the potential for the provision of funds to neglected public sectors. Nor is there any question that cybernation would make possible the abolition of poverty at home and abroad. But the industrial system does not possess any adequate mechanisms to permit these potentials to become realities. The industrial system was designed to produce an ever-increasing quantity of goods as efficiently as possible, and it was assumed that the distribution of the power to purchase these goods would occur almost automatically. The continuance of the income-through-jobs link as the only major mechanism for distributing effective demand—for granting the right to consume—now acts as the main brake on the almost unlimited capacity of a cybernated productive system.

Secretary of Labor Willard Wirtz recently summarized these trends.

The confluence of surging population and driving technology is splitting the American labor force into tens of millions of "haves" and millions of "have-nots." In our economy of 69 million jobs, those with wanted skills enjoy opportunity and earning power. But the others face a new and stark problem—exclusion on a permanent basis, both as producers and consumers, from economic life. This division of people threatens to create a human slag heap. We cannot tolerate the development of a separate nation of the poor, the unskilled, the jobless, living within another nation of the well-off, the trained and the employed.

As a first step to a new consensus it is essential to recognize that the traditional link between jobs and incomes is being broken. The economy of abundance can sustain all citizens in comfort and economic security whether or not they engage in what is commonly reckoned as work. Wealth produced by machines rather than by men is still wealth. We urge, therefore, that society, through its appropriate legal and governmental institutions, undertake an unqualified commitment to provide every individual and every family with an adequate income as a matter of right. This undertaking we consider to be essential to the emerging economic, social and political order in this country. We regard it as the only policy by which the quarter of the nation now dispossessed and soon-to-be dispossessed by lack of employment can be brought within the abundant society. The unqualified right to an income would take the place of the patchwork of welfare measures—from unemployment insurance to relief—designed to ensure that no citizen or resident of the United States actually starves.

We do not pretend to visualize all of the consequences of this change in our values. It is clear, however, that the distribution of abundance in a cybernated society must be based on criteria strikingly different from those of an economic system based on scarcity. In retrospect, the establishment of the right to an income will prove to have been only the first step in the reconstruction of the value system of our society brought on by the triple revolution.

The Alleviation of Poverty

MILTON FRIEDMAN

Professor Friedman in his section on poverty in Capitalism and Freedom *was perhaps the first to propose the widely discussed negative income tax plan.*

THE EXTRAORDINARY ECONOMIC GROWTH experienced by Western countries during the past two centuries and the wide distribution of the benefits of free enterprise have enormously reduced the extent of poverty in any absolute sense in the capitalistic countries of the West. But poverty is in part a relative matter, and even in these countries, there are clearly many people living under conditions that the rest of us label as poverty.

One recourse, and in many ways the most desirable, is private charity. It is noteworthy that the heyday of *laissez faire,* the middle and late nineteenth century in Britain and the United States, saw an extraordinary proliferation of private eleemosynary organizations and institutions. One of the major costs of the extension of governmental welfare activities has been the corresponding decline in private charitable activities.

It can be argued that private charity is insufficient because the benefits from it accrue to people other than those who make the gifts—a neighborhood effect. I am distressed by the sight of poverty; I am benefited by its alleviation; but I am benefited equally whether I or someone else pays for its alleviation; the benefits of other people's charity therefore partly accrue to me. To put it differently, we might all of us be willing to contribute to the relief of poverty, *provided* everyone else did. We might not be willing to contribute the same amount without such assurance. In small communities, public pressure can suffice to realize the proviso even with private charity. In the large impersonal communities that are increasingly coming to dominate our society, it is much more difficult for it to do so.

Suppose one accepts, as I do, this line of reasoning as justifying governmental action to alleviate poverty; to set, as it were, a floor under the standard of life of every person in the community. There remain the questions, how much and how. I see no way of deciding "how much" except in terms of the amount of taxes we —by which I mean the great bulk of us—are willing to impose on ourselves for the purpose. The question, "how," affords more room for speculation.

Two things seem clear. First, if the objective is to alleviate poverty, we should have a program directed at helping the poor. There is every reason to help the poor man who happens to be a farmer, not because he is a farmer but because he is poor. The program, that is, should be designed to help people as people not as members of particular occupational groups or age groups or wage-rate groups or labor organizations or industries. This is a defect of farm programs, general old-age benefits, minimum-wage laws, pro-union legislation, tariffs, licensing provisions of crafts or professions, and so on in seemingly endless profusion. Second, so far as possible the program should, while operating through the market, not distort the market or impede its functioning. This is a defect of price supports, minimum-wage laws, tariffs and the like.

The arrangement that recommends itself on purely mechanical grounds is a negative income tax. We now have an exemption of $600 per person under the federal income tax (plus a minimum 10 per cent flat deduction). If an individual receives $100 taxable income, i.e., an income of $100 in excess of the exemption and deductions, he pays tax. Under the proposal, if his taxable income were minus $100, i.e., $100 less than the exemption plus deductions, he would pay a negative tax, i.e., receive a subsidy. If the rate of subsidy were, say, 50 per cent, he would receive $50. If he had no income at all, and, for simplicity, no deductions, and the rate were constant, he would receive $300. He might receive more than this if he had deductions, for example, for medical expenses, so that his income less deductions, was negative even before subtracting the exemption. The rates of subsidy could, of course, be graduated just as the rates of tax above the exemption are. In this way, it would be possible to set a floor below which no man's net income (defined now to include the subsidy) could fall—in the simple example $300 per person. The precise floor set would depend on what the community could afford.

The advantages of this arrangement are clear. It is directed specifically at the problem of poverty. It gives help in the form most useful to the individual, namely, cash. It is general and could be substituted for the host of special measures now in effect. It makes explicit the cost borne by society. It operates outside the market. Like any other measures to alleviate poverty, it reduces the incentives of those helped to help themselves, but it does not eliminate that incentive entirely, as a system of supplementing incomes up to some fixed minimum would. An extra dollar earned always means more money available for expenditure.

No doubt there would be problems of administration, but these seem to me a minor disadvantage, if they be a disadvantage at all. The system would fit directly into our current income tax system and could be administered along with it. The present tax system covers the bulk of income recipients and the necessity of covering all would have the by-product of improving the operation of the present income tax. More important, if enacted as a substitute for the present rag bag of measures directed at the same end, the total administrative burden would surely be reduced.

A few brief calculations suggest also that this proposal could be far less costly in money, let alone in the degree of governmental intervention involved, than our present collection of welfare measures. Alternatively, these calculations can be regarded as showing how wasteful our present measures are, judged as measures for helping the poor.

In 1961, government amounted to something like $33 billion (federal, state, and local) on direct welfare payments and programs of all kinds: old age assistance, social security benefit payments, aid to dependent children, general assistance, farm price support programs, public housing, etc.[1] I have excluded veterans'

1. This figure is equal to government transfer payments ($31.1 billion) less veterans' benefits ($4.8 billion), both from the Department of Com-

benefits in making this calculation. I have also made no allowance for the direct and indirect costs of such measures as minimum-wage laws, tariffs, licensing provisions, and so on, or for the costs of public health activities, state and local expenditures on hospitals, mental institutions, and the like.

There are approximately 57 million consumer units (unattached individuals and families) in the United States. The 1961 expenditures of $33 billion would have financed outright cash grants of nearly $6,000 per consumer unit to the 10 per cent with the lowest incomes. Such grants would have raised their incomes above the average for all units in the United States. Alternatively, these expenditures would have financed grants of nearly $3,000 per consumer unit to the 20 per cent with the lowest incomes. Even if one went so far as that one-third whom New Dealers were fond of calling ill-fed, ill-housed, and ill-clothed, 1961 expenditures would have financed grants of nearly $2,000 per consumer unit, roughly the sum which, after allowing for the change in the level of prices, was the income which separated the lower one-third in the middle 1930's from the upper two-thirds. Today, fewer than one-eighth of consumer units have an income, adjusted for the change in the level of prices, as low as that of the lowest third in the middle 1930's.

Clearly, these are all far more extravagant programs than can be justified to "alleviate poverty" even by a rather generous interpretation of that term. A program which *supplemented* the incomes of the 20 per cent of the consumer units with the lowest incomes so as to raise them to the lowest income of the rest would cost less than half of what we are now spending.

The major disadvantage of the proposed negative income tax is its political implications. It establishes a system under which taxes are imposed on some to pay subsidies to others. And presumably, these others have a vote. There is always the danger

---

merce national income accounts, plus federal expenditures on the agricultural program ($5.5 billion) plus federal expenditures on public housing and other aids to housing ($0.5 billion), both for year ending June 30, 1961 from Treasury accounts, plus a rough allowance of $0.7 billion to raise it to even billions and to allow for administrative costs of federal programs, omitted state and local programs, and miscellaneous items. My guess is that this figure is a substantial underestimate.

that instead of being an arrangement under which the great majority tax themselves willingly to help an unfortunate minority, it will be converted into one under which a majority imposes taxes for its own benefit on an unwilling minority. Because this proposal makes the process so explicit, the danger is perhaps greater than with other measures. I see no solution to this problem except to rely on the self-restraint and good will of the electorate.

On Improving the Economic Status of the Negro

JAMES TOBIN

James Tobin, Sterling Professor of Economics at Yale University, contributed this paper to the Fall 1965 issue of Daedalus *on "The Negro American." While emphasizing the problems of the Negro poor, most of his analysis is applicable to the entire poverty problem. Professor Tobin was a member of the Council of Economic Advisers from 1961 to 1962.*

THE ECONOMIC PLIGHT OF INDIVIDUALS, Negroes and whites alike, can always be attributed to specific handicaps and circumstances: discrimination, immobility, lack of education and experience, ill health, weak motivation, poor neighborhood, large family size, burdensome family responsibilities. Such diagnoses suggest a host of specific remedies, some in the domain of civil rights, others in the war on poverty. Important as these remedies are, there is a danger that the diagnoses are myopic. They explain why certain individuals rather than others suffer from the economic maladies of the time. They do not explain why the over-all incidence of the maladies varies dramatically from time to time—for example, why personal attributes which seemed to doom a man to unemployment in 1932 or even in 1954 or 1961 did not so handicap him in 1944 or 1951 or 1956.

Public health measures to improve the environment are often more productive in conquering disease than a succession of individual treatments. Malaria was conquered by oiling and draining swamps, not by quinine. The analogy holds for economic maladies. Unless the global incidence of these misfortunes can be diminished, every individual problem successfully solved will be replaced by a similar problem somewhere else. That is why an economist is led to emphasize the importance of the over-all economic climate.

Over the decades, general economic progress has been the major factor in the gradual conquest of poverty. Recently some observers, John Kenneth Galbraith and Michael Harrington most eloquently, have contended that this process no longer operates. The economy may prosper and labor may become steadily more productive as in the past, but "the other America" will be stranded. Prosperity and progress have already eliminated almost all the easy cases of poverty, leaving a hard core beyond the reach of national economic trends. There may be something to the "backwash" thesis as far as whites are concerned.[1] But it definitely does not apply to Negroes. Too many of them are poor. It cannot be true that half of a race of twenty million human beings are victims of specific disabilities which insulate them from the national economic climate. It cannot be true, and it is not. Locke Anderson has shown that the pace of Negro economic progress is peculiarly sensitive to general economic growth. He estimates that if nationwide per capita personal income is stationary, nonwhite median family income falls by .5 per cent per year, while if national per capita income grows 5 per cent, nonwhite income grows nearly 7.5 per cent.[2]

National prosperity and economic growth are still powerful engines for improving the economic status of Negroes. They are not doing enough and they are not doing it fast enough. There is ample room for a focused attack on the specific sources of Negro poverty. But a favorable over-all economic climate is a necessary condition for the global success—as distinguished from success in individual cases—of specific efforts to remedy the handicaps associated with Negro poverty.

1. As Locke Anderson shows, one would expect advances in median income to run into diminishing returns in reducing the number of people below some fixed poverty-level income. W. H. Locke Anderson, "Trickling Down: The Relationship between Economic Growth and the Extent of Poverty Among American Families," *Quarterly Journal of Economics*, Vol. 78 (November 1964), pp. 511–524. However, for the economy as a whole, estimates by Lowell Gallaway suggest that advances in median income still result in a substantial reduction in the fraction of the population below poverty-level incomes. "The Foundations of the War on Poverty," *American Economic Review*, Vol. 55 (March 1965), pp. 122–131.

2. Anderson, *op. cit.*, Table IV, p. 522.

THE IMPORTANCE OF A TIGHT LABOR MARKET

The economy has not operated with reasonably full utilization of its manpower and plant capacity since 1957. Even now, after four and one-half years of uninterrupted expansion, the economy has not regained the ground lost in the recessions of 1958 and 1960. The current expansion has whittled away at unemployment, reducing it from 6.5 to 7 per cent to 4.5 to 5 per cent. It has diminished idle plant capacity correspondingly. The rest of the gains since 1960 in employment, production, and income have just offset the normal growth of population, capacity, and productivity.

The magnitude of America's poverty problem already reflects the failure of the economy in the second postwar decade to match its performance in the first.[3] Had the 1947–56 rate of growth of median family income been maintained since 1957, and had unemployment been steadily limited to 4 per cent, it is estimated that the fraction of the population with poverty incomes in 1963 would have been 16.6 per cent instead of 18.5 per cent.[4] The educational qualifications of the labor force have continued to improve. The principle of racial equality, in employment as in other activities, has gained ground both in law and in the national conscience. If, despite all this, dropouts, inequalities in educational attainment, and discrimination in employment seem more serious today rather than less, the reason is that the over-all economic climate has not been favorable after all.

3. This point, and others made in this section, have been eloquently argued by Harry G. Johnson, "Unemployment and Poverty," in Leo Fishman, ed., *Poverty Amid Affluence* (New Haven, 1966), pp. 182–199.

4. Gallaway, *op. cit.* Gallaway used the definitions of poverty originally suggested by the Council of Economic Advisers in its 1964 Economic Report, that is: incomes below $3000 a year for families and below $1500 a year for single individuals. The Social Security Administration has refined these measures to take better account of family size and of income in kind available to farmers. Mollie Orshansky, "Counting the Poor: Another Look at the Poverty Profile," *Social Security Bulletin*, Vol. 28 (January 1965), pp. 3–29. These refinements change the composition of the "poor" but affect very little their total number; it is doubtful they would alter Gallaway's results.

The most important dimension of the overall economic climate is the tightness of the labor market. In a tight labor market unemployment is low and short in duration, and job vacancies are plentiful. People who stand at the end of the hiring line and the top of the layoff list have the most to gain from a tight labor market. It is not surprising that the position of Negroes relative to that of whites improves in a tight labor market and declines in a slack market. Unemployment itself is only one way in which a slack labor market hurts Negroes and other disadvantaged groups, and the gains from reduction in unemployment are by no means confined to the employment of persons counted as unemployed.[5] A tight labor market means not just jobs, but better jobs, longer hours, higher wages. Because of the heavy demands for labor during the second world war and its economic aftermath, Negroes made dramatic relative gains between 1940 and 1950. Unfortunately this momentum has not been maintained, and the blame falls largely on the weakness of labor markets since 1957.

The shortage of jobs has hit Negro men particularly hard and thus has contributed mightily to the ordeal of the Negro family, which is in turn the cumulative source of so many other social disorders. The unemployment rate of Negro men is more sensitive than that of Negro women to the national rate. Since 1949 Negro women have gained in median income relative to white women, but Negro men have lost ground to white males.[6] In a society which stresses breadwinning as the expected role of the mature male and occupational achievement as his proper goal, failure to find and to keep work is devastating to the man's self-respect and family status. Matriarchy is in any case a strong tradition in Negro society, and the man's role is further downgraded when the family must and can depend on the woman for its liveli-

5. Gallaway, *op cit.*, shows that postwar experience suggests that, other things equal, every point by which unemployment is diminished lowers the national incidence of poverty by .5 per cent of itself. And this does not include the effects of the accompanying increase in median family income, which would be of the order of 3 per cent and reduce the poverty fraction another 1.8 per cent.

6. Differences between Negro men and women with respect to unemployment and income progress are reported and analyzed by Alan Batchelder, "Decline in the Relative Income of Negro Men," *Quarterly Journal of Economics*, Vol. 78 (Nov. 1964), pp. 525–548.

hood. It is very important to increase the proportion of Negro children who grow up in stable families with two parents. Without a strong labor market it will be extremely difficult to do so.

Unemployment · It is well known that Negro unemployment rates are multiples of the general unemployment rate. This fact reflects both the lesser skills, seniority, and experience of Negroes and employers' discrimination against Negroes. These conditions are a deplorable reflection on American society, but as long as they exist Negroes suffer much more than others from a general increase in unemployment and gain much more from a general reduction. A rule of thumb is that changes in the nonwhite unemployment rate are twice those in the white rate. The rule works both ways. Nonwhite unemployment went from 4.1 per cent in 1953, a tight labor market year, to 12.5 per cent in 1961, while the white rate rose from 2.3 per cent to 6 per cent. Since then, the Negro rate has declined by 2.4 per cent, the white rate by 1.2. Even the Negro teenage unemployment rate shows some sensitivity to general economic conditions.

Part-time Work · Persons who are involuntarily forced to work part time instead of full time are not counted as unemployed, but their number goes up and down with the unemployment rate. Just as Negroes bear a disproportionate share of unemployment, they bear more than their share of involuntary part-time unemployment. A tight labor market will not only employ more Negroes; it will also give more of those who are employed full-time jobs. In both respects, it will reduce disparities between whites and Negroes.

Labor-force Participation · In a tight market, of which a low unemployment rate is a barometer, the labor force itself is larger. Job opportunities draw into the labor force individuals who, simply because the prospects were dim, did not previously regard themselves as seeking work and were therefore not enumerated as unemployed. For the economy as a whole, it appears that an expansion of job opportunities enough to reduce unemployment by one worker will bring another worker into the labor force.

This phenomenon is important for many Negro families. Statistically, their poverty now appears to be due more often to the lack of a breadwinner in the labor force than to unemployment.[7] But in a tight labor market many members of these families, including families now on public assistance, would be drawn into employment. Labor-force participation rates are roughly 2 per cent lower for nonwhite men than for white men, and the disparity increases in years of slack labor markets.[8]

Duration of Unemployment · In a tight labor market, such unemployment as does exist is likely to be of short duration. Short-term unemployment is less damaging to the economic welfare of the unemployed. More will have earned and fewer will have exhausted private and public unemployment benefits.

As Rashi Fein has pointed out, one more dimension of society's inequity to the Negro is that an unemployed Negro is more likely to stay unemployed than an unemployed white.[9] But Fein's figures also show that Negroes share in the reduction of long-term unemployment accompanying economic expansion.

Migration from Agriculture · A tight labor market draws the surplus rural population to higher paying nonagricultural jobs. Southern Negroes are a large part of this surplus rural population. Migration is the only hope for improving their lot, or their children's. In spite of the vast migration of past decades, there are still about 775,000 Negroes, 11 per cent of the Negro labor force of the country, who depend on the land for their living and that of their families.[10] Almost a half million live in the South, and almost all of them are poor.

Migration from agriculture and from the South is the Negroes'

7. In 34 per cent of poor Negro families, the head is not in the labor force; in 6 per cent, the head is unemployed. These figures relate to the Social Security Administration's "economy-level" poverty index: Mollie Orshansky, *op. cit.*

8. See *Manpower Report of the President,* March 1964, Table A-3, p. 197.

9. [Rashi Fein, "An Economic and Social Profile of the American Negro," *Daedalus,* Vol. 94 (Fall 1965), pp. 828–829).—*Editor.*]

10. Dale Hiestand, *Economic Growth and Employment Opportunities for Minorities* (New York, 1964), Table 1, pp. 7–9.

historic path toward economic improvement and equality. It is a smooth path for Negroes and for the urban communities to which they move only if there is a strong demand for labor in towns and cities North and South. In the 1940's the number of Negro farmers and farm laborers in the nation fell by 450,000 and one-and-a-half-million Negroes (net) left the South. This was the great decade of Negro economic advance. In the 1950's the same occupational and geographical migration continued undiminished. The movement to higher-income occupations and locations should have raised the relative economic status of Negroes. But in the 1950's Negroes were moving into increasingly weak job markets. Too often disguised unemployment in the countryside was simply transformed into enumerated unemployment, and rural poverty into urban poverty.[11]

Quality of Jobs · In a slack labor market, employers can pick and choose, both in recruiting and in promoting. They exaggerate the skill, education, and experience requirements of their jobs. They use diplomas, or color, or personal histories as convenient screening devices. In a tight market, they are forced to be realistic, to tailor job specifications to the available supply, and to give on-the-job-training. They recruit and train applicants whom they would otherwise screen out, and they upgrade employees whom they would in slack times consign to low-wage, low-skill, and part-time jobs.

Wartime and other experience shows that job requirements are adjustable and that men and women are trainable. It is only in slack times that people worry about a mismatch between supposedly rigid occupational requirements and supposedly unchangeable qualifications of the labor force. As already noted, the relative status of Negroes improves in a tight labor market not only in respect to unemployment, but also in respect to wages and occupations.

11. Batchelder, *op. cit.*, shows that the incomes of Negro men declined relative to those of white men in every region of the country. For the country as a whole, nevertheless, the median income of Negro men stayed close to half that of white men. The reason is that migration from the South, where the Negro-white income ratio is particularly low, just offset the declines in the regional ratios.

Cyclical Fluctuations · Sustaining a high demand for labor is important. The in-and-out status of the Negro in the business cycle damages his long-term position because periodic unemployment robs him of experience and seniority.

Restrictive Practices · A slack labor market probably accentuates the discriminatory and protectionist proclivities of certain crafts and unions. When jobs are scarce, opening the door to Negroes is a real threat. Of course prosperity will not automatically dissolve the barriers, but it will make it more difficult to oppose efforts to do so.

I conclude that the single most important step the nation could take to improve the economic position of the Negro is to operate the economy steadily at a low rate of unemployment. We cannot expect to restore the labor market conditions of the Second World War, and we do not need to. In the years 1951–1953, unemployment was roughly 3 per cent, teenage unemployment around 7 per cent, Negro unemployment about 4.5 per cent, long-term unemployment negligible. In the years 1955–1957, general unemployment was roughly 4 per cent, and the other measures correspondingly higher. Four per cent is the official target of the Kennedy-Johnson administration. It has not been achieved since 1957.[12] Reaching and maintaining 4 per cent would be a tremendous improvement over the performance of the last eight years. But we should not stop there; the society and the Negro can benefit immensely from tightening the labor market still further, to 3.5 or 3 per cent unemployment. The administration itself has never defined 4 per cent as anything other than an "interim" target.

12. [This was written in 1965. Unemployment averaged 4.7 per cent for the first nine months of 1965; 3.9 per cent for the corresponding period in 1966.—*Editor.*]

WHY DON'T WE HAVE A TIGHT LABOR MARKET?

We know how to operate the economy so that there is a tight labor market. By fiscal and monetary measures the federal government can control aggregate spending in the economy. The government could choose to control it so that unemployment *averaged* 3.5 or 3 per cent instead of remaining over 4.5 per cent except at occasional business cycle peaks. Moreover, recent experience here and abroad shows that we can probably narrow the amplitude of fluctuations around whatever average we select as a target.

Some observers have cynically concluded that a society like ours can achieve full employment only in wartime. But aside from conscription into the armed services, government action creates jobs in wartime by exactly the same mechanism as in peacetime —the government spends more money and stimulates private firms and citizens to spend more too. It is the *amount* of spending, not its purpose, that does the trick. Public or private spending to go to the moon, build schools, or conquer poverty can be just as effective in reducing unemployment as spending to build airplanes and submarines—if there is enough of it. There may be more political constraints and ideological inhibitions in peacetime, but the same techniques of economic policy are available if we want badly enough to use them. The two main reasons we do not take this relatively simple way out are two obsessive fears, inflation and balance of payments deficits.

Running the economy with a tight labor market would mean a somewhat faster upward creep in the price level. The disadvantages of this are, in my view, exaggerated and are scarcely commensurable with the real economic and social gains of higher output and employment. But fear of inflation is strong both in the United States financial establishment and in the public at large. The vast comfortable white middle class who are never touched by unemployment prefer to safeguard the purchasing power of their life insurance and pension rights than to expand opportunities for the disadvantaged and unemployed.

The fear of inflation would operate anyway, but it is accentuated by United States difficulties with its international balance of payments. These difficulties have seriously constrained and hampered United States fiscal and monetary policy in recent years. Any rise in prices might enlarge the deficit. An aggressively expansionary monetary policy, lowering interest rates, might push money out of the country.

In the final analysis what we fear is that we might not be able to defend the parity of the dollar with gold, that is, to sell gold at thirty-five dollars an ounce to any government that wants to buy. So great is the gold mystique that this objective has come to occupy a niche in the hierarchy of United States goals second only to the military defense of the country, and not always to that. It is not fanciful to link the plight of Negro teenagers in Harlem to the monetary whims of General de Gaulle. But it is only our own attachment to "the dollar" as an abstraction which makes us cringe before the European appetite for gold.

The connection between gold and the plight of the Negro is no less real for being subtle. We are paying much too high a social price for avoiding creeping inflation and for protecting our gold stock and "the dollar." But it will not be easy to alter these national priorities. The interests of the unemployed, the poor, and the Negroes are underrepresented in the comfortable consensus which supports and confines current policy.

Another approach, which can be pursued simultaneously, is to diminish the conflicts among these competing objectives, in particular to reduce the degree of inflation associated with low levels of unemployment. This can be done in two ways. One way is to improve the mobility of labor and other resources to occupations, locations, and industries where bottlenecks would otherwise lead to wage and price increases. This is where many specific programs, such as the training and retraining of manpower and policies to improve the technical functioning of labor markets, come into their own.

A second task is to break down the barriers to competition which now restrict the entry of labor and enterprise into certain occupations and industries. These lead to wage- and price-increasing bottlenecks even when resources are not really short. Many barriers are created by public policy itself, in response to the vested interests concerned. Many reflect concentration of economic power in unions and in industry. These barriers represent another way in which the advantaged and the employed purchase their standards of living and their security at the expense of unprivileged minorities.

In the best of circumstances, structural reforms of these kinds will be slow and gradual. They will encounter determined economic and political resistance from special interests which are powerful in Congress and state legislatures. Moreover, Congressmen and legislators represent places rather than people and are likely to oppose, not facilitate, the increased geographical mobility which is required. It is no accident that our manpower programs do not include relocation allowances.

INCREASING THE EARNING CAPACITY OF NEGROES

Given the proper over-all economic climate, in particular a steadily tight labor market, the Negro's economic condition can be expected to improve, indeed to improve dramatically. But not fast enough. Not as fast as his aspirations or as the aspirations he has taught the rest of us to have for him. What else can be done? I shall confine myself to a few comments and suggestions that occur to a general economist.

Even in a tight labor market, the Negro's relative status will suffer both from current discrimination and from his lower earning capacity, the result of inferior acquired skill. In a real sense both factors reflect discrimination, since the Negro's handicaps in earning capacity are the residue of decades of discrimination in education and employment. Nevertheless for both analysis and policy it is useful to distinguish the two.

Discrimination means that the Negro is denied access to certain markets where he might sell his labor, and to certain markets where he might purchase goods and services. Elementary application of "supply and demand" makes it clear that these restrictions are bound to result in his selling his labor for less and buying his livelihood for more than if these barriers did not exist. If Negro women can be clerks only in certain stores, those storekeepers will not need to pay them so much as they pay whites. If Negroes can live only in certain houses, the prices and rents they have to pay will be high for the quality of accommodation provided.

Upgrading the earning capacity of Negroes will be difficult, but the economic effects are easy to analyze. Economists have long held that the way to reduce disparities in earned incomes is to eliminate disparities in earning capacities. If college-trained people earn more money than those who left school after eight years, the remedy is to send a larger proportion of young people to college. If machine operators earn more than ditchdiggers, the remedy is to give more people the capacity and opportunity to be machine operators. These changes in relative supplies reduce the disparity both by competing down the pay in the favored line of work and by raising the pay in the less remunerative line. When there are only a few people left in the population whose capacities are confined to garbage-collecting, it will be a high-paid calling. The same is true of domestic service and all kinds of menial work.

This classical economic strategy will be hampered if discrimination, union barriers, and the like stand in the way. It will not help to increase the supply of Negro plumbers if the local unions and contractors will not let them join. But experience also shows that barriers give way more easily when the pressures of unsatisfied demand and supply pile up.

It should therefore be the task of educational and manpower policy to engineer over the next two decades a massive change in the relative supplies of people of different educational and professional attainments and degrees of skill and training. It must be a more rapid change than has occurred in the past two decades, because that has not been fast enough to alter income differentials. We should try particularly to increase supplies in those fields where salaries and wages are already high and rising. In this process we should be very skeptical of self-serving arguments and calculations—that an increase in supply in this or that profession would be bound to reduce quality, or that there are some mechanical relations of "need" to population or to Gross National Product that cannot be exceeded.

Such a policy would be appropriate to the "war on poverty" even if there were no racial problem. Indeed, our objective is to raise the earning capacities of low-income whites as well as of Negroes. But Negroes have the most to gain, and even those who because of age or irreversible environmental handicaps must inevitably be left behind will benefit by reduction in the number of whites and other Negroes who are competing with them.

ASSURING LIVING STANDARDS IN THE ABSENCE OF EARNING CAPACITY

The reduction of inequality in earning capacity is the fundamental solution, and in a sense anything else is stopgap. Some stopgaps are useless and even counterproductive. People who lack the capacity to earn a decent living need to be helped, but they will not be helped by minimum wage laws, trade union wage pressures, or other devices which seek to compel employers to pay them more than their work is worth. The more likely outcome of such regulations is that the intended beneficiaries are not employed at all.

A far better approach is to supplement earnings from the public fisc. But assistance can and should be given in a way that does not force the recipients out of the labor force or give them incentive to withdraw. Our present system of welfare payments does just that, causing needless waste and demoralization. This application of the means test is bad economics as well as bad sociology. It is almost as if our present programs of public assistance had been consciously contrived to perpetuate the conditions they are supposed to alleviate.

These programs apply a strict means test. The amount of assistance is an estimate of minimal needs, less the resources of the family from earnings. The purpose of the means test seems innocuous enough. It is to avoid wasting taxpayers' money on people who do not really need help. But another way to describe the means test is to note that it taxes earnings at a rate of 100 per cent. A person on public assistance cannot add to his family's standard of living by working. Of course, the means test provides a certain incentive to work in order to get off public assistance altogether. But in many cases, especially where there is only one adult to provide for and take care of several children, the adult simply does not have enough time and earning opportunities to get by without financial help. He, or more likely she, is essentially forced to be both idle and on a dole. The means test also involves limitations on property holdings which deprive anyone who is or expects to be on public assistance of incentive to save.

In a society which prizes incentives for work and thrift, these are surprising regulations. They deny the country useful productive services, but that economic loss is minor in the present context. They deprive individuals and families both of work experience which could teach them skills, habits, and self-discipline of future value and of the self-respect and satisfaction which comes from improving their own lot by their own efforts.

Public assistance encourages the disintegration of the family, the key to so many of the economic and social problems of the American Negro. The main assistance program, Aid for Dependent Children, is not available if there is an able-bodied employed male in the house. In most states it is not available if there is an able-bodied man in the house, even if he is not working. All too often it is necessary for the father to leave his children so that they can eat. It is bad enough to provide incentives for idleness but even worse to legislate incentives for desertion.[13]

The bureaucratic surveillance and guidance to which recipients of public assistance are subject undermine both their self-respect and their capacity to manage their own affairs. In the administration of assistance there is much concern to detect "cheating" against the means tests and to ensure approved prudent use of the public's money. Case loads are frequently too great and administrative regulations too confining to permit the talents of social workers to treat the roots rather than the symptoms of the social maladies of their clients.

The defects of present categorical assistance programs could

13. The official Advisory Council on Public Assistance recommended in 1960 that children be aided even if there are two parents or relatives *in loco parentis* in their household, but Congress has ignored this proposal. *Public Assistance: A Report of the Findings and Recommendations of the Advisory Council on Public Assistance*, Department of Health, Education, and Welfare, January 1960. The Advisory Council also wrestled somewhat inconclusively with the problem of the means test and suggested that states be allowed to experiment with dropping or modifying it for five years. This suggestion too has been ignored.

be, in my opinion, greatly reduced by adopting a system of basic income allowances, integrated with and administered in conjunction with the federal income tax. In a sense the proposal is to make the income tax symmetrical. At present the federal government takes a share of family income in excess of a certain amount (for example, a married couple with three children pays no tax unless their income exceeds $3700). The proposal is that the Treasury pay any family who falls below a certain income a fraction of the shortfall. The idea has sometimes been called a negative income tax.

The payment would be a matter of right, like an income tax refund. Individuals expecting to be entitled to payments from the government during the year could receive them in periodic installments by making a declaration of expected income and expected tax withholdings. But there would be a final settlement between the individual and the government based on a "tax" return after the year was over, just as there is now for taxpayers on April 15.

A family with no other income at all would receive a basic allowance scaled to the number of persons in the family. For a concrete example, take the basic allowance to be $400 per year per person. It might be desirable and equitable, however, to reduce the additional basic allowance for children after, say, the fourth. Once sufficient effort is being made to disseminate birth control knowledge and technique, the scale of allowances by family size certainly should provide some disincentive to the creation of large families.

A family's allowance would be reduced by a certain fraction of every dollar of other income it received. For a concrete example, take this fraction to be one-third. This means that the family has considerable incentive to earn income, because its total income including allowances will be increased by two-thirds of whatever it earns. In contrast, the means test connected with present public assistance is a 100 per cent "tax" on earnings. With a one-third "tax" a family will be on the receiving end of the allowance and income tax system until its regular income equals three times its basic allowance.[14]

14. Adjusting the size of a government benefit to the amount of other in-

Families above this "break-even" point would be taxpayers. But the less well-off among them would pay less taxes than they do now. The first dollars of income in excess of this break-even point would be taxed at the same rate as below, one-third in the example. At some income level, the tax liability so computed would be the same as the tax under the present income tax law. From that point up, the present law would take over; taxpayers with incomes above this point would not be affected by the plan.

The best way to summarize the proposal is to give a concrete

FIGURE 1. *Illustration of Proposed Income Allowance Plan (married couple with three children)*

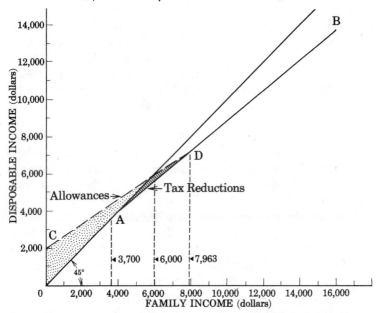

graphical illustration. On the horizontal axis of Figure 1 is measured family income from wages and salaries, interest, dividends,

come is not without precedent. Recipients of Old Age Survivors and Disability Insurance benefits under the age of seventy-two lose one dollar of benefits and only one dollar for every two dollars of earned income above $1200 but below $1700 a year.

rents, and so forth—"adjusted gross income" for the Internal Revenue Service. On the vertical axis is measured the corresponding "disposable income," that is, income after federal taxes and allowances. If the family neither paid taxes nor received allowance, disposable income would be equal to family income; in the diagram this equality would be shown by the 45° line from the origin. Disposable income above this 45° line means the family receives allowances; disposable income below this line means the family pays taxes. The broken line OAB describes the present income tax law for a married couple with three children, allowing the standard deductions. The line CD is the revision which the proposed allowance system would make for incomes below $7963. For incomes above $7963, the old tax schedule applies.

Beneficiaries under Federal Old Age Survivors and Disability Insurance would not be eligible for the new allowances. Congress should make sure that minimum benefits under OASDI are at least as high as the allowances. Some government payments, especially those for categorical public assistance, would eventually be replaced by basic allowances. Others, like unemployment insurance and veterans' pensions, are intended to be rights earned by past services regardless of current need. It would therefore be wrong to withhold allowances from the beneficiaries of these payments, but it would be reasonable to count them as income in determining the size of allowances, even though they are not subject to tax.

Although the numbers used above are illustrative, they are indicative of what is needed for an effective program. It would be expensive for the federal budget, involving an expenditure of perhaps fifteen billion dollars a year. Partially offsetting this budgetary cost are the savings in public assistance, on which governments now spent five and six-tenths billion dollars a year, of which three and two-tenths billion are federal funds. In addition, savings are possible in a host of other income maintenance programs, notably in agriculture.

The program is expensive, but it need not be introduced all at once. The size of allowances can be gradually increased as room in the budget becomes available. This is likely to happen fairly rapidly. First of all, there is room right now. The budget, and the budget deficit, can and should be larger in order to create a tight labor market. Second, the normal growth of the economy increases federal revenues from existing tax rates by some six to seven billion dollars a year. This is a drag on the economy, threatening a stagnation and rising unemployment unless it is matched by a similar rise in federal spending or avoided by cutting taxes. With defense spending stable or declining, there is room both for increases in civilian spending, as in the war on poverty, and for further tax cuts. Indeed, periodic tax reduction is official administration policy, and President Johnson agrees that the next turn belongs to low-income families. Gradually building an allowance system into the federal income tax would be the best way to lower the net yield of the tax—fairer and more far reaching than further cuts in tax rates.

I referred to programs which make up for lack of earning capacity as stopgaps, but that is not entirely fair. Poverty itself saps earning capacity. The welfare way of life, on the edge of subsistence, does not provide motivation or useful work experience either to parents or to children. A better system, one which enables people to retain their self-respect and initiative, would in itself help to break the vicious circle.

The proposed allowance system is of course not the only thing which needs to be done. Without attempting to be exhaustive, I shall mention three other measures for the assistance of families without adequate earning capacity.

It hardly needs emphasizing that the large size of Negro families or non-families is one of the principal causes of Negro poverty. There are too many mouths to feed per breadwinner, and frequently the care of children keeps the mother, the only possible breadwinner, at home. A program of day care and pre-school education for children five and under could meet several objectives at once—enriching the experience of the children and freeing the mother for training or for work.

The quality of the medical care of Negroes is a disgrace in itself and contributes to their other economic handicaps. Even so the financing of the care of "the medically indigent" is inadequate and chaotic. Sooner or later we will extend the principle of Medicare to citizens under sixty-five. Why not sooner?

As mentioned above, much Negro poverty in the South reflects the inability of Negroes to make a livelihood in agriculture. As far as the traditional cash crop, cotton, is concerned, mechanization and the competition of larger-scale units in the Southwest are undermining the plantation and share-cropping system of the Southeast. The Negro subsistence farmer has too little land, equipment, and know-how to make a decent income. Current government agricultural programs, expensive as they are to the taxpayer, do very little to help the sharecropper or subsistence farmer. Our whole agricultural policy needs to be recast, to give income support to people rather than price support to crops and to take people off the land rather than to take land out of cultivation. The effects on the social system of the South may be revolutionary, but they can only be salutary. Obviously there will be a tremendous burden on educational and training facilities to fit people for urban and industrial life. And I must emphasize again that substantial migration from agriculture is only possible, without disaster in the cities, in a booming economy with a tight labor market.

CONCLUSION

By far the most powerful factor determining the economic status of Negroes is the over-all state of the United States economy. A vigorously expanding economy with a steadily tight labor market will rapidly raise the position of the Negro, both absolutely and relatively. Favored by such a climate, the host of specific measures to eliminate discrimination, improve education and training, provide housing, and strengthen the family can yield substantial additional results. In a less beneficent economic climate, where jobs are short rather than men, the wars against racial inequality and poverty will be uphill battles, and some highly touted weapons may turn out to be dangerously futile.

The forces of the market place, the incentives of private self-interest, the pressures of supply and demand—these can be powerful allies or stubborn opponents. Properly harnessed, they quietly and impersonally accomplish objectives which may elude detailed legislation and administration. To harness them to the cause of the American Negro is entirely possible. It requires simply that the federal government dedicate its fiscal and monetary policies more wholeheartedly and singlemindedly to achieving and maintaining genuinely full employment. The obstacles are not technical or economic. One obstacle is a general lack of understanding that unemployment and related evils are remediable by national fiscal and monetary measures. The other is the high priority now given to competing financial objectives.

The goal of racial equality suggests that the federal government should provide more stimulus to the economy. Fortunately, it also suggests constructive ways to give the stimulus. We can kill two birds with one stone. The economy needs additional spending in general; the wars on poverty and racial inequality need additional spending of particular kinds. The needed spending falls into two categories: government programs to diminish economic inequalities by building up the earning capacities of the poor and their children, and humane public assistance to citizens who temporarily or permanently lack the capacity to earn a decent living for themselves and their families. In both categories the nation, its conscience aroused by the plight of the Negro, has the chance to make reforms which will benefit the whole society.

Suggested Further Readings

Adler, J. H., and E. R. Schlesinger, "The Fiscal System, the Distribution of Income, and Public Welfare," K. E. Poole, ed., *Fiscal Policies and the American Economy* (Prentice-Hall, 1951), pp. 359–421.

Blum, Walter J., and Harry Kalven, Jr., *The Uneasy Case for Progressive Taxation* (University of Chicago Press: Phoenix Books, 1963).

Boulding, Kenneth E., *The Principles of Economic Policy* (Prentice-Hall, 1958), ch. 4.

Bowen, Howard R., *Toward Social Economy* (Rinehart, 1948), chs. 14, 19.

Bowman, Mary Jean, "A Graphical Analysis of Personal Income Distribution in the United States," American Economic Association, *Readings in the Theory of Income Distribution* (Blakiston, 1951), pp. 72–99.

Brady, Dorothy, "Research on the Size Distribution of Income," *Studies in Income and Wealth*, vol. 13 (N.B.E.R., 1951), Part I.

Cartter, Allan M., *The Redistribution of Income in Postwar Britain* (Yale University Press, 1955).

———, "Income Shares of Upper Income Groups in Great Britain and the U. S.," *American Economic Review*, vol. 44 (Dec. 1954), pp. 875–83.

Council of Economic Advisers, *Economic Report of the President* (U. S. Government Printing Office), 1964, ch. 2; 1965, pp. 161–7.

Dahl, Robert A., and Charles E. Lindblom, *Politics, Economics, and Welfare* (Harper and Row, 1953), chs. 2, 5.

Dalton, Hugh, *Some Aspects of Inequality of Incomes in Modern Communities* (Macmillan, 1921).

Denison, E. F., "Income Types and Size Distribution," *American Economic Review*, vol. 44 (May 1954), pp. 254–69.

Fisher, A. G. B., "Alternative Techniques for Promoting Equality in a Capitalist Society," *American Economic Review*, vol. 40 (May 1950), pp. 356–70.

Fishman, Leo, ed., *Poverty amid Affluence* (Yale University Press, 1965).

Friedman, Milton, "Choice, Chance, and the Personal Distribution of Income," *Journal of Political Economy*, vol. 41 (Sept. 1953), pp. 277–90.

Galbraith, J. K., *The Affluent Society* (Houghton-Mifflin, 1958), chs. 7, 23.

Gallaway, Lowell, "The Foundations of the War on Poverty," *American Economic Review*, vol. 55 (March 1965), pp. 122–31.

Garvy, George, "Inequality of Income: Causes and Measurement," *Studies in Income and Wealth*, vol. 15 (N.B.E.R., 1952), Part II.

———, "Functional and Size Distributions of Income and their Meaning," *American Economic Review*, vol. 44 (May 1954), pp. 236–53.

Goldsmith, Selma F., George Jaszi, Maurice Liebenberg, and Hyman Kaitz, "Size Distribution of Income since the Mid-Thirties," *Review of Economics and Statistics*, vol. 36 (Feb. 1954), pp. 1–32.

Goldsmith, Selma F., "The Relation of Census Income Distribution Statistics to Other Income Data," *An Appraisal of the 1950 Census Income Data*, Studies in Income and Wealth, vol. 23 (N.B.E.R., 1958), pp. 65–107.

——, "Impact of the Income Tax on Socioeconomic Groups of Families in the United States," *Income Redistribution and the Statistical Foundations of Economic Policy*, Income and Wealth, Series X (Bowes and Bowes, 1964), pp. 248–79.

Gordon, Margaret S., ed., *Poverty in America* (Chandler Publishing Co., 1965).

Jenkins, Roy, "Equality," in R. H. S. Crossman, ed., *New Fabian Essays* (Praeger, 1952), pp. 69–90.

Keyserling, Leon H., *Progress or Poverty* (Conference on Economic Progress, 1964).

——, *Poverty and Deprivation in the U. S.* (Conference on Economic Progress, 1962).

Kolko, Gabriel, *Wealth and Power in America* (Praeger, 1962).

Kravis, Irving B., *The Structure of Income* (University of Pennsylvania, 1962).

Kuznets, Simon, *Shares of Upper Income Groups in Income and Savings* (N.B.E.R., 1953).

——, "Economic Growth and Income Inequality," *American Economic Review*, vol. 45 (March 1955), pp. 1–28.

Knight, Frank H., *The Ethics of Competition* (Harper Bros., 1935), ch. 2.

Lampman, Robert J., "Recent Changes in Income Inequality Reconsidered," *American Economic Review*, vol. 44 (June 1954), pp. 251–68.

——, "Recent Thought on Egalitarianism," *Quarterly Journal of Economics*, vol. 71 (May 1957), pp. 234–66.

——, *The Low Income Population and Economic Growth*, Study Paper No. 12, U. S. Congress, Joint Economic Committee (1959).

Lerner, A. P., *The Economics of Control* (Macmillan, 1944), ch. 3.

Little, I. M. D., *A Critique of Welfare Economics* (Oxford University Press, 2nd edition, 1957), chs. 1, 4, 5.

Lydall, Harold, and John B. Lansing, "A Comparison of the Distribution of Personal Income and Wealth in the U. S. and Great Britain," *American Economic Review*, vol. 49 (March 1959), pp. 43–67.

Mincer, Jacob, "Investment in Human Capital and Personal Income Distribution," *Journal of Political Economy*, vol. 66 (Aug. 1958), pp. 281–302.

Miller, Herman P., *Income of the American People* (Wiley, 1955).

——, *Trends in the Income of Families and Persons in the United States: 1947 to 1960*, Bureau of the Census (U. S. Government Printing Office, 1963).

——, *Rich Man, Poor Man* (Crowell, 1964).

——, *Income Distribution in the United States*, Bureau of the Census (U.S. Government Printing Office, 1966).

Moore, G. H., "Secular Changes in the Distribution of Income," *American Economic Review*, vol. 42 (May 1952), pp. 527–44.

Morgan, James N., "The Anatomy of Income Distribution," *Review of Economics and Statistics*, vol. 44 (Aug. 1962), pp. 270–83.

Morgan, James N., Martin H. David, Wilbur J. Cohen, and Harvey E. Brazer, *Income and Welfare in the United States* (McGraw-Hill, 1962).

Musgrave, R. A., "The Incidence of the Tax Structure and its Effect on Consumption," *Federal Tax Policy for Growth and Stability*, U. S. Congress, Joint Economic Committee (1955), pp. 96–113.

——, "Estimating the Distribution of the Tax Burden," *Income Redistribution and the Statistical Foundations of Economic Policy*, Series X (Bowes and Bowes, 1964), pp. 186–219.

Orshansky, Mollie, "Counting the Poor: Another Look at the Poverty Profile," *Social Security Bulletin*, vol. 28 (Jan. 1965), pp. 3–29.

Office of Business Economics, *Income Distribution in the United States* (U. S. Government Printing Office, 1953) and subsequent issues of the *Survey of Current Business*.

Peacock, Allan T., ed., *Income Redistribution and Social Policy* (Jonathan Cape, 1954).

Schultz, T. Paul, *The Distribution of Personal Income*, U. S. Congress: Joint Economic Committee (U. S. Government Printing Office, 1965).

Schultz, T. W., "Investment in Human Capital," *American Economic Review*, vol. 51 (March 1961), pp. 1–17.

——, "Investing in Poor People: An Economist's View," *American Economic Review*, vol. 55 (May 1965), pp. 510–20.

Stigler, George, *Five Lectures on Economic Problems* (Macmillan, 1950), Lecture 1.

Theobald, Robert, *Free Men and Free Markets* (Anchor, 1965).

Theobald, Robert, ed., *A Guaranteed Income* (Doubleday, 1966).

Thomson, David, *Equality* (Cambridge University Press, 1949).

U. S. Congress, Joint Economic Committee, *Materials on the Problems of Low Income Families* (1950), *Making Ends Meet on Less Than $2,000 a Year* (1951), *Hearings on Low-Income Families* (1955), *Characteristics of the Low-Income Population and Related Federal Programs* (1955), U. S. Government Printing Office.

Wright, David McCord, "Income Redistribution Reconsidered," *Income, Employment, and Public Policy* (W. W. Norton, 1948), pp. 159–76.

Yntema, Dwight, "Measures of Inequality in Personal Distribution of Income or Wealth," *Journal of American Statistical Association*, vol. 27 (1933), pp. 423–33.